Heart at the Center

An Educator's Guide to Sustaining Love, Hope, and Community Through Nonviolence Pedagogy

Mike Tinoco

Routledge
Taylor & Francis Group

NEW YORK AND LONDON

A Stenhouse Book

Cover art: Malisa Suchanya
Interior illustrations: Keilani Mae Jasmin

First published 2025
by Routledge
605 Third Avenue, New York, NY 10158

and by Routledge
4 Park Square, Milton Park, Abingdon, Oxon, OX14 4RN

Routledge is an imprint of the Taylor & Francis Group, an informa business

Library of Congress Cataloging-in-Publication Data
Names: Tinoco, Mike, author.
Title: Heart at the center : an educator's guide to sustaining love, hope, and community through
     nonviolence pedagogy / Mike Tinoco.
Description: New York : Routledge, 2024. | Includes bibliographical references and index. |
     Summary: "In Heart at the Center: An Educator's Guide to Sustaining Love, Hope, and
     Community through Nonviolence Pedagogy, high school teacher Mike Tinoco examines
     what it means to reimagine classrooms and schools as spaces that humanize, resist violence
     and injustice, and center love. Offering both a framework and a set of practices that are
     grounded in different nonviolence traditions, Heart at the Center asks readers to consider
     what a pedagogy of nonviolence looks like, sounds like, and feels like in the classroom"—
     Provided by publisher.
Identifiers: LCCN 2023052266 (print) | LCCN 2023052267 (ebook) | ISBN 9781625316288
     (pbk) | ISBN 9781032681221 (ebk)
Subjects: LCSH: Affective education—United States. | Nonviolence—Study and teaching—
     United States. | Peace—Study and teaching—United States. | Social change—Study and
     teaching—United States. | Classroom environment—Social aspects—United States. |
     Inclusive education—United States. | Critical pedagogy.
Classification: LCC LB1072 .T56 2024 (print) | LCC LB1072 (ebook) |
     DDC 370.15/34—dc23/eng/20240229
LC record available at https://lccn.loc.gov/2023052266
LC ebook record available at https://lccn.loc.gov/2023052267

ISBN: 978-1-625-31628-8 (pbk)
ISBN: 978-1-032-68122-1 (ebk)

DOI: 10.4324/9781032681221

Designed and typeset in Adobe Garamond Pro and URW DIN by Alex Lazarou

Given the current state of our world, we need a (re)centering of love more than ever. In this very important book, Mike Tinoco helps educators to (re)imagine a different and better world—moving readers toward the inner, reflective, and pedagogical work. *Heart at the Center* is an urgent call for truth, love, and justice for every educator and community member who deeply dreams of and seeks peace. Beauty is manifested on each page.

Gholnecsar (Gholdy) Muhammad,
Associate Professor of Curriculum & Instruction at the University of Illinois Chicago

Dr. Vincent Harding, civil rights leader, author, historian, pastor, and professor is known for drafting the 1967 anti-war Beyond Vietnam speech given by his beloved friend Dr. Martin Luther King Jr. He was also my cousin-in-law, my family. Vincent shared that before Dr. King was killed, he was thinking about what it means to create nonviolent revolutionary change. Today, as we bear witness to horrendous acts of violence locally, nationally, and globally, I wonder what Vincent and Dr. King might say. What does it mean to dedicate ourselves to the work of nonviolence? *Heart at the Center: An Educator's Guide to Sustaining Love, Hope, and Community Through Nonviolence Pedagogy* addresses this call. Mike Tinoco builds upon the tools provided by educators and activists of the past and helps us recognize the historical and holistic pathways that can move us forward. I urge educators to read this book so we can radically reorient ourselves away from the conditions and mindsets that cause violence and turn toward a lifetime commitment to caring for ourselves, the collective, and to love.

Dr. Sonja Cherry-Paul,
Founder, Red Clay Educators, adapter of the #1 NYT bestselling
Stamped (For Kids): Racism, Antiracism, and You

Mike Tinoco is one of the most grounded and visionary teachers I have ever met. He has built a way of being in the classroom that reflects a holistic and loving embodiment of justice and care through a framework of nonviolence that is tangible, visceral, and possible. *Heart at the Center* is a gift to all teachers, as Mike provides a path for us to both heal and develop clarity in our evolving visions for our classrooms, schools, and communities. The book guides us through a process of deep reflection and urges us toward realistic possibilities for love and justice in classrooms that are too often devalued and discouraged in school systems. I am grateful to have this book as a tool for transformation for myself and for the teachers and future teachers I support.

Marcos Pizarro,
Dean, College of Education, California State University, Los Angeles

Heart at the Center is not just the book I wanted to read; it is the person I hope to become. In an age where the world expects teachers to do everything, Mike Tinoco's recognition of our shared humanity and the importance of our mission is such a welcome part of our professional discourse.

Cornelius Minor,
author of *We Got This: Equity, Access,*
and the Quest to Be Who Our Students Need Us to Be

Written with vulnerability, humility, and powerful examples of his own classroom practice, Mike Tinoco offers a brilliant nonviolence framework to re-imagine our schools as spaces of hope, love, possibility, and vehicles for radical change. This book is a must-read for anyone in education, a space where we can dream collectively of a world that centers love, justice, and humanity.

Ruchi Agarwal-Rangnath,
Associate Professor in Teacher Education at the University of
San Francisco and author of *Social Studies, Literacy, and Social Justice*
in the Elementary Classroom: A Guide for Teachers

Courageous, yet humble. Theoretical, yet practical. *Heart at the Center* is a love letter on loving ourselves, our communities, and our young people.

Aldrich Limpin Sabac,
ELD, English, & Ethnic Studies Teacher, Stockton, California

Mixing personal story and applicable classroom strategies, Mike Tinoco inspires educators to reach for their authentic selves in the classroom and create opportunities for young people to find their own beat within. Mike encourages us to slow down and focus on the things that really matter: relationships, creativity and communication.

KZ Zapata,
co-founder, Teachers 4 Social Justice

If you are a teacher trying to build a culture of nonviolence in your classroom, look no further. In this inspirational work, Mike Tinoco skillfully weaves together wisdom from historical sources, examples from his classroom, and even practices from martial arts to offer a comprehensive playbook in the art of nonviolent pedagogy.

K.M. DiColandrea,
cofounder of Brooklyn Debate League

For Tala
and the youth of yesterday, today, and tomorrow

CONTENTS

OUTER PRACTICE   224

APPENDICES   300

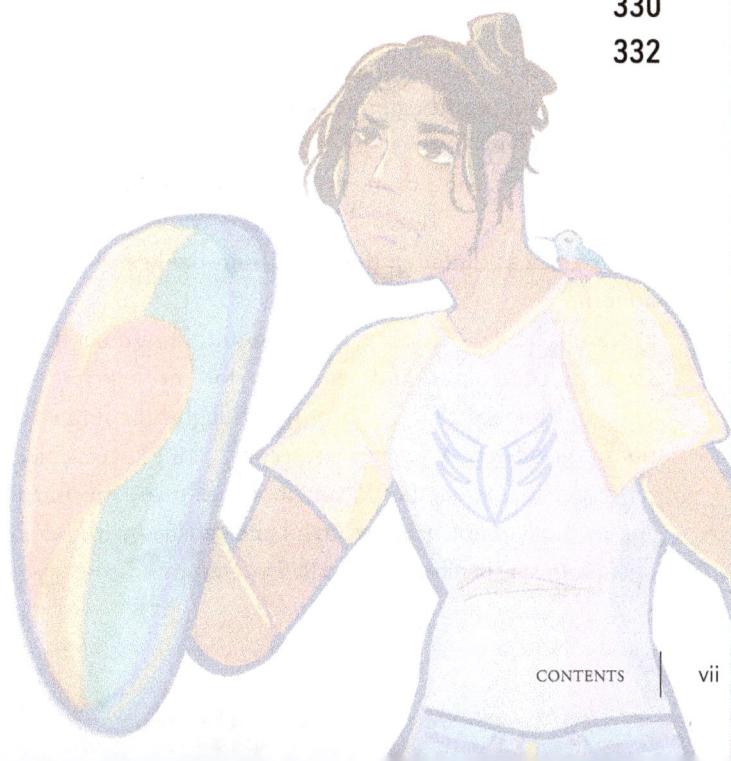

ACKNOWLEDGMENTS

The late political activist Yuri Kochiyama once said, "Life is not what you alone make it. Life is the input of everyone who touched your life and every experience that entered it. We are all part of one another" (2004, xxi).

I would not be the educator, parent, and human being I strive to be were it not for the innumerable experiences and individuals that have touched my life. This book, too, is not what I, alone, have made it. It is the result of many people and experiences that have touched it in some way. And so, I want to express my deepest gratitude to those who directly and indirectly contributed to my being able to write it.

To my partner, Rachelle, thank you for your unwavering love, encouragement, and support. When I first brought up the idea of wanting to write a book, you believed in and encouraged me as you always do. You helped me give myself permission to venture into a project I had never done before. Thank you for helping me think through parts where I felt stuck, offering perspective when I needed it, and celebrating milestones with me. Thank you for the countless times you watched Tala and lay with her in the early mornings and during naptime so I could write. I love you so much and am eternally grateful to have you in my life.

To Lola, Lolo, Mom, Dad, James, and my siblings—Maisie, Will, Ben, and Michelle—thank you for your love and support. Lola and Lolo, thank you for the many times when you watched Tala, picked her up from school, and played with her so I could write. Mom, thank you for your loving ear and open heart; you helped me think through one of the hardest sections of the book. Dad, thank you for your undying enthusiasm for this book and for always believing in me. Maisie, thank you for being a thought partner early on when I was choosing a publisher.

To my editor, Kassia Omohundro Wedekind, thank you for taking a chance on me and championing this book from the beginning. I especially appreciate you honoring my vision and trusting me as a writer to, as you told me, "bend the genre of teacher books." Thank you for the untold number of times you read and reread chapters, paragraphs, and sentences; for the many text messages, emails, zoom calls, and phone calls; for all of the thoughtful comments, questions, and suggestions you offered. Your eye for keeping things accessible, connected, and concise for readers has strengthened my book and made me a better writer. As a first-time author, I could not be more joyful and satisfied with my experience of writing this book. I am so thankful to have had you as my editor.

To those who read portions of my manuscript and offered feedback; were a thought partner; shared advice; or helped me get in touch with people, thank you: Roxy Manning, Matthew Kay, Carl Ponzio, Jessica Cohen, Ray Ramirez, Alejandra Delgado, Kazu Haga, Emily (Ems) La, Dani Wadlington, Ana Benderas, Mike Espinoza, Marcos Pizarro, Edmundo Norte, Rachel deLahunta, Aayesha Nangia, Kate Flowers Rossner, Jane Martin-Gilmore, Marty Brandt, Tobey Antao, Holly Kim Price, Cornelius Minor, Kwame Sarfo-Mensah, Kelly Gallagher, Nawal Qarooni, Whitney La Rocca, Sarah Zerwin, Tony Santa Ana, James Kass, Sarah Peyton, Ruchi Rangnath, Emily Spangler, Mayra Quezada, Stephanie Foo, Josh Walters, Rita Kohli, Candace-Omnira LaFayette, Jane Felts Osgerby, Marbella Romero, Cristobal Van Breen, David Jensen, and Nick Patterson.

To the elders from the civil rights movement who've dedicated their lives to building the Beloved Community and who shared their time and stories with me, thank you: Gloria Washington Lewis-Randall, Bernard LaFayette, and Ronald English. And to the freedom fighters no longer here but whose stories live on in this book and elsewhere, thank you for your courage, sacrifice, and leadership: Autherine Lucy, Mary Hamilton, Septima Clark, and Ella Baker.

To Martin Luther King Jr., who embodied and modeled an alternate way of being in the world and whose teachings on nonviolence have transformed my pedagogy and life, thank you.

To my students, whom I am honored to be in community with, learn from, and build alongside every day, thank you. And to the students, current and former, who gave their blessing for me to include their stories, writing, and pictures in this book, thank you.

To Malisa Suchanya, thank you for creating such beautiful cover art for this book. You captured the spirit of what I envisioned and hoped for.

To my former student Keilani Mae Jasmin, thank you for creating the lovely illustrations that accompany the opening of each section of this book.

To my advisors and cohorts from the Teacher Education Program at UCLA, thank you for helping me see and imagine what is possible in classrooms and schools. I will forever be thankful for the learning and unlearning I experienced with you. (Shout out to Team Lee!)

To the education and nonviolence groups, organizations, and spaces that have contributed to my learning and growth over the years, thank you: South Bay Critical Friends; Maestrx: A Movement for Raza Liberation through Educación; the Institute for Teachers of Color Committed to Racial Justice; Teachers 4 Social Justice; Free Minds, Free People; Rock The School Bells; the Nonviolent Leadership for Social Justice retreat; East Point Peace Academy; the International Nonviolence Summer Institute; and aikido of San José.

FOREWORD

What an honor it was for me to be asked to write a foreword for *Heart at the Center*. As I reviewed the manuscript, I was deeply moved to see how my friend and colleague Mike Tinoco fully manifests the values and consciousness of nonviolence that he has modeled since our very first interaction.

As a psychologist and a Nonviolent Communication trainer and certification assessor, I meet hundreds of people a year. I met Mike ten years into my efforts to integrate Nonviolent Communication and anti-oppression work. From our very first interaction, his way of being ignited a beacon of hope for me. A young teacher at the time, Mike emailed my colleague Edmundo, one of the trainers of the Nonviolent Leadership for Social Justice retreat and a Dean of Intercultural and International Studies at a local community college, to ask if they could chat over coffee about the work that Edmundo and our team were doing. In his note, Mike mourned the way those advocating for social change vilified administrators and those with structural power. He shared how much he dreamed of reconciliation, of finding ways to bridge differences and move toward collaboration and a world where everyone could thrive. Looking back, this small request from Mike provided a significant foreshadowing of who Mike is and the deeply held values that culminated in this book. If every person who reads it learns to show up in the uniquely powerful way that Mike does, our schools would be transformed.

As I write this, I'm struck again by the powerful, deceptive simplicity with which Mike embodies the values of the three disciplines that form the core of his approach—Kingian Nonviolence, Nonviolent Communication, and aikido. You're probably reading my words and thinking, *he wrote an email. Not a big deal.* That letter was so much more. Mike did something I still rarely experience. He reached out across lines of power and status and made a human connection. How many of you have written a note to someone you admire, someone with stature in your field, asking them out to coffee? If you're a teacher, how often have you had a student reach out to you with admiration for your work and ask to meet to talk about it? Mike's thirst for knowledge and inspiration, his trust in his own value, and his ability to see the human behind the role empowered him to make a seemingly simple request for connection that so few of us do. That small gesture led to his becoming deeply involved in the Nonviolent Leadership for Social Justice retreat, initially as a participant and eventually as an organizer and trainer. His request for connection manifested into strong bonds, continual learning, and leadership that have endured since.

And now we as readers benefit from Mike's capacity to do that over and over again. Throughout his book, we are gifted with gems of learning and hope gleaned from direct conversations Mike had with so many people—from leaders of the US civil rights movement to the most disenfranchised student in the class. Mike shows us what we can gain—as teachers, students, humans—when we look beyond social labels and connect to the human essence in each person.

Mike's simple letter also foreshadowed another quality he infuses into his book—his commitment to calling out harm with love. Through poignant stories of his own journey and his interactions with students and colleagues, Mike makes clear the damage we all experience when we vilify others interpersonally, and the cost of systems and ways of advocating for change that pit teachers against students, administrators against teachers, and teachers against each other. Instead, Mike shows us what is possible, demonstrating how the wisdom gleaned from the US civil rights movement is still deeply applicable today, still sorely needed if we seek to transform our systems, rather than simply replace who is in power. Each inspiring story from the civil rights era, which he connects to current episodes in the news and in his classroom, offers a model of a different world.

Heart at the Center is more than just a visionary, inspirational text. It's also a practical, hands-on guide that supports anyone wanting to transform their classroom and their school. Mike draws on his vast classroom experience with students from diverse socioeconomic classes, in addition to his own lived experience as a student who was almost a statistic, to show us how love can transform the student–teacher relationship, and he gives us concrete steps to get there.

Mike's ability to support teachers and administrators through the integration of Nonviolent Communication—both the consciousness of nonviolence at the heart of the model and its structured communication form—is a reflection of his deep commitment and practice. Anyone who picks up this book and dives deep into the many exercises he offers will experience a shift—in their reconnection to the values that led them to enter the profession, in their ability to connect from a genuine place with the students in their lives, and in their capacity to forge supportive, collaborative relationships with their peers.

Thank you for reading *Heart at the Center.* May you leave inspired, reinvigorated, and most of all, full of love.

ROXY MANNING, PhD
Assessor and certified trainer with the Center for Nonviolent Communication; author of *How to Have Antiracist Conversations* and co-author with Sarah Peyton of *The Antiracist Heart.*

Introduction

As a parent and educator, I feel deep anguish and mourning over the turbulent state of our country and world. Ongoing mass shootings in and beyond our schools. A rise in hate crimes against BIPOC and LGBTQIA+ communities. White supremacists as the largest domestic terrorist threat in the United States. Deepening polarization and normalization of violent rhetoric in political discourse. Denial of truth and erasing of history. A worsening climate crisis and efforts to address it being stymied.

Sometimes, I cannot help but agonize about the mess my child and future generations will inherit due to our collective failures to create a just, loving, and sustainable planet where the needs of all people and living things are held with care. Sometimes, I cannot help but despair when I feel the weight of multiple catastrophes unfolding and worsening.

But then I think about one of my teachers, Dr. Bernard LaFayette Jr., a civil rights leader who co-founded the Student Nonviolent Coordinating Committee and later served as the program director for Dr. Martin Luther King Jr.'s Southern Christian Leadership Conference. LaFayette was a student leader during the lunch counter sit-in movement in Nashville, participated in the Freedom Rides, led voting rights efforts in Selma, Alabama, and more. He knows full well what it is like to be confronted with dire and seemingly insurmountable obstacles.

LaFayette once said of his experience during the sit-ins: "We protested because *we* had changed. We continued to give them the opportunity to also change because we believed that it was possible" (Porter 2020). He and the other brave individuals who put their bodies and lives on the line for the sake of freedom were working toward creating a world that did *not yet exist*. They attempted to eradicate hatred and violence within themselves and never lost hope that those who opposed them, too, could change—that the *world* could change. People are never the enemy, he said. Violence, injustice, and oppression are what need to be defeated.

LaFayette's profound faith in humanity, guided by an unwavering commitment to nonviolence and deep ethic of love, helps sustain my hope. And one of my hopes is that we can respond collectively to the current moment with our hearts as our compass.

Addressing the ubiquitous violence in our society and schools is a moral imperative that demands urgency. If schools do not serve as reservoirs of hope, sites of love and possibility, and vehicles for radical change, then what's the point of public education?

The painful truth is that schools have historically served, and continue to serve, as sites of bodily, mental, emotional, and spiritual harm, particularly toward Black, Brown, indigenous, migrant, LGBTQIA+, neurodiverse, and disabled youth. So long as scores of young people go through school feeling disconnected from themselves and each other, unable to imagine, let alone believe they can create, a world fundamentally different than the one that currently exists, the collective challenges we are confronted with will persist if not worsen. But we do not have to accept the current state of the world. We do not have to succumb to despondence. Through love, hope, community, and collective action, we sustain our hearts and sustain each other.

Heart at the Center is for educators who believe or want to believe that a different world is possible. Drawing from global and long-standing nonviolence traditions that I have studied, trained in, and integrated into my teaching and life—namely Kingian Nonviolence, Nonviolent Communication, and aikido—this book offers educators a framework and set of practices to *embody* nonviolence within and beyond the classroom.

Maybe you are a preservice or first-year teacher wanting to maintain hope and joy as you start out. Maybe you are a veteran teacher who feels disillusioned by the school system and what's happening in the world, and you are yearning for some inspiration. Maybe you feel isolated at your school and are longing for companionship, wanting to know that you are not alone in your experience. Maybe your staff or department are close with each other and are looking to read, reflect, and grow together. Maybe you picked this book up on a whim and are just curious about expanding your practice and trying something different. Wherever you are in your journey, this book is for you.

So, you might be wondering: What does classroom practice rooted in nonviolence even mean? What does it look like? Let's begin by first digging into some important understandings about violence and nonviolence that inform everything else in this book.

UNDERSTANDING VIOLENCE

The Center for Disease and Control and the World Health Organization (WHO) characterize violence as:

> the intentional use of physical force or power—threatened or actual—against oneself, another person, or against a group or community—that either results in or has a high likelihood of resulting in injury, death, psychological harm, maldevelopment or deprivation (n.d.).

While helpful for understanding some of the impact of *physical* violence, this definition leaves out other ways in which violence inflicts harm, and it fails to mention that violence can still exist even if it is **un**intentional.

Dr. Hongyu Wang, a nonviolence practitioner, writer, and professor of curriculum studies at Oklahoma State University, defines violence as "the result of the collapse of relationality, whether the relationship is human or ecological, physical or psychic, material or spiritual" (2013, 494). My understanding of violence aligns with hers, and I similarly think of violence as a violation of the body, mind, heart, and/or spirit that results in or from disconnection. Whether it's words, action, or policy inflicted upon a person, community, animal, plant, living system, organism, or the earth, ultimately, violence destroys.

With regard to violence in schools, what generally comes to mind for people is how it plays out among students (e.g., fights, bullying, use of weapons, etc.). While certainly important, we must also concern ourselves with and attend to pernicious forms of violence that transpire every day in schools and classrooms. It is violence when curriculum erases, distorts, or does not represent the truth of racism, enslavement, and stories of resistance. It is violence when adults abuse their power and squelch young people's autonomy in service of "managing" them. It is violence when schools enact policies that deny the humanity and rights of trans and queer students such as restricting bathroom access, participation in sports, and access to gender and sexuality education. It is violence when we feed into hustle culture and don't allow ourselves to slow down. It is violence when academics and rigor are prioritized over students' spiritual, emotional, mental, and physical well-being. It is violence when educators are punished for speaking out and fighting for just education.

We can, and we must, disrupt these forms of violence through both individual and collective efforts. The beautiful thing is that we already have within us the power to do so; it is only a matter of having the will and developing the skills to practice nonviolence.

UNDERSTANDING NONVIOLENCE

For the longest time, I conceived of nonviolence in terms of what I thought it was *not*—not violent, not aggressive, not hateful. And while nonviolence, indeed, seeks to avoid violence and enacting harm, its power really derives from its **engagement** with life: creating, bridging, restoring, disrupting.

Wang writes that "the underlying basis of nonviolence is the mutual embeddedness of everything and everybody in the cycle of life" (2014, 12). That is, nonviolence calls on us to recognize that we are part of the same web and fabric of life. Embracing our interconnectedness is a global idea that has spanned generations and cultures and is reflected in the African teaching of Ubuntu, Pilipinx value of Kapwa, Maya precept of In Lak'Ech, Buddhist concept of nondual relationality (what Thich Nhat Hanh often referred to as inter-being), among others. Nurturing our relationality builds and sustains "loving, compassionate, and constructive" communities, of which all people want to be part (Wang 2014, 12).

Similarly, Martin Luther King Jr. wrote and spoke frequently on the importance of recognizing our interdependence. He articulated this point eloquently in his 1961 sermon "The Man Who Was a Fool":

> [A]ll life is interrelated. We are tied in a single garment of destiny, caught in an inescapable network of mutuality. And whatever affects one directly affects all indirectly…I can never be what I ought to be until you are what you ought to be, and you can never be what you ought to be until I am what I ought to be (1961).

King believed that *we* cannot be what *we* ought to be so long as poverty, racism, militarism, and other forms of injustice and oppression exist. Nonviolence calls on us to collectively confront and transform violence so that we can *be* in the fullest sense of the word.

Wang adds that "nonviolence works at the site of relationality within and between individuals or groups or institutions to work through difficulty and transform both individuality and communality" (2013, 489). In its focus on relationality, nonviolence aims to disrupt all that inhibits us from being fully in touch with life, with ourselves, and with each other. We do this through both individual and collective acts of resistance all the while bringing people together and bringing out the best in one another.

I share Wang's view that "educators have a unique opportunity to practice nonviolence from an authority position and thus to model how to establish nonviolent relationships" (2014, 14). Both within and beyond our classrooms, when we practice and model nonviolence, we emanate life-affirming energy that touches those around us. When people are positively influenced by each other, they are more likely to generate healthy relationships. It is from healthy relationships that people come together and create strong communities. And from these strong communities emerge possibilities to forge humanizing institutions and systems.

TOWARD A PEDAGOGY OF NONVIOLENCE

The framework offered in this book for practicing nonviolence pedagogy is based primarily on three enduring traditions, philosophies, and approaches that have global reach: Kingian Nonviolence, Nonviolent Communication, and the martial art aikido. Whether these are new to you or you already have intimate knowledge of or experience with one or more of them, there is room for everyone to practice and expand on what they already know.

Kingian Nonviolence is a philosophy and methodology of nonviolence grounded in Black resistance, culture, and history of the civil rights movement. Specifically, Kingian Nonviolence draws from the leadership of Dr. King as well as the leadership and organizing strategies of Black women, young people, and accomplices who made the movement possible. Following King's assassination, Bernard LaFayette and social change activist David Jehnsen co-developed the Kingian Nonviolence Conflict Reconciliation training curriculum. It offers ways of understanding and approaching conflict, solving community issues including violence, and developing leadership. The name "Kingian" is used not to idolize King but to refer to a historical period during which King's example offered hope to many and helped materialize social change. The use of Kingian also reclaims King's radical legacy of agitating the status quo, demanding justice, and moving us closer to his vision of the Beloved Community.

Nonviolent Communication (NVC), originally developed by Dr. Marshall Rosenberg, is a powerful approach to engaging with ourselves and others and moving through the world more authentically. NVC assumes that all human beings share universal needs and that every single behavior is an attempt to meet needs. NVC also rests on the premise that we experience emotions in relation to needs that are either met or unmet. If, for instance, I feel joyful or content, I am likely experiencing needs that are being met. Conversely, if I feel lonely or angry, I am likely experiencing those feelings in response to unmet needs. When we can be more attuned to both our own and others' feelings and underlying needs through empathy, we "can create a shared basis for connection, cooperation, and more globally—peace" (Kashtan and Kashtan n.d.). In this way, NVC can be considered a consciousness practice, as well as a spiritual and communicative one, that seeks to foster social change and enrich life.

Aikido is a Japanese martial art developed by Morihei Ueshiba in the early twentieth century. Ueshiba drew from and synthesized techniques from various martial arts to create aikido, which translates to "way of the harmonious spirit," "way of unifying with life energy," or "way of uniting opposite powers in harmony" (Roedel 2011). The goal of aikido is not to defeat or hurt one's opponent but to literally connect with them through movements that create harmony. As a martial art, there are practical techniques that can incapacitate and injure an opponent if doing so seems necessary, but the goal is to aim for unification.

An understanding of Kingian Nonviolence, Nonviolent Communication, and aikido offer a path for an alternate way of being in the world, and they have transformed my teaching and life. The nonviolence framework that I offer in this book includes:

1. aligning vision with values and action,
2. relational nurturing,
3. love for self and humanity,
4. honoring slowness,
5. nonviolent leadership.

Without a doubt, you already have your own ideas and practices that you bring to your teaching and work as an educator. It is my hope that you use the nonviolence framework offered in this book in a way that makes sense for your context and builds on what you are already doing.

This framework, when implemented and practiced holistically, will benefit you, your students, and perhaps even your colleagues by helping address forms of violence that can exist in classrooms and schools. Doubtless, the more people in a school who adopt such a framework, the more potential it has for transforming relationships, culture, and systems. But even if it's just you reading this book, I promise that you and your students will reap learning, growth, and hope.

HOW THIS BOOK IS ORGANIZED

This book is divided into three broad parts: inner practice, classroom practice, and outer practice. While there is overlap between these areas, it is helpful for our purposes to have a general distinction between practices that focus on ourselves (**inner**), instructional and pedagogical practices (**classroom**), and practices outside of our classroom that involve colleagues (**outer**). As you may have noticed in the Table of Contents, each part contains one or more sections that detail the nonviolence framework. Each section presents a particular form of violence in classrooms and schools that we can disrupt through a nonviolent approach.

Section I: Rethinking Nonviolence invites you to articulate your vision for the kind of world you dream of as an educator and human being. Chapter 1 focuses on the importance of reclaiming our stories from when we were younger by practicing self-empathy. Doing so can provide us clarity about the kind of classrooms we want for our students. Chapter 2 offers guidance for articulating your vision, identifying the core needs and values that undergird that vision, and developing classroom strategies that would fulfill those needs and values.

Section II: Relational Nurturing, Not Classroom Management challenges the conventional view that teachers should "manage" young people through forced compliance and, instead, offers an alternate way of building strong relationships. Rather than relying on traditional classroom management tactics, this chapter asserts that creating classroom spaces that welcome and lovingly respond to conflict disrupts power dynamics that tend to dehumanize and create disconnection. Chapter 3 explores the difference between positive and negative peace and why that matters to our classroom practice. Chapter 4 differentiates between being in control of others and being in command of ourselves and offers space for educators to work through a conflict involving a student by practicing empathy.

Section III: Life as Text, Love as Ink focuses on the importance of centering a love that heals, demands justice, and treats students' lives as primary texts. When we provide students multiple opportunities through our curriculum to practice love, we create robust learning spaces where students come together and celebrate one another. Chapter 5 explores what it means to curricularize love and offers examples of, and space to brainstorm, what it can look like to help students practice self-love. Chapter 6 focuses on the importance of practicing love for humanity by creating learning spaces and opportunities that center community, healing, and justice.

Section IV: Slow Urgency explores how the nonstop pace of school and incessant pressure to produce and quantify perpetuates scarcity in mentality and practice that damages the well-being of both educators and students. Chapter 7 focuses on how to slow down, both in our classrooms and personal lives, in order to be more present and more sustainably care for ourselves and our students. Chapter 8 explores the role of voluntary suffering in our work as educators and grapples with the seeming paradox of slowing down while not compromising the urgency to act for justice.

Section V: Tending the Whole Garden looks at ways we can practice and model leadership beyond our classrooms that is non-hierarchical, grounded in nonviolence, and in service of sustaining relationality. Chapter 9 explores how to maintain connection with ourselves and colleagues in the midst of conflict.

Chapter 10 focuses on how teachers can create their own professional development opportunities that support collective care.

THE STORIES IN THIS BOOK

Each section of this book opens with a story from my own life as a student, teacher, or parent. I do this to both introduce the theme and focus of that section and to illustrate how my thinking or practice has evolved. I do not want to give the false impression that I've had nonviolence figured out since Day One and that I'm not still learning. I've experienced tremendous struggle and setbacks in my journey as an educator—as well as enormous joy, growth, and gratitude.

I also include anecdotes and examples from my classroom, where I show *how* I practice what I preach, both individually and with my students. In offering a glimpse of my journey toward and practice of nonviolence, I hope you feel accompanied as you reflect upon and continue along your own journey. All of the stories and artifacts in this book from colleagues and students have been shared with their consent. At times, I have shared their real names (with their permission), and in other instances I have changed their names to protect their privacy.

Also woven throughout the book are some of Martin Luther King Jr.'s most radical teachings on nonviolence, many of which are seldom taught in schools. King's legacy has been heavily sanitized and distorted, and we do a disservice to him, the civil rights movement, and ourselves when we perpetuate the shallow idea that he just wanted people to hold hands, be nice, and love each other. It is critical that we and our students understand the *radical* King who spoke out against racism, war, and poverty and who never wavered on his belief in nonviolence despite constant criticism, numerous death threats, FBI surveillance, and isolation at the end of his life.

That said, I am deliberate about not perpetuating the iconization of King as if he were an unimpeachable saint. He was a person with flaws. He plagiarized portions of his doctoral dissertation. He used gendered language in his speeches, sermons, and writings that frequently left out women. He cheated numerous times on his wife. His top-down leadership style often excluded women from the kind of respect and opportunities afforded to his straight, male counterparts. Sexism was rampant in the civil rights movement, and King was no exception to its upholding.

Moreover, although the success of the civil rights movement would not have happened without the extraordinary vision and nonviolent leadership of King, there would have been no civil rights movement at all nor a Martin Luther King Jr. we celebrate today, were it not for the courage, labor, and power of countless unsung heroes and heroines. Black women, especially, were often on the ground as foot soldiers and organizers, who "ran the mimeograph machines, made sandwiches, placed phone calls, and passed out flyers with information on gatherings" (Bates 2013). But they were also leaders in their own right, who brought people together and effected change. Although many of their stories have, unfortunately, been eclipsed and forgotten, they have not been lost, and they deserve to be told.

The stories of Gloria Washington Lewis-Randall, Autherine Lucy, Mary Hamilton, Septima Clark, Bernard LaFayette, Ronald English, and Ella Baker included in this book are but a fraction of countless unsung freedom fighters who made the civil rights movement possible. As a Kingian Nonviolence trainer, educator, and person who cares about history, I believe I have a responsibility to continue learning and help elevate their stories so that we have an accurate account of our history, which is under assault right now. The contributions and stories of Black women, in particular, must be remembered if we are to have a fuller and richer understanding of our past—and how it can shape our present and future. Some of the elders I've named are still with us as of the time of this writing, and it has been a great honor getting to interview them and hear about their experiences in the movement.

In sharing their stories with you, however, I humbly ask that you see them as a sacred gift and integral part of how to embody and practice nonviolence. While there are certainly examples and strategies of nonviolence I share within and beyond the classroom, this book is not *just* a collection of classroom approaches. The stories in this book are not intended to be rushed through or skipped over in order to get to the "classroom stuff"; they help illuminate the *how* and *why* of nonviolence. We pay homage to those who have put their bodies and lives on the line for our freedom when we understand who they were and are.

Moreover, for those of us who are non-Black POC, white, or mixed race, we can educate ourselves about and lift up the stories of the Black freedom dreamers whose names are not as well known as the likes of King. Doing so alleviates the burden of others having to "teach" us what we don't already know and allows us to engage in an ongoing process of learning.

EMBRACING OUR INCOMPLETENESS

"I don't want to seem to sound as if I feel so self-righteous, or absolutist, that I think I have the only truth, the only way. Maybe he does have some of the answer." These words were said by Martin Luther King Jr. when writer Alex Haley asked for King's thoughts on Malcolm X during a 1965 interview with *Playboy* magazine

(Eig 2023a, 423). The quote, recently discovered from a transcript of the interview, shines important new light on King's view of himself and nonviolence. For decades, writers and historians pointed to an oft-quoted line from the originally published interview in which King supposedly said, "in [Malcom's] litany of articulating the despair of the Negro without offering any positive, creative alternative, I feel that Malcolm has done himself and our people a great disservice" (Eig 2023a, 422). But that quote appears to have been a mischaracterization of what King actually said, which was, "in [Malcom's] litany of expressing the despair of the Negro, without offering a positive, creative approach, I think that he falls into a rut sometimes."

Doubtless, King was critical of violence, saying that Malcolm X's "[f]iery, demagogic oratory in the black ghettos, urging Negroes to arm themselves and prepare to engage in violence can achieve nothing but negative results." But he also tried to be open-minded and recognized that he and Malcolm X shared common ground (Eig 2023a, 422–423). In stating that he does not have "the only truth, the only way," King acknowledges his *incompleteness*—that is, the idea that no one possesses all the answers and that there is *always* more to learn. There is great power in recognizing the limits of what we know and finding ways to expand our understanding, consciousness, and practice. When we learn from and grow with each other, we generate more expansive truths. In King's time, patriarchy and LGBTQIA+ phobia were not centered in the civil rights struggle as forces of injustice for the country to confront. Given the historical time period and context, it is understandable why that was, but, nonetheless, those issues were and remain very much alive.

I, too, do not claim to know it all nor have all the answers when it comes to nonviolence and teaching. I strive to always be in a state of learning and unlearning. Moreover, what I offer in this book is not "new." The wisdom and teachings from across nonviolence traditions have been passed down through generations and speak to a fundamental aspect of who we are: that we long to be in community and to give and receive love. This book is one educator's humble attempt to bring more attention to the need for nonviolence in ourselves, in our classrooms, and in our world. I hope that more practitioners can build on and strengthen what I offer here.

The last words Martin Luther King Jr. said to his friend and associate Bernard LaFayette were, "Now Bernard, the next and most important campaign we need to focus on is institutionalizing and internationalizing nonviolence" (LaFayette and Johnson 2015, 148). In the decades since King's death, LaFayette has made it his life's mission to carry out those last words he heard from his dear friend. He has brought King's teachings of nonviolence into schools, communities, prisons, law enforcement agencies, and other institutions in order to both "institutionalize and internationalize" nonviolence.

As a student of LaFayette's, as an educator, as a parent, and as someone who cares about the present state and future of our world, I, too, see it as my duty to help teach and preserve this sacred work and vision.

May this book contribute to and help advance the efforts of the many educators and young people working together to create spaces that sustain love, hope, and community.

May we, together, manifest the Beloved Community.

INNER
PRACTICE

"The Way of the Warrior has been misunderstood as a means to kill and destroy others....To smash, injure, or destroy is the worst sin a human being can commit. The real Way of the Warrior is to prevent such slaughter—it is the Art of Peace, the power of love."

MORIHEI UESHIBA, creator of aikido

Rethinking Nonviolence

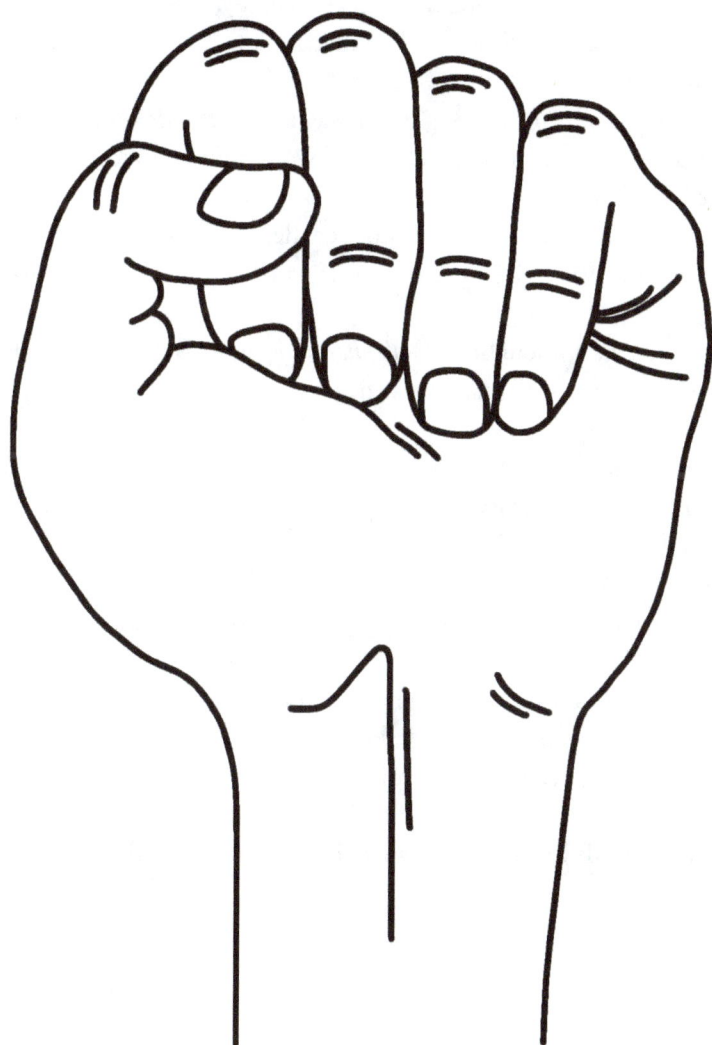

CHAPTER 1

Reclaiming Our Stories

"**Michael Tinoco**, please report to the principal's office. Michael Tinoco, please report to the principal's office."

I was sitting in class, caught off guard slightly, but not entirely surprised, to hear my name called over the intercom one day in late April of my eighth-grade year.

What'd I do this time? I thought as I walked casually down the hallway, my fingertips dragging along the lockers and worn out skate shoes squeaking on the checker-tiled floor.

When I turned the corner, I stopped dead in my tracks. Through the office window was a sight I hadn't anticipated: my mom talking to the principal.

What the...?!? I thought. *What's she doing here?* My mom, perpetually busy with raising five kids, almost never came to my school, basketball games, and parent conferences.

And then I remembered.

My breathing quickened and my heart pounded so strongly I could feel the blood pumping in my ears.

"Mom?" I asked hesitantly as I entered the office slowly.

She turned around with red, teary eyes and a bunched up tissue in one hand and said, "I'm so sorry, Mikey, but we have to go now."

"Go where?!?" I asked with panic and confusion, not wanting to hear what she was about to say.

"To the airport," she said, her voice tinged with regret and frayed from hours of crying.

I was stupefied. I hadn't even had a chance to pack my things, let alone say goodbye to anyone.

"*Right now?*" I asked. She nodded while dabbing her cheeks with the tissue.

"I packed a bag for you," she said.

My heart sank and tears began flooding my eyes like a dam bursting, no longer able to hold back the water.

A few nights before, I had been wrestling with my brother. But apparently I was too rough because he started yelling and called for my mom—a pattern that occurred with so much frequency, I could almost always predict her exact response and my correlating punishment.

But this time was different. She thought I had hurt him and yelled, "I'm done! I can't put up with this anymore. I'm sending you back to California to live with your dad."

My brother and I looked at each other, stunned. In recent months, my mom had threatened to send me to live with my dad whenever I had gotten into trouble, but hearing her say it would happen with such conviction now perplexed and shocked me.

"We were just playing, Mom," I said with flabbergast. "I'll leave him alone."

My brother jumped in, "Yeah, Mom, Mike was just messing around."

But my mom wouldn't budge. She was firm in her decision, and she listed the reasons why she thought I had to go: The incessant shoplifting. Multiple suspensions from school. Grades plummeting. Bullying. Sneaking out in the middle of the night. Stealing money from her. Burning things at home. Smoking weed and packs of cigarettes. Constantly fighting with her and my step dad. Nearly getting arrested more than once.

And she wasn't wrong. I was, indeed, engaging in self-destructive behavior that was only intensifying. But what she did not know, did not see, did not ask about—nor did anyone at school or anywhere else—was that I felt so utterly alone and subsumed by deep self-loathing, seeds of which were planted only a few years earlier. Around my tenth birthday, we moved away from San José, California, the place I called home, to Eugene, Oregon, a supposed bastion of liberalism that was predominantly white.

"Will I be able to come back and graduate with my friends?" I asked the principal, wiping my eyes with the back of my hands. "There's only one month left of eighth grade."

The principal rubbed his neck and shifted his gaze toward the floor. "Let's…let's see how it goes for you in California first, and then maybe we can look into it," he said with an air of forced optimism, as if he was trying to convince himself.

"We're worried about the path you're going down," my mom interjected, tears streaming down her face. "I know this is really hard for you, and it pains me to do this, but I believe it's the best thing for you."

I knew my mom felt desperate and wanted to help. But the intention behind those words did little to assuage the immense heartbreak I felt in that moment because the message I interpreted was a familiar one: I did not belong—not here in this city, not at this school, not at home, not even in my own skin.

Uprooted

Growing up, I was fully aware of the fact that I had brown skin and came from a mixed-race family. My maternal grandparents were immigrants from Peru and Hungary who married in the early 1950s. My father's side of the family came from Mexico, though both his parents were born and raised in California. I have several fond memories of my grandparents expressing their love for us and love of where they came from.

I remember Grandma Nilda's savory saltado that kept her memory of Lima alive and gave us a taste of home.

I remember the warm, handmade tortillas Grandpa Rudy made for us when we'd visit him at his farm in Manteca, and the distinctly sweet, raspy sound of his voice when he'd call me and my siblings mijito and mijita.

I remember Grandpa Tom's fingers dancing on the piano, creating a vibrant kaleidoscope of classical music whose primary hues came from Budapest.

I remember the black and white family album photos of Grandma Rachel, whom I never met but came to know through my father's stories.

What I don't have memory of, though, is sharing their language. Despite all of my grandparents being bilingual—three of them were fluent in Spanish—my mom and dad grew up speaking only English. Consequently, I did not learn what was not taught to me. Consciously or not, my grandparents' attempts to buy into the American Dream in the mid-twentieth century and forgo teaching my parents their native tongues contributed to an erasure of familial and cultural identity that would directly impact how I—and others—saw my Brownness.

Without having access to my grandparents' home languages, conduits through which culture and history are kept alive, I did not feel Mexican and Peruvian "enough." And this confused me because I looked like my paternal grandfather, Rudy, who had deep brown skin the color of the earth, distinctly thick eyebrows, and high cheekbones that made his eyes smile. I had

1.1

Me and my siblings with our mom, circa 1999. Personal collection.

the darkest skin out of everyone in my immediate family [Figure 1.1], and my phenotype and complexion were a constant reminder that I wasn't *really* white to the world around me even though I had European blood.

But where I felt a link to my grandfather in resemblance, there were vast gaps in what I knew of his and my other grandparents' early lives and respective cultural traditions. Aside from a few family recipes and stories passed down, their origins were largely a mystery to me—until adulthood, when I did research, conducted interviews, and met relatives I didn't know I had.

Moreover, we rarely, if ever, talked about our racial identities as a family; they just existed, like a painting in the background that everyone knows is there but doesn't stop to acknowledge and discuss. Connection to my family's heritage felt more peripheral than central to my identity growing up. Without a deep sense of knowing who and where I came from, I was like a tree, beautiful and unique in its own right, but susceptible to harm without roots firm enough to keep it tethered to the earth and to other trees. When the time came for us to relocate to Oregon, there was zero preparation for the culture shock I would experience, zero conversation about how to navigate white spaces as a Brown person.

Lost

Shortly after moving to Oregon, it was incredibly confusing to me when, for the first time, I was followed in stores by adults while the white kids were left alone. It was disconcerting to be asked, incessantly, "What *are* you?" because my ethnically ambiguous complexion was a site of constant curiosity. *Am I Latino? Just mixed? Do I get to claim more of my Mexican side since I'm technically half? But I don't speak Spanish and we don't practice Mexican traditions, so what does that make me? Am I more white than Brown?*

It was strange to notice that there were no other kids who looked like me in class; I was often one of few, or the only, Brown kid there. But most perplexing and painful was being called racist slurs by some of my own family, only to be called the same names, and worse, by the few friends—all white—I had at school. I would pretend to laugh it off in their presence, but internally, their words pierced me and led me to believe that there was something genuinely wrong with me.

Eventually, the pain imploded. I grew resentful for being Brown and hated who I saw in the mirror [Figure 1.2]. I internalized that I was an ugly, bad kid undeserving of others' affection. Save for my father who lived hundreds of miles away and was accessible primarily by the telephone, I believed that I did not matter to anyone. There was no one in my family, including my dad, who shared my experience, and, therefore, no one who could relate. My mom and step dad were busy caring for two very young children while simultaneously trying to raise three adolescents; the stress of their being overwhelmed parents, compounded by financial strain, led to frequent arguments and strife at home.

There was no wellness center at school, no social workers from whom to seek counseling. There were no assignments nor opportunities offered to write about my life, let alone help me process my experience. It was difficult to prioritize school when school didn't

1.2
My eighth-grade yearbook photo.
Personal collection.

prioritize me, so I gradually checked out and thought I wasn't smart enough to do well. All but one of my teachers were white, and I didn't know any of them well enough to confide in. I don't recall a single teacher ever inviting students to do so, either. Even if they had made themselves available, I'm not sure that I would have taken the initiative to approach them and had the courage to open up.

The Cost of Shame

"If you put shame in a petri dish, it needs three ingredients to grow exponentially: secrecy, silence, and judgment," says Brené Brown, a writer and researcher of shame and resilience (2012, 18:55).

The shame I carried was monstrous, and hiding it beneath a cloak of rage and "bad behavior" felt safer than revealing it. But this safety came at an immense cost, as my body was in a constant state of stress and anxiety: I developed anxious tics; I slept poorly and couldn't focus at school; I damaged my lungs with cigarettes, believing they would soothe my anxiety; I developed a short fuse and sometimes alarmed myself when I blew up at people (e.g., swearing at and almost hitting a teacher).

I once heard someone say that "when language is suppressed, sickness kicks in." I did not have the words to name what, exactly, I was experiencing; even *thinking* about it was something I tried to avoid. The story I told myself was that, somehow, I had brought this pain upon myself, and, thus, deserved it. Why would anyone come to my aid if the shame was merited? *Don't think about it. Don't talk about it. Just hide it and maybe it will go away*, I remember thinking.

But what if I had named it instead of suppressing it and projecting my woundedness onto others? What if I had named the emotions encased within the pain?

"If you put the same amount of shame in the Petri dish and douse it with empathy, it can't survive," Brené Brown adds (2012, 19:02).

I can't help but wonder how markedly different my younger—and future—self would have felt had I been shown how to douse myself with empathy. To connect with what my heart felt and yearned for, free of self-judgment and self-blame. To disrupt an all-too-common story many of us tell ourselves, especially when we're younger—that our needs and deepest yearnings don't matter when they go unseen, seem unattainable, and/or remain unmet.

Similarly, as educators, we are not immune from the effects of working in institutions that seldom center the humanity and holistic needs of both youth and adults. How many of us have ever felt as though our ideas, concerns, and experiences were not acknowledged? Not respected? Not valued? It is utterly demoralizing when it happens repeatedly.

Given that many of us work in school settings where there are polarizing political viewpoints, divergent teaching philosophies and practices, and a range of social identities with varying degrees of privilege and power, there are bound to be moments when we clash with and feel disconnected from others. Sometimes, we may even question the extent to which our experience is even real when it is neither shared nor recognized by others. If we feel isolated enough, perhaps some of us internalize self-judgments, such as:

- *Maybe I'm making too big a deal out of _____.*
- *Since no one else is speaking up about _____, maybe I shouldn't either.*
- *That was really stupid of me to _____.*
- *It didn't make any difference when I did/said _____, so why bother?*

But accurately naming and deeply connecting with our internal experience, whether we are young people or adults, enables us to be attuned to what is alive within us—and doing so reminds us that our experience is valid. This attunement can offer great clarity about what truly matters to us and help us come back to ourselves when we feel disconnected from others and even ourselves.

In this chapter, we will reclaim part of our story of when we were younger by practicing self-empathy. The purpose of doing so is to help us connect with the needs we yearned to fulfill when we were younger. This process, in turn, is intended to support us in creating (or strengthening already existing) classrooms that center needs, thereby honoring the humanity of our students and ourselves.

accurately naming and deeply connecting with our internal experience, whether we are young people or adults, enables us to be attuned to what is alive within us

CONNECTING WITH OUR YOUNGER SELVES

I would like to present a framework and consciousness practice mentioned in the Introduction that we will draw from and use throughout this book. Nonviolent Communication (NVC) is a powerful approach to engaging with ourselves and others through empathy and moving through the world more authentically. As my friend, mentor, and NVC trainer Dr. Roxy Manning says, Nonviolent Communication gives people "permission and freedom to be themselves"—permission to *feel* (2020, 0:23).

For our purposes here, I will demonstrate how to apply NVC by connecting with my younger self, and then I'll invite you to do the same. The intention is twofold. First, by empathizing with your younger self, you are practicing an integral skill that you can continue to use for yourself now, as an adult. Second, empathizing with your younger self will also, I hope, support you in centering the needs of the students in your classroom, school, or whatever context you may be working in.

NVC rests on the assumption that every single human behavior is an attempt to meet one or more needs (Kashtan and Kashtan n.d.). Through deep listening, in part, to feelings that arise in relation to needs that are either met or unmet in any given moment, NVC helps us to better understand the motivations behind our behavior and offers tremendous opportunity for building and sustaining connection (Manning 2020, 0:30–4:20). According to renowned NVC teacher and leader Miki Kashtan, "needs are the fundamental motivators for all our actions, as well as what gives meaning to all our experiences"—that is, they "provide the 'why' for everything we do" (2014a, 10).

NVC also supports us in noticing and unlearning patterned thoughts and habitual responses that do not necessarily serve us in the most helpful ways but that we have nonetheless been conditioned to rely on. NVC creator Marshall Rosenberg once said, "While we may not consider the way we talk to be 'violent,' words often lead to hurt and pain, whether for others or ourselves" (2015, 2–3). Even if we do not say the words aloud, negative judgments we formulate about ourselves (or others) that lead to hurt or suffering are ultimately not life-serving, especially when we are younger and more vulnerable.

In the following section, I invite you to reflect on your younger self and describe a difficult or painful moment in which you experienced self-blame or self-judgment. Perhaps you felt unseen, unheard, misunderstood, alone, or harmed in some way. By drawing from NVC and continuing to weave in my own story alongside yours, the goal here is to connect with the heart of your younger self, to be in touch with feelings you experienced in relation to needs of yours that weren't met.

If, as discussed in the Introduction, nonviolence centers relationality, then part of that practice must entail connecting with ourselves; we cannot practice nonviolence if we do not practice self-connection. This is a starting point for us to disrupt harmful stories we've told ourselves in order to create alternate stories of who we are and want the world to be, particularly in our role as educators.

Connecting with Your Younger Self

▷ What is a difficult or painful experience from your childhood or adolescence that significantly affected how you showed up in the world?

▷ What kinds of judgments did you receive from others and/or tell yourself?

▷ What role did school play in how you interpreted or felt about the experience?

Identify Feelings

Feelings represent our emotional state and bodily sensations and help us experience life in a meaningful way (Kashtan and Kashtan n.d.). NVC holds that feelings surface when needs are either met or unmet. For example, if I am reuniting with a sibling I have not seen in a long time, I may feel *joyful* because I am connecting with someone I care deeply about. If I slept for a full eight hours overnight, I may feel *energized* because I got adequate rest.

When I was at my lowest point in Oregon, I remember feeling *dejected* a lot of the time because there was little fulfillment in my life, and I did not sense any prospect of my circumstances improving. I also remember feeling *lonely* because I believed I had no one to talk to about my experience; I seldom smiled or laughed and found little reason to engage with most people. My body was often *tense* and *tired*, and I rarely felt relaxed. Despite the discomfort of the stress and compounding pain, I did not know how to cope in a way that was not self-defeating. Both at home and at school, I wore alternating masks of *anger* and *sadness* to hide the massive insecurity and shame that pervaded my being.

The Feelings Inventory [Figure 1.3], available in Appendix A, is a partial list of some of the many emotions that we experience. The list is adapted from the Feelings Inventory developed by the Center for Nonviolent Communication. It is deliberately presented as only a *partial* list of the many emotions we experience as people and is intended to serve as an accessible resource that my high school students can refer to continually throughout the year. They keep a copy in their notebook, and there are multiple occasions when they reflect on their own feelings and those of others (subsequent chapters will share examples of what this looks like).

Please take a moment to review the Feelings Inventory and identify the feeling(s) associated with the experience about which you wrote.

Peaceful	Happy	Compassionate
Calm	Glad	Affectionate
Content	Excited	Warm
Satisfied	Joyful	Tender
Relaxed	Pleased	Appreciative
Quiet, still	Amused	Friendly
Secure	Encouraged	Moved
Tranquil	Confident	Passionate
Centered	Hopeful	Loving
Safe	Proud	Sympathetic
Serene	Blissful	Open-hearted

Frustrated	Sad	Scared
Impatient	Lonely	Terrified
Annoyed	Hurt	Afraid
Irritable	Heavy	Nervous
Agitated	Broken-hearted	Desperate
Disgusted	Disappointed	Cautious
Furious	Helpless	Insecure
Enraged	Hopeless	Confused
Mad/bitter	Discouraged	Uncertain
Anxious	Overwhelmed	Stressed
Cranky	Tired	Shocked

1.3

Feelings Inventory. Emojis designed by my former student Keilani Mae Jasmin.

▷ What feelings did you experience during the moment you wrote about?
Please list or describe them here.

Identify Unmet Needs

As human beings, we all have needs—such as water, food, rest, belonging, purpose, to name a few—which are necessary for our survival. They are universal and underlie everything we say and do. When needs are met, our quality of life is enriched and we are more likely to thrive than if our needs were to remain unmet, especially over prolonged periods of time.

As painful as it was to experience the emotions I felt as a youth, I now recognize that they were teachers eliciting wisdom. They were pointing to unmet needs of mine that I was yearning to have fulfilled, even if I did not consciously realize it.

One of the needs I yearned for was *to matter*—to know that my existence meant something and that I was worthy of other people's time, attention, and care. Without these things, it makes complete sense why I regularly felt dejected and lonely. In hindsight, I don't doubt that I was loved by my mom and step dad; however, their preoccupation with caring for my two younger siblings while simultaneously trying to raise us three older kids eclipsed their ability to be present and express their love in a manner that actually felt *loving* for me.

As for the group of white kids I hung out with, I was so desperate for *friendship* that I would rather subject myself, daily, to racist taunts, ridicule, and illicit activity than be alone. I also wanted some semblance of *control* since I often felt so powerless; I was willing to engage in (self-)destructive behavior, even if it meant compromising my own well-being. I now realize how toxic and tragic that line of thinking is, but I am holding abundant compassion for my younger self, who was merely in survival mode.

Another core need of mine that was largely unmet during that time was *support*. While the lectures and punishments I received at home and school may have been intended to redirect my behavior, I did not at all experience them as supportive in helping me understand the source of my pain. It was convenient, I believe, for the adults to simply see a disobedient youth who was "going down the wrong path." According to this logic, I was the source of my own problems because I exercised poor judgment in making bad choices. But such choices were born from having so little worth and being bombarded with messages that to be Brown was to not belong. What other "path" was there for me? There was no one to help guide my fourteen-year-old wounded self toward a different way.

Furthermore, I think the anger I felt was largely due to my intuitive sense that there was *something* beyond my control causing me great distress, even if I could neither recognize nor articulate it. I remember also feeling sad and frustrated every time I was admonished for getting in trouble because, while I "knew better," I did not know how to make my circumstances better. It was as though *I* was an undiagnosable problem needing to be fixed.

The Needs Inventory [Figure 1.4], available in Appendix B, is a partial list of the many needs and values that we share as human beings. I adapted this visual representation of human needs from the Needs Inventory developed by the Center for Nonviolent Communication. Similar to the list of feelings introduced earlier, my students have a copy of this list in their notebooks which they refer to regularly throughout the year (subsequent chapters will share examples). Please take a moment to review the Needs Inventory and write down the needs associated with the feelings you identified earlier.

Purpose, Growth, Meaning
awareness/consciousness,
understanding, learning, discovery, truth,
making sense of life, mattering, service,
creativity, expression, contribution,
achievement, aliveness, faith, hope,
inspiration, effectiveness

**Security and Safety
(physical or emotional)**
consistency
predictability
structure
stability
protection
peace of mind
trust

Connection and Belonging
presence, trust, love, friendship,
companionship, community,
acceptance, empathy, affection,
appreciation, support,
communication, openness,
respect, care,
shared values,
being seen/heard/understood

Peace, Freedom, Justice
dignity, respect
harmony, beauty, ease
kindness, warmth
peace/respect for others
choice, independence
empowerment
cooperation
partnership, shared values
mattering

Sustenance and Well-Being
food, air, water
space, spaciousness
shelter, survival
rest, sleep
play, movement
clothing
health, nutrition
healing (physical or emotional)
expression (joy, anger, etc.)

1.4

Needs Inventory.

▷ Thinking back to the difficult childhood or adolescent experience
you reflected on earlier, which of your needs seemed hindered,
unattainable, or were otherwise unmet? Please list / describe them
here.

As you reflect back on this experience from when you were younger, here are some
reflection questions for consideration:

- What insights or new understandings emerge for you?
- Do you feel more compassion for your younger self?
- What do you wish you or others would have done differently?
- What would you say to the adults who were around at that time?
- What would you say to the younger you?

If I could talk to my younger self, I would say:

Mikey,

You are hurting right now, but you did not create your own wounds.

The anger you're feeling and acting upon is due to not having the support you need.

When you lash out at people, you feel helpless because you want to be understood but don't know how to be.

Beneath the sadness and loneliness is a deep yearning to know that you matter.

And while you might not be hearing it from others right now, hear it from me:

You are beautiful. Your brown skin is sacred. You are enough as you are.

You simply want to *be* in this world.

During those moments of intense hurt, give yourself space to be alone, to breathe, to rest.

It is completely okay to be by yourself.

Mom and Jim love you, but they are also hurting and don't know how to help.

They might listen if you tell them that you are in pain—even if they are part of it.

Dad might be 600 miles away, but his voice is within reach.

He'll listen if you tell him what's in your heart.

Hop back on those rollerblades that used to make you feel alive.

Keep moving even if you don't know where, exactly, to go.

I'll be here waiting for you.

Thank you for being you, for being me, for being here.

I love you,

Mike

▷ If you feel moved to do so, I invite you to write a message to your younger self, giving the younger you the compassion, encouragement, and/or advice you needed to hear at that time. If it is helpful, here is an optional sentence starter:

When you experienced _____ , you felt _____ because you needed _____

_____
_____
_____
_____
_____
_____
_____
_____
_____
_____
_____
_____
_____
_____
_____
_____
_____
_____
_____
_____
_____
_____
_____
_____
_____
_____
_____
_____
_____
_____
_____

CREATING A NEW STORY

When we disrupt the self-judgments we may have internalized when we were younger, we create an alternate narrative of who we were, who we are. As we practice becoming more attuned to our unmet needs, we increase the likelihood of stepping into our power, in any given moment, and imagining ways to *interrupt* stories that others have created for us. That is, we interrupt stories that distort who we are and inhibit who we can be.

We, as educators, may sometimes feel as though the systems within which we work are so rigid and the status quo so entrenched in school culture that things cannot change. Perhaps we have been told such by well-meaning administrators, fellow teachers, friends, or family—or maybe we've told that to ourselves. Maybe you have heard, said, or thought the following:

- "People may come and go, but the system will always be the same."
- "A corrupt system cannot be changed from the inside."
- "That idealism will wear off once you've been here as long as I have."
- "Things never change around here."

During moments of doubt or when we feel as though we've lost our way, it is essential that we do not lose sight of *why* we started teaching in the first place. There was something that pulled you, me, and our fellow teachers to this beautiful calling, and chances are, the reason was innately connected to your core values and what you want to contribute to the world. Connected to what you dream(ed) of for yourself and others. If we become jaded to the point where our hope for creating more loving and humanizing schools dims, then that can rub off on our students. And I can think of few things more tragic than young people believing that the world as it is cannot be changed.

In the next chapter, we will look at a moment in history when youth against insurmountable odds disrupted a harmful narrative about how others saw them and freedom-dreamed their way into writing their *own* story, demanding to be seen for who they actually were. This story will then guide us into thinking more deeply about the vision each of us holds as educators and how to manifest it with our students.

CHAPTER 2

A Conscious(ness) Shift

Gloria Washington Lewis-Randall was a student at A.H. Parker High School in Birmingham, Alabama in 1963 [Figure 2.1] when she and thousands of other youth grew tired of the violence and dehumanizing grip of white supremacy that they, their families, and communities were subjected to every day.

Segregation was a fact of life in Birmingham, which, at that time, had experienced over fifty racially motivated and unsolved bombings, earning the moniker "Bombingham." The Ku Klux Klan had members in the city's police department and throughout city hall, reifying institutional racism (Houston 2005). In staunch opposition to civil rights activists' efforts to integrate, then-Governor of Alabama, George Wallace, infamously said in his inaugural address in January of 1963, "segregation now, segregation tomorrow, and segregation forever." Dr. Martin Luther King Jr. himself called Birmingham "the most thoroughly segregated city in the United States" (King 2015a, 129).

"As a kid I always wanted to eat at Newberry's downtown, and I always wanted the big hamburger plate...we couldn't have that," recounts Lewis-Randall in the 2004 documentary *The Children's March* about an experience shared by many Black youth at the time (Houston 2005). Segregation was dumbfounding to her, and she recalls asking her mother, "'Ma, why I got to sit in the back of this bus?' or 'Why can't I go to the zoo and ride a train?'" to which her mother would respond, "'That's just the way it is'" (Patterson 2014, chap. "Gloria Washington Lewis-Randall").

Who can blame her mother for responding this way? On more than one occasion, her family had faced terror at the hands of the police. In a conversation I had with Lewis-Randall, she told me about such an encounter she and her parents experienced one Sunday. As they often did after church, the family drove around the city for fun, and on this particular day, they drove by East Lake Park, one of many segregated areas, when young Gloria "saw a duck in the beautiful water, swimming around" and said, "I gotta see the duck!" (Lewis-Randall 2022).

Her mother "started hollering and screaming," telling her father, "'No! You know she can't go to that park—*you* can't go to that park. That park's not for us.'" Upon hearing this, young Gloria thought to herself, "Then who's the park for? When you say 'us,' who are you talking about?" (2022).

Her father, wanting to indulge his daughter's innocent wish—even if just for a moment—stopped the car, got them out, and let her look at the duck. Seconds later, however, two white police officers approached the family, castigating them while hurling the n-word, before hitting her father in the head with a billy club right in front of her.

Lewis-Randall's mother was not alone in her desire to not "trouble the waters." Many Black people were employed by whites, and fear of retaliation (i.e., unemployment, loss of income, violence, even death) for participating in integration efforts was prevalent. There were adults, including parents, who attended mass meetings, participated in protests, or even went to jail, but early efforts by the Southern Christian Leadership Conference (SCLC), the organization for which King served as President, to mobilize mass support for and involvement in the movement did not result in the numbers they had hoped for (Gilmore 2021). Even King's arrest, holding in solitary confinement, and eventual release from jail "barely caused a ripple" (Houston 2005).

Similarly, at school, the issue of segregation and activism was not broached in class, as far as Lewis-Randall recalls. "I can't ever remember…it didn't come out of civics, it didn't come out of social studies, it didn't come out of government," she said. If teachers were to bring it up, the ramifications were stark and well-understood:

> They were told that if any of the kids were involved in the civil rights movement or talked about the civil rights movement and it came from them and their classes, then they would be dismissed from the school system.…Everybody had to take care of their families and had to eat, so they needed their jobs (Lewis-Randall 2022).

Although such discussions may not have occurred inside Lewis-Randall's classes, they most certainly took place with her friends. In particular, they discussed a degrading sentiment they shared of being forced to use segregated, lower quality amenities downtown:

A lot of the conversations that were taking place between my friends and I were, 'Have you noticed, girl, that you can't go to the bathroom when we go to town at Newberry's or change at Woolworth's? And when you do, you have to go downstairs where the bathrooms are nasty and filthy…nobody wants to use them' (2022).

The absence of these discussions at school notwithstanding, Lewis-Randall fondly remembers her teachers, all of whom were Black, as "wonderful" and "the cream of the crop," who "always went the extra step to help the kids." She excelled academically and was in advanced placement courses. Her achievement was undergirded by the knowledge that she was supported and loved by her teachers, who encouraged the students to envision their life trajectory and consider the kind of legacy they wanted to leave behind. "Our teachers talked about the future," she recalls. They would ask the students, "'What have you decided to do with your life? How can you make a

2.1

Gloria Washington Lewis-Randall at age sixteen, from her school yearbook. Photo courtesy of Lewis-Randall.

difference? What will *you* do to make sure your epitaph reads that you were here?'" (2022).

And make a difference she felt inspired and determined to do, yet the gulf between the push for her to attend college to attain success and the brutality of segregated life frustrated her. In his book *Birmingham Foot Soldiers: Voices from the Civil Rights Movement*, journalist Nick Patterson featured a profile of Lewis-Randall in which she said, "I wanted to make a difference [but] I could not understand why my parents were dead-bound on me going to college, achieving and being all I can be—and I'm a second-class citizen, probably a third-class citizen" (2014, chap. "Gloria Washington Lewis-Randall"). A recurring and potent thought that ran through her mind was, *"Something's wrong with this picture"* (2022).

She did not, however, think "negatively" of individuals who avoided discussing or involving themselves in the civil rights struggle, as she understood the fear that segregation instilled and the psychological toll it had; still, to her, "silence simply means consent." Other participants in the movement, like Gwendolyn Webb, echoed a similar sentiment: "As a kid we always wanted to think that these things would stop soon…and mom and dad, since they fixed everything else, that they would fix it" (Houston 2005). To young people like Gloria and Gwendolyn, the older they got, the more tired they grew of hearing that their circumstances were more fixed than fixable.

And so, with discontent brewing at the material conditions of segregated life and feeling buttressed by the love and "sanctity of the community" in which they were raised, Lewis-Randall and scores of other young people heeded the call to participate in the movement when most adults could not or would not—to dismantle the oppressive story that they were *less than* by fighting to meet their needs for freedom, dignity, and justice.

Lewis-Randall attended mass meetings at 16th Street Baptist Church, where Rev. James Bevel, one of SCLC's leaders, mobilized and trained young people in nonviolent tactics. Then, on May 2, 1963, known as "D-Day," Gloria and her peers walked out of class and took to the streets as planned [Figure 2.2]. She walked "hand in hand" with a classmate toward city hall, where upon arriving, she turned around, pulled out a sign from her pants that read "We shall overcome," knelt down, prayed, and then waited to be arrested.

The nearly 1,000 arrests of kids on the first day did nothing to stop the momentum of resistance that was building, so the police and fire department, at the order of Commissioner of Public Safety, Eugene "Bull" Connor, ratcheted up their efforts to intimidate and contain the protests.

2.2

Students and supporters outside of 16th Street Baptist Church, the central meeting location for the youth participating in the Birmingham Campaign.

One of their violent tactics was spraying the kids with high-powered "water cannons," as Lewis-Randall called them. The water pressure was so intense that, in addition to knocking her over, the blast rendered her deaf in her left ear when she was hit. "I never could rectify that," she said (2022).

When the jails were filled to capacity, law enforcement resorted to detaining kids at the fairgrounds. While there, Lewis-Randall recalled a horrifying incident in which a police officer attempted to sexually assault a young woman in the middle of the night. Lewis-Randall and several other girls "jumped on him and took his billy club," using it to effectively ward him off.

She was subsequently transferred to Jefferson County Jail, where she was subjected to humiliating treatment, like being told to scrub the floor with a toothbrush. On another occasion, she mentioned to a guard that she had rheumatic fever as a child and was worried that her heart would give out, to which the guard responded, "'We'll throw you in the sweatbox until your heart gets better.'" The sweatbox—a confining metal contraption with several locks—was "made like an oven. You had to slide backwards into it,"

Lewis-Randall described to Wyatt Cenac on his HBO show *Problem Areas* (Hawkins 2018).

Whereas many of the kids were released from jail within a few days, Lewis-Randall was ultimately held for nearly a *month*. Understandably, the experience was traumatizing to her and still affects her today. When, for instance, HBO producers were able to find photographs of her in jail and of the sweatbox—the latter of which prison officials had previously denied the existence of, according to her—she said, "I had flashbacks, and I had to go to the emergency room" (2022).

But her involvement in the Children's Crusade of 1963 also equipped her with invaluable wisdom for which she will forever be grateful. "Sometimes, you have to try to turn tragedy into something positive," she told me. "We can't hate; don't teach your children to hate. Babies are like sponges—they soak up everything. *Knowledge* is your power. Knowledge is what you use [to fight]. No one can take that from you." It was advice humbly given by a warrior to a teacher and father, but she might just as well have been talking directly to my hurting, younger self in Eugene, Oregon, who did not know my own worth and power nor how to be in kinship with myself. Might just as well have been talking to my parents, educators, and all other adults who care for young people about the importance of *knowing* and *loving* ourselves—and each other. About never losing hope, no matter how hard the circumstances. About believing in one's own capacity to meet needs, effect change, and create the kind of world that one dreams of.

The profound impact of the Children's Crusade on national legislation and local institutions was not a result of spontaneous nonviolent demonstrations that just happened to work out. "The movement was scientific, educational, and spiritual," says Lewis-Randall. "It was a combination of all three. And all those things were involved in the planning and strategy." The young people believed—and *felt*—that they were part of something much larger than themselves, and committing to nonviolence enabled them to embody values that were not reflected in the society in which they lived. They and the adults who participated literally forged an alternate way of being by holding to a shared vision and aligning their action to that vision. Nonviolence wasn't and isn't about *not* doing; it is about engaging deeply with problems and conflict and taking an active stance against injustice in order to effect change.

The Children's March is one of many historical examples that greatly inspires me, especially as a teacher. So often, youth are told what to do, what not to do, and reprimanded when they do something we adults don't like. But what if we and our students were to hold a shared vision and work toward building it, together? Working together to disrupt forms of violence that may exist in our classroom, school, and beyond?

In this chapter, we will focus on articulating the vision each of us holds as educators and how to move toward that vision with our students. In particular, this chapter will support us in identifying the core needs and values that undergird our vision and in developing classroom approaches that would fulfill those needs and values. I will also share with you my vision as an educator, how it came to be, and how it informs my teaching.

Reflecting on this Historical Moment

▷ Where do you see young people today exercising similar power and agency as Gloria Washington Lewis-Randall and other youth from the Children's March?

A RADICAL SHIFT

NVC trainer Miki Kashtan writes in her book *Spinning Threads of Radical Aliveness: Transcending the Legacy of Separation in Our Individual Lives* that "[w]e need vision in order to be able to see outside of what we have been told is the only possibility that exists" (2014b, 199). Sometimes our vision can be obscured by our own pain, internalized oppression, or lack of awareness. But when we are able to move "outside of the normative story of the society into which we were born," centering and practicing nonviolence in such a way that it "affects our habits of action and even our emotional responses in addition to our beliefs," we cultivate what she calls "radical consciousness" (2014b, 200, 208).

It is the kind of consciousness that fueled Martin Luther King Jr.'s vision of the Beloved Community, which radically and unapologetically challenged a culture of normalized violence by offering a fundamentally different path forward for society. Originally coined by theologian and founder of the Fellowship of Reconciliation, Josiah Royce, and popularized by King, the Beloved Community is a vision of society in which relationships are elevated to a degree where injustice is not tolerated for anyone, and liberation from all forms of oppression is a collective effort. Conflicts are able to be resolved and reconciled, offering a path of healing, rather than become sources of strife, division, and violence (The King Center n.d.). King believed that a culture of violence cannot sustain and must necessarily give way to a culture of nonviolence when we recognize and celebrate our interdependence and collectively build institutions that actually meet everyone's needs. The Beloved Community was a kind of North Star that guided the vision and heart of the civil rights movement.

Many educators, too, believe that a different world is possible. Classrooms can be, and often are, sites of immense possibility, hope, and change when we trust that what we are doing with our young people is in service of something larger than the subject and standards we teach. Larger than academic performance. Larger than college and career readiness.

Even for those who are not necessarily driven by a vision of an alternate world, I have never met a teacher who did not hold the intention of wanting to help their students do well in some capacity. I *have* met plenty of disillusioned ones, some of whom had questionable, even harmful, classroom practices and ways of trying to support their students, but even then, those were mere strategies— albeit problematic ones—to meet needs.

And at the end of the day, isn't that, ultimately, what we are doing with and for our students and for ourselves as teachers—attempting to meet needs? If the suppression, neglect, violation, or impediment of needs is what allows violence to exist, then, too, the centering of needs exponentially increases the capacity for nonviolence to flourish in our classroom, school, and beyond so long as the focus on needs is aligned to a vision grounded in nonviolence.

HONORING OUR VISION

In a moment, I will share with you the journey of how I came to hold the vision that shapes who I am and how I teach, as well as the values that underpin this vision. First, though, I invite you to think about your own vision, even if it is not necessarily explicitly grounded in nonviolence or the concept of Beloved Community. We will return to this vision of yours soon.

Your Vision

▷ In your school community, what do you most yearn for as an educator? Consider your hopes for yourself, your students, the school, and the world.

▷ Why is this vision important to you?

Growing Pains

When I first started teaching, my vision was nascent in form and more abstract than concrete. I knew that I wanted to create a space where students could flourish academically, socially, and emotionally and feel supported on their respective paths. Popular ideas like social justice, culturally responsive teaching, social and emotional learning, to name a few, were concepts that I deeply valued—and certainly still do—but at the time, I did not have an overarching framework that cohered them together. I generally had a clear sense of the skills, texts, and essential questions I wanted to teach, but I couldn't satisfactorily answer for myself, on a consistent basis, three questions that loomed:

- *Toward what ends am I teaching this?*
- *Am I doing it as effectively, creatively, and engaging as I can?*
- *How is this helping students, right now, in their lives?*

The lack of clarity sometimes resulted in inconsistent efficacy of and engagement with lessons. There were days that felt as though we were on top of the world, right there from our classroom. And there were plenty of others when lessons fell flat or when we were just going through the motions. Plenty of days when I struggled to bridge the gap between what I envisioned for my students and how to get there. When I questioned if I was really cut out for teaching at all.

It was around this time that I read Dr. Jeff Duncan-Andrade's book *What a Coach Can Teach a Teacher: Lessons Urban Schools Can Learn from a Successful Sports Program* (2010). In it, he describes a set of twelve principles he developed for his students in East Oakland, adapted from legendary college basketball coach Pat Summitt's twelve rules to live by. Named the Definite Dozen, these principles constitute a kind of code that embodies the mentality of a "warrior scholar," a concept Duncan-Andrade borrows from *Hagakure: The Book of the Samurai* (2014, 12:30–13:33). In addition to achieving academic excellence, warrior scholars aspire to develop self-discipline, honesty, loyalty, critical awareness of and solutions to injustice, among other qualities, in order to see themselves as agents of change in their schools and communities.

Duncan-Andrade's students would commit the Definite Dozen to memory, and, together, they would recite them every day in class as a reminder of their collective purpose. It was a "rite of passage" that supported his goal of "teach[ing] students to understand the ways in which school can be unfair, how to navigate those injustices, and how to take advantage of the places where school can offer them opportunity" (2010, 117). I felt deeply inspired and pulled to create my own set of principles, but I lacked confidence to emulate such a strong framework as a novice teacher. So I put it off.

Shortly thereafter, a former colleague shared with me a similar set of principles they adopted in their own classroom. Inspired by Duncan-Andrade's Definite Dozen, this colleague's principles focused on self-love, self-respect, self-discipline, and community regeneration. I appreciated the emphasis on developing character to empower themselves and their communities, and I saw how students gravitated toward a collective identity and purpose they felt invested in. Again, I felt pulled and thought more deeply about creating my own, but I did not yet know how to *integrate* them in the classroom. It was one thing to have them posted in the room and referenced; it was another thing entirely to effectively embody them with students, putting them into practice.

And then I read, really for the first time, some of Martin Luther King Jr.'s most thought-provoking sermons, speeches, and essays [Figure 2.3]. I read the ones typically *not* taught in school because I wanted to understand how nonviolence could be applied today as a driving force for social change, especially within the education system. Up until that point, I had thought nonviolence simply meant being "not violent"—being passive in the face of violence. Little did I know how sorely misguided I was.

Pilgrimage to Nonviolence

Particularly illuminating for me was learning about King's journey to nonviolence and the six tenets of his philosophy, which was critical to the success of the Montgomery Movement and subsequent campaigns. In "Pilgrimage to Nonviolence" from his book *Stride Toward Freedom*, King said, "Living through the actual experience of the protest, nonviolence became more than a method to which I gave intellectual assent; it became a commitment to a way of life" (1958, 101). *A way of life*. I could not recall ever having heard someone characterize nonviolence as such. I was intrigued by the notion that it could be anything but a passive tactic for protesting, anything but "turning the other cheek."

King then illustrates how it can be a way of life by laying out the six principles that define his philosophy of nonviolence.

First, nonviolence is the way of the strong person, for it draws from and strengthens our creative, emotional, mental, and spiritual capacities.

Second, it challenges us to see all people as redeemable and worthy of being part of the Beloved Community; if the fruition of such a community is our goal—our vision—then the means must be consistent with the ends.

Third, nonviolence focuses on attacking forces of injustice and oppression rather than individuals perpetuating these destructive forces; systems and ideas, not people, are what need to be changed.

Fourth, nonviolence invites those who are willing and have the capacity to suffer voluntarily. Doing so, King argues, has "tremendous educational and transforming possibilities" in garnering support, galvanizing communities, and effecting change (1958, 103).

Fifth, nonviolence "avoids not only external physical violence but also internal violence of the spirit" by projecting an "ethic of love to the center of our lives" (1958, 103–104). King calls this love agape (pronounced uh-gah-pay), which seeks to win the "friendship and understanding" of one's opponent rather than "defeat or humiliate" them. It is a kind of "love in action" that aims to "preserve and create community…even when one seeks to break it" (1958, 102, 105).

And sixth, nonviolence calls on us to have "deep faith in the future"—to trust that our efforts will not be in vain because "the universe is on the side of justice" (1958, 106–107). This principle is about being willing and able to endure short-term setbacks and disappointments and staying invested in the long-term struggle.

Heretofore, I did not fully grasp nor appreciate the potency that nonviolence could have on an individual, community, and society. Reading the six tenets of

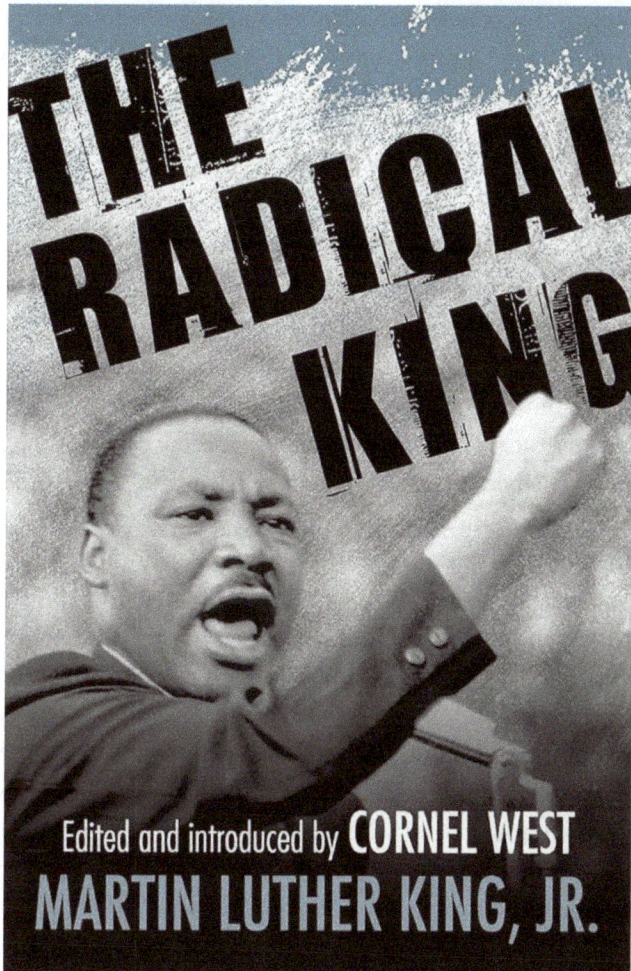

2.3

The Radical King, edited by Dr. Cornel West, contains some of King's most radical writings, speeches, and sermons. They are thematically organized and show the progression of King's thinking and radicalism.

King's philosophy of nonviolence, however, helped me understand that it was a powerful force that could be practiced internally and interpersonally and applied institutionally.

As I continued reading and listening to King's speeches and writings, I was surprised by what I had not known previously and was bothered that this history had not been taught to me as a student in school. I did not know how vehemently King had chastised the United States for its "triple evils" of racism, militarism, *and* poverty—and how harshly he was rebuked for it, especially when he condemned the war in Vietnam. I was not aware that he once applied for a gun permit. I had no idea how increasingly outspoken, and subsequently isolated, he was near the end of his life. I had no clue that the FBI surveilled him and suggested that he should die by suicide. I was ignorant of just how unyieldingly radical and visionary he was in spite of the hatred and violence continually leveled at him, his family, and his people.

Nonviolence, more than anything else I knew of, seemed truly revolutionary, and I was eager to figure out how to embody and cultivate an ethic of nonviolence within and beyond my classroom—and invite my students to do the same. And so, I searched for trainings and groups, hoping to find a space where I could practice nonviolence in community and not just read about it. The Nonviolent Leadership for Social Justice retreat (NLSJ) was one such space. Focusing on integrating NVC and anti-oppressive, liberatory, and social change work, NLSJ brought together people of diverse backgrounds and identities.

From emerging and seasoned activists to novice and fluent NVC practitioners, the NLSJ retreat supported participants in building, sustaining, and repairing connections with each other. We shared our stories, hopes, and mournings and discussed how to dismantle systems of oppression. We had empathy groups where we got to practice receiving each other with empathic listening. When conflicts inevitably arose within the community, the trainers, with great skill, grace, and humility, modeled how to prioritize those who were negatively impacted while holding care for everyone's needs. It was a life-changing experience unlike anything I had ever been part of before. I went back year after year and eventually became an organizer and trainer.

Shortly after my first NLSJ retreat, I found out about an upcoming Kingian Nonviolence workshop that focused on King's philosophy and methodology of nonviolence. I was unaware that such a training even existed; I registered immediately and could not wait to learn more. Similar to my experience with NLSJ, the Kingian Nonviolence workshop was transformative. I learned even more about King's radical philosophy of nonviolence and how his teachings and example could be applied today. And, as I did with NLSJ, I returned to several subsequent workshops before eventually becoming a certified Kingian Nonviolence trainer myself.

The Way of the Warrior

At the time that I had begun learning about Kingian Nonviolence and NVC, I did not yet consciously know, but intuitively felt, that nonviolence was what I had been seeking and needing for much of my life. As I continued studying and practicing NVC and Kingian Nonviolence, I soon learned about the Japanese martial art aikido.

When I started practicing aikido at a nearby dojo, I was introduced to writings and teachings by its creator, Morihei Ueshiba. One of the teachings that profoundly resonated with me early on was his belief that to be a warrior is, first and foremost, to love:

> The Way of the Warrior has been misunderstood as a means to kill and destroy others....To smash, injure, or destroy is the worst sin a human being can commit. The real Way of the Warrior is to prevent such slaughter—it is the Art of Peace, the power of love (1992, 8).

Ueshiba believed that we already possess the wisdom and wherewithal to create peace—to be true warriors—so long as we are willing to be guided by love for humanity, "put ourselves in tune with the universe, maintain peace in our own realms, nurture life, and prevent death and destruction" (1992, 45). I was awestruck because this definition of a warrior was so antithetical to the ubiquitous messages I grew up hearing about what it means to be a fighter: to defeat, overpower, and destroy.

The moment I embarked on my own pilgrimage to nonviolence is the moment when my consciousness and pedagogy fundamentally shifted—when my vision crystalized and tenets of that vision were born.

A Moment for Reflection

- How do you define nonviolence?
- How do King's, Ueshiba's, and/or Kashtan's ideas add to or challenge your understanding of nonviolence?

ALIGNING MEANS WITH ENDS

Let's now take a look at my vision and classroom principles [Figure 2.4], which are grounded in King's vision of the Beloved Community, Ueshiba's teachings of the way of the warrior, and Miki Kashtan's concept of radical consciousness. These are named the principles of a warrior scholar, based on my own interpretation of what a warrior scholar is [Figure 2.5].

> ### Mike's Vision
>
> I yearn for a world that values the humanity of all people; takes an active stance against injustice; centers human needs; values interconnectedness and collective liberation from all forms of oppression.

Principles of a Warrior Scholar

1. Love myself and others
(My thoughts, words, and actions can build or destroy)

2. Discipline myself so that no one else has to
(I am in control of my own life)

3. Stay committed and grow
(Never, ever give up)

4. Speak & listen with an open heart and mind
(Honor differences and see people's humanity)

5. Be of service to others
(Help people succeed and thrive)

6. Fight for what's right
(Be on the side of justice)

2.4
Principles of a Warrior Scholar, grounded in King's vision of the Beloved Community, Ueshiba's teachings of the way of the warrior, and Kashtan's concept of radical consciousness.

2.5
Designed by Jazmine Basa, a former student of mine, this is a visual representation of a Warrior Scholar. They are equipped with love as their shield, knowledge as their tool for change, and wings for growth. The hummingbird represents beauty, freedom, and movement. The warrior scholar's gender is intentionally ambiguous so that any of my students can see themselves in the individual.

These principles are not rules or norms; rather, they constitute a philosophy and a way of being that draws out the best in me and my students. I invite my students to say them with me at the beginning of class each day, before jumping into any content or agenda items. Doing so serves as a reminder that, above all else, our collective purpose during our finite time together is to grow as human beings and create a more loving and just world. By reciting and committing them to memory, the principles become reinforced and part of the fabric of our space; we refer back to them throughout the year, reflect on areas of growth and struggle, and hold ourselves to a high standard individually and communally. To be clear, this is not to say that the specific subject matter is not of importance; on the contrary, the subject matter is given even *more* relevance and significance when students understand and trust that what we are doing is grounded in honoring their humanity and not just focusing on "academics."

I tell my students, both at the start of the school year and throughout, "These principles are not about changing who you are; they are about strengthening who you *already* are." I explain that they are both aspirational and needs-centered, thus allowing us to put them into practice—through activities, assignments, rituals, and how we engage with each other. They are foundational to the space and greatly contribute to what, how, and why I teach. They also remind me about the young person I once was and help me intentionally design the kind of classroom environment that likely would have helped me immensely. By the end of the year, the majority of my students say them with conviction and pride because they have applied them regularly and know they have grown.

I typically introduce the principles at the start of the second week of school to allow for students to ease into the space and get to know each other. Depending on the class, sometimes it can take students a little while to warm up to the principles; others gravitate immediately, especially if there are returning students, whose excitement and zeal help garner buy-in more quickly. Students have a copy of these principles in their notebook, and they're also posted in the front of my classroom. After a few weeks, most students have them memorized, and nearly all participate in saying them. But even when some don't, that's okay with me; sometimes kids are tired or prefer to follow along mentally. The heart of the work is in *practicing* the principles.

What follows is a brief description of each of our warrior scholar principles, underlying needs that each principle aims to meet, and a glimpse of what they look like in the classroom. It is impossible to fully capture in bullet points the complex and nuanced ways in which we practice these throughout a school year, but I hope that what I've shared here gives you an idea. Subsequent chapters in this book will touch on some of these principles a bit more; for now, my intention is to support you in thinking about how you would put your own into practice.

PRINCIPLE 1

Love myself and others (my thoughts, words, and actions can build or destroy)

Description

At the heart of this principle are interdependence and love for humanity. It is the first principle for a reason—valuing ourselves and each other and recognizing our impact are necessary prerequisites to bringing more love into the world.

Needs underlying this principle

Care, connection, community, companionship

What this looks like in the classroom (strategies to meet underlying needs)

- Presenting/sharing personal stories with class (e.g., poetry, narrative, persona pieces)
- Writing positive notes and gratitude cards (e.g., during poetry reading, end of term)
- Reflective community circles at beginning/end of terms, marking periods
- Representing students' cultures, experiences, interests in the curriculum

PRINCIPLE 2

Discipline myself so that no one else has to (I am in control of my own life)

Description

Many young people believe that they don't have much power and feel controlled in many aspects of their daily lives. Some comply out of fear or intimidation, not from a conscious, empowered decision to meet needs. Self-discipline supports students in attending to their needs with awareness while also being mindful of others' needs. When we are self-disciplined, we focus on learning to hold ourselves accountable to prevent others from having to do so.

Needs underlying this principle

Choice, autonomy, respect

What this looks like in the classroom (strategies to meet underlying needs)

- Periodic self-reflections (i.e., behavioral, academic, relational, etc.)
- Opportunities for students to exercise autonomy (e.g., open restroom policy)
- Using cell phone with discretion and mindfulness (e.g., not during discussions)
- Modeling, at all times, how I would like students to treat me and each other

PRINCIPLE 3

Stay committed and grow (never, ever give up)

Description

There can be a helpful distinction, I think, between failing and giving up. Sometimes, we may put effort into something and still fail at whatever it is we are trying to accomplish. We can learn from that failure. In contrast, giving up, whether it's on ourselves or a larger purpose, can inhibit growth and signal that there are unmet needs at play. I tell my students that it's okay, maybe even necessary at times, to fail in the short-term; what matters is staying engaged in the long-term effort of reaching our goals. This principle recognizes the importance of resilience *and* attention to systemic factors contributing to students' well-being and success.

Needs underlying this principle

Learning, discovery, growth, achievement

What this looks like in the classroom (strategies to meet underlying needs)

- Goal-setting and revisiting of goals (e.g., vision boards, annotated life maps)
- Self-assessments (e.g., identifying areas of growth, areas of challenge)
- Reading and writing stories of resilience (esp. as related to class subject)
- Celebrating areas of growth and recognizing areas for growth as opportunities

PRINCIPLE 4

Speak & listen with an open heart and mind (honor differences and see people's humanity)

Description

At the heart of this principle is empathy. It encourages students to speak their truth while also asking them to recognize that others may hold a different truth. When we consider the underlying needs of people's views and actions, it opens up room for more understanding and compassion.

Needs underlying this principle

Empathy, respect, expression

What this looks like in the classroom (strategies to meet underlying needs)

- Discussion activities with conflicting viewpoints (e.g., debates, Socratic Seminars)
- Understanding people's motivations from a needs perspective (e.g., empathy letters, character analysis, perspective writing)
- Intentional design of mixed groups to allow for a variety of viewpoints

PRINCIPLE 5

Be of service to others (help people succeed and thrive)

Description

This principle seeks to counter the hyper-competitiveness and rugged individualism so ubiquitous in schools and society. It emphasizes the importance of interconnectedness and valuing the unique gifts that each person brings into the world. Students lean on each other regularly in class to support one another's learning and growth.

Needs underlying this principle

Support, ease, contribution

What this looks like in the classroom (strategies to meet underlying needs)

- Ample opportunities for students to learn from each other (e.g., co-creating a project, solving or answering a problem, constructing a question, etc.)
- Intentional design of groups, triads, or pairs (e.g., emergent bilingual learners sitting together with fluent language speakers)
- Community engagement projects (e.g., showcasing learning in community, teaching/learning from members of community, etc.)

PRINCIPLE 6

Fight for what's right (be on the side of justice)

Description

This principle is about taking a stand, about fighting for what one believes in. It is about trusting that we have the individual and collective power to effect change. A commitment to nonviolence demands that we as educators interrupt ways in which violence and injustice exist because there is no such thing as neutral teaching; to be neutral is to pretend that schools are not politicized institutions that shape and are shaped by politics.

Needs underlying this principle

Peace, harmony, fairness

What this looks like in the classroom (strategies to meet underlying needs)

- Learning and telling stories of freedom fighters, past and present (i.e., unsung heroes, heroines, and siblings from historically targeted groups)
- Intentionally designing units that address systemic or social problems
- Helping students practice advocating for self and others (e.g., writing a letter, creating a video, multimedia project, etc.)
- Disrupting school policies or practices that result in harm or lack of fairness

YOUR TURN

After having now taken a look at my vision and classroom principles, let's now turn to your own vision and think about how you might articulate it to your students and put it into practice.

Step 1: Revisit Your Vision

Review the vision that you wrote earlier. Does the concept of Beloved Community or something similar align with what you yearn for? What kind of classroom space would the younger you have needed during the difficult time you wrote about? If there is anything that you would like to change or refine in the vision you wrote on page 42, I invite you to do so in the following space.

Your (refined) vision:

▷ Is there anything else you would like to add or change to your vision? What, if anything, might that be?

Step 2: Distill Your Vision

Next, I invite you to distill this vision into different principles using the following graphic organizer. The number of principles is, of course, entirely up to you. Maybe you'd find it helpful to start small and try out even just one or two principles for now. Here are some guiding questions to support you:

- What ways of being (in your classroom) would support the fruition of this vision?
- What values of yours guide how you live?
- What values guide or inform what, how, and why you teach?

Step 3: Identify Underlying Needs

Next, please review the list of needs on page 29 (or Appendix B). Then consider: What are the underlying needs for each principle? Is there balance in the needs that are represented across the principles (e.g., intellectual, emotional, etc.)?

Step 4: Brainstorm Classroom Practices

Finally, what would it sound/look like for you to practice these principles (with students)? What do you and your students already do well that you could build off of? What would help to meet the needs you identified?

Principle

Optional sentence starter: A behavior/ mindset that would support the fruition of my vision is _____

Needs underlying this principle
Optional sentence starter: Some needs that this value would fulfill are...

What we're already doing or what we could do to practice this (to meet needs)

Principle

Optional sentence starter: Another behavior/mindset that would support the fruition of my vision is _____

Needs underlying this principle
Optional sentence starter: Some needs that this value would fulfill are...

What we're already doing or what we could do to practice this (to meet needs)

Principle

Optional sentence starter: Another behavior/mindset that would support the fruition of my vision is _____

Needs underlying this principle
Optional sentence starter: Some needs that this value would fulfill are...

What we're already doing or what we could do to practice this (to meet needs)

Principle

Optional sentence starter: Another behavior/mindset that would support the fruition of my vision is _____

Needs underlying this principle
Optional sentence starter: Some needs that this value would fulfill are...

What we're already doing or what we could do to practice this (to meet needs)

Principle

Optional sentence starter: Another behavior/mindset that would support the fruition of my vision is _____

Needs underlying this principle
Optional sentence starter: Some needs that this value would fulfill are...

What we're already doing or what we could do to practice this (to meet needs)

Principle

Optional sentence starter: Another behavior/mindset that would support the fruition of my vision is _____

Needs underlying this principle
Optional sentence starter: Some needs that this value would fulfill are...

What we're already doing or what we could do to practice this (to meet needs)

As you think about your vision and underlying principles or values, here are a few other questions for consideration:

- How would you share these with your students?
- Would you say them aloud as a class?
- Would you have them posted in the classroom or printed via handout?

It is my hope that this process serves as more than just an exercise on paper. I genuinely hope that reflecting on and constructing your vision and principles support you individually as a teacher, interpersonally with your students, and potentially contribute to meaningful conversations and change in your school community.

That said, there are times when we may feel limited in our capacity to effect significant change within and beyond our classrooms, especially when we are already very busy attending to the myriad demands of school. Moments when we may feel disillusioned, complacent, even hopeless. That is all the more reason for us to concretize our vision so that we can remind ourselves of what we are working *toward* and not just working *against*.

I am sometimes asked: "I'm inspired by the warrior scholar principles, but how do you fit them in on top of the subject matter you teach? Isn't it a lot more work to incorporate these?"

My response is two-part. First: ideating, practicing, and reflecting on my vision and principles do require time and effort, especially at first. But doing so ensures that the *foundation* from which I teach is solid. I remember how much harder it was to teach when my vision and principles did *not* exist, when I frequently second-guessed what, how, and why I taught the way I did. And to be clear, excellent pedagogy requires ongoing self-reflection and inquiry. But if I am in a constant state of floundering—or, conversely, if I believe "I've got it down" because things in my classroom tend to run smoothly with little to no disruption—it may be worthwhile to revisit my foundation. It is always good practice to ask ourselves: *Toward what ends am I teaching this? Is what we're doing in class disrupting the status quo or maintaining it?* (More on nonviolence in relation to curriculum will be explored in Chapters 5 and 6.)

Second, the beauty of embedding principles into our practice is that they are a reflection of who we already are. If we are bringing our authentic selves into our classroom space and earnestly trying to embody the values that matter to us, then we *will* see our principles flourish and vision begin to manifest, however infinitesimal in scale it may seem at times. Moreover, because we are constantly evolving beings, our vision and principles are not likely to remain static. I am not the same teacher I was five years ago, last year, or even yesterday.

My principles have evolved over time and will continue to do so. What used to be "stand on the side of justice" is now "be on the side of justice," as I am striving to use language that is as inclusive as possible. Originally, that principle didn't even exist, as I was still figuring out, as a novice teacher, how to embed social justice throughout all aspects of my pedagogy, particularly in the curriculum. But even then, I felt that something was missing; I soon realized that practicing nonviolence in its fullness could not happen without an explicit commitment to fighting against injustice—both within and beyond the classroom.

If you find that a principle you're trying out is not working, let it go and try adopting a different one. Again, it's okay to start with three, two, or maybe even one principle so that you don't feel as though you have to figure it all out at once. Give yourself time and grace.

Embarking on the path of nonviolence begins with ourselves—knowing who we are, embracing our stories, and trusting our capacity to create what does not yet exist. And to practice nonviolence is just that: a *practice*. It is not a destination. We will fall short at times of living up to our values and vision. What's important is that we provide ourselves opportunities to keep learning and keep trying in order to bring our vision to life. And as we consciously work toward building and sustaining our vision with our students, the vision symbiotically sustains *us* as well, bringing us closer to one another and to the world we dream of [Figure 2.6].

2.6

Me and some of my Warrior Scholars. Personal collection.

CLASSROOM PRACTICE

"When I remember that you are sovereign,
I release my need to dictate and rule...
I not only awaken my own humanity,
I give space for yours to flourish as it fully
deserves."

DR. SHEFALI TSABARY, from *The Awakened Family*

Relational Nurturing, Not Classroom Management

CHAPTER 3

Negative and Positive Peace

"**One way** you can start off your narrative essay is by setting a scene with strong sensory details. Would someone like to read the example?"

Teresa threw her hand up. "I'll do it!"

"Cool, thanks, Teresa," I said, adjusting the sheet beneath the document camera.

As she read, I noticed Xavier turn to a classmate and start up a conversation. I waited a few seconds, hoping he'd wrap it up, but he did not seem to take his peer's cue that they weren't interested.

"Hey, Xavier," I said, in an unsuccessful attempt to get his attention.

"*Xavier,*" I repeated louder. "Do you have a question or something?"

"Nope," he said, popping the p-sound as he shook his head side to side.

"Okay, well can you please not talk while someone else is reading? It's distracting."

He rolled his eyes and nodded silently, his head bobbing slowly and somewhat dramatically.

"Sorry, Teresa," I continued. "Do you mind reading that again?"

No sooner had she gotten through the first sentence than Xavier turned to his classmate again, presumably picking up where he left off.

"Seriously, Xavier? I already asked you to not talk over someone else," I said, annoyed.

"Wow, that's nice," Xavier uttered with sarcasm that was nearly palpable.

I let out a sigh. "You're really testing my patience. I don't want to ask you again."

We stared at each other briefly before I cleared my throat and looked at the projector screen, attempting to compose myself before continuing with the lesson. But before I could say another word, Xavier belted out, "That's *NICE*!"

"Alright, dude, that's it." I said with exasperation. "I don't want to be *that* kind of teacher, but I'm done asking. Please take your stuff and go to the office."

"For *what*?!" he asked incredulously. "I was just talking."

"I already asked you to stop talking, but now you're just being straight-up disrespectful. Please take your things and go."

"Nah, I'm good," he said matter-of-factly, leaning back in his chair with his arms crossed.

My face got hot and the top of my head started to tingle like it was covered in pine needles. I glanced around the room and saw some students looking down at their desks while others shifted awkwardly in their seats. The rest of the class looked on silently, awaiting my response.

"I'm waiting, Xavier."

Nothing.

I could feel sweat dripping down from my armpits. "Fine. If you're not going to leave, then I'll have someone come and get you."

I picked up my classroom phone and dialed the campus monitor, Jerry, whose swift arrival was announced with heavy footsteps up the ramp outside my portable classroom.

The door swung open and Jerry boomed, "What's the problem here?!"

Xavier jumped slightly before sinking into his seat.

"I asked Xavier to go to the office for disrupting the lesson, but he's refusing to leave."

Jerry glared at Xavier from the doorway before yelling, "If the teacher tells you to do something, then you *do* it, kid—period!"

"But I didn't do anything wrong. I was just talking," Xavier pleaded.

Jerry marched toward Xavier and hovered momentarily, hands on hips, before shouting, "Come on, man! Get your stuff and LET'S GO. NOW!"

With a dejected slump, Xavier slipped out of his chair, grabbed his backpack, and followed Jerry out the door, his head held low.

In that moment, I thought I had handled the situation appropriately. The student had acted defiantly, and I tried multiple times to redirect his behavior but to no avail. I didn't *want* to call the campus monitor, but Xavier's actions left me with no other choice, right?

Later that afternoon, I ran into the vice principal in the hallway.

"Mike, I'm not sure what exactly happened in your class with Xavier today, but just so you know—" she scanned the hall, ensuring no other students were within earshot before continuing in a lowered voice, "He was crying when he got to the office." Her eyebrows furrowed slightly, painting her countenance with concern. "I mean, just...literally *bawling*."

I took a moment to register her words, and when I visualized Xavier sitting in the office, his tear-strewn face drenched with humiliation, my heart sank.

I felt guilty for having him escorted out of class for something so seemingly insignificant. Mostly, though, I felt ashamed for allowing myself to be "that" kind of teacher. The kind who tries to utilize power over to force compliance. The kind who punishes students who display resistant behavior. The kind who believes that learning always necessitates a quiet and orderly classroom.

I became the kind of teacher I feared and held little respect for when I was a student but had nonetheless come to embody in that moment with Xavier.

Admittedly, it *was* my first year in the classroom and I had a gargantuan workload and demanding schedule with graduate courses in the evening. Adequate sleep was perpetually elusive, capacity invariably stretched thin, and patience often in short supply. Consequently, I did not always respond to difficult or unexpected moments from a centered place.

My credentialing program espoused the importance of cultivating classrooms and schools that center connection, love, and justice, especially for our most wounded and marginalized youth. Of course, in my heart I believed this and vowed to create that space. And for the most part, I did—with lots of stumbling along the way.

> when power is wielded to instill intimidation, control people, or quell real or perceived disturbances—in the name of maintaining peace and at the expense of relationships—it perpetuates a culture of violence

And yet, I chose to ostracize Xavier from the classroom because I had internalized the idea that I, as the teacher, had more power than he did. This stance was bolstered by the fact that kicking "misbehaving" kids out of class was part of the culture of the school, at least while I was there. In my misguided naïveté, I thought creating classroom spaces that center joy, belonging, and community sometimes came with occasional costs like sending students out of class. But I didn't fully grasp how punishing and excluding a member of a community, especially when done publicly, can damage a relationship. My actions did absolutely nothing to support our connection. If anything, it undermined whatever respect and trust that I had been building with him—and it took time for us to repair that.

Moreover, I doubt our confrontation resulted in any valuable lesson but instead reinforced a pervasive message that so many generations of both youth and adults alike have internalized: those with power and authority are to be obeyed or else.

And when power is wielded to instill intimidation, control people, or quell real or perceived disturbances—in the name of maintaining peace and at the expense of relationships—it perpetuates a culture of violence. In this chapter, we will look at the difference between negative and positive peace and how welcoming conflict can actually be a helpful part of creating peace in our classrooms. We will also return to Xavier at the end of this chapter.

OBNOXIOUS PEACE

I first learned of the following story about the late Autherine Lucy [Figure 3.1] from my friend Kazu Haga, a nonviolence trainer and activist. My telling of Autherine's story honors the spirit of how I've heard Kazu tell it, which has been instrumental in helping shape my understanding of peace.

In March of 1956, Dr. Martin Luther King Jr. delivered a sermon, "When Peace Becomes Obnoxious," at Dexter Avenue Baptist Church. In this sermon, he referenced Autherine Lucy, a twenty-seven-year-old Black woman who enrolled at the University of Alabama that February.

When Lucy initially applied with her friend Pollie Myers Hudson, both were not allowed to enroll because they were Black. The women took the matter to

3.1

An undated portrait of Autherine Lucy.

court, and the university subsequently admitted Lucy but not Hudson due to the latter's having a child out-of-wedlock, which violated the university's moral code (Taylor 2022).

Lucy became the first-ever Black student to be accepted into the university, although she was denied the opportunity to use the dining facilities and dormitory. As one might expect, her presence on the campus was swiftly met with white backlash.

A mob soon assembled at the campus during which some individuals burned crosses, invoking fear and terror of the KKK, while others harassed Lucy with hate-filled taunts. She had to be escorted to her classes by car, which was pelted with eggs, rocks, rotten produce, and bricks and even jumped on top of.

"'At that point, it was almost all people in the white race didn't want me,'" said Lucy in an interview from 2022, shortly before her death at age ninety-two. "'I just said, 'Oh well, I haven't done anything to them. I have to learn to do like my dad.' My dad didn't care what color they were'" (Taylor 2022).

The university's response? The Board of Trustees suspended *Lucy*, claiming that removing her from the campus was for her own safety. When her lawyers called out the school for not doing more to protect her nor putting a stop to the mob's behavior, the university "accuse[d] Lucy of defaming the school and its administration" and eventually expelled her (Smithsonian n.d.). Autherine Lucy would eventually return to the university to earn a master's degree in education, but not until the university lifted a ban on her in 1988. In 2019, the university awarded her an honorary doctorate, and in 2022, shortly before she passed away, the university named one of its buildings after her.

Immediately following Lucy's removal from the school in 1956, a local newspaper ran the following headline: "Things are quiet in Tuscaloosa today. There is peace on the campus of the University of Alabama." The university was ostensibly quieter and calmer, at least optically. But to what extent does "peace" exist when a person is punished for something they were not responsible for in the first place and the primary injustice goes unaddressed?

King described this so-called peace as "obnoxious" because it "had been purchased at the price of capitulating to the forces of darkness" (King 1956). Any semblance of peace that resulted from Lucy's removal from the university came at the expense of justice for *her*.

King goes on to say that he would rather reject peace than have his dignity and personhood compromised by accepting a degrading, false sense of peace:

> If peace means accepting second class citizenship I don't want it. If peace means keeping my mouth shut in the midst of injustice and evil, I don't want it. If peace means being complacently adjusted to a

deadening status quo, I don't want peace. If peace means a willingness to be exploited economically, dominated politically, humiliated and segregated, I don't want peace (King 1956).

This "obnoxious," harmful peace King speaks of is a *negative* peace, a term popularized by Norwegian sociologist and theorist Johan Galtung. With negative peace, visible signs of direct, interpersonal violence may appear to be absent, yet structural and institutional violence persist, causing "actual human physical or psychological capabilities to be below their potential realization" (Orosco 2008, 73).

It is the kind of peace that so many classrooms and schools have reinforced, often through extreme measures like zero-tolerance policies and punitive responses, in the name of creating "safe," "orderly," and "respectful" spaces to purportedly maximize student learning. Such as when sixteen-year-old Kiera Wilmot brought a science experiment to school that resulted in a small explosion. No one was harmed and no property destroyed, yet the school recommended her for expulsion and she was charged with two felonies (McCray 2013).

In other instances, such approaches have led to overt, physical violence. Several years ago, a white school resource officer in South Carolina forcefully flipped over the desk of a sixteen-year-old student named Shakara—while she was sitting in it—and violently dragged her across the classroom for allegedly refusing to give up her cell phone to the teacher. One of Shakara's classmates, Niya, was also "arrested for encouraging other classmates to record the violent encounter and yelling at the officer to stop" and for "'disturbing a school'" (Changa 2022, 45).

It is not difficult to surmise what likely immediately followed in that classroom: shock, fear, and silence, leaving the teacher with the non-disruptive kids who would stay in their place. Problem solved. Order restored. "Peace" once again. It is also not beyond reason to entertain the possibility that that *could have* been my student Xavier, had it been a school resource officer who came to my classroom instead of the campus monitor.

A growing number of schools have been shifting away from zero tolerance and moving toward restorative justice practices and social-emotional learning in order to build and sustain strong relationships among students and adults. Additionally, anti-racism work and abolitionist teaching have garnered significant attention in recent years, especially after the killings of Breonna Taylor, Ahmaud Arbery, and George Floyd in 2020, when protests erupted across the country that summer. Dismantling racist policies and practices and creating humanizing and liberatory learning spaces are necessary and hopeful shifts that I hope more and more schools will embrace.

And yet, when students, especially Black and Brown youth, display or engage in real or perceived transgressive behavior, it is still normalized for many schools to nonetheless rely on punitive approaches when social-emotional learning and restorative justice "don't work." For example, some school districts who, in the wake of the 2020 uprising for Black lives, initially voted against renewing contracts with their cities' police departments, reversed course and are bringing police officers *back* onto campuses. Even progressive schools that tout social justice values sometimes rely on the same disciplinary practices—behavioral referrals, office visits, suspensions, expulsions, and arrests—that schools with high incidents of discipline problems and police involvement utilize.

But the presence of negative peace is not limited to matters involving law enforcement, overt power struggles, and harsh, punitive responses to real or perceived student resistance. In our efforts to maximize ease for teaching and learning, we may impose seemingly innocuous rules and expectations that nonetheless subordinate students by positioning ourselves as having ultimate power over them. The following are but a few examples of statements I've heard teachers say about and to their students:

> "Leave your cell phone in [the sleeve pocket/drawer/box] when you enter my room."
> "I don't accept late work for any reason."
> "You only get three bathroom passes per semester."
> "It wouldn't be fair for me to make an exception for you."
> "I'm going to teach the kids who want to learn."
> "The bell doesn't dismiss you; I do."

Perhaps these sound familiar to you, too. I believe that they come from a well-intentioned place and I can understand why one might adopt certain rules if they result in smoother facilitation of learning and minimizing disruptive behavior. Especially now, as we navigate teaching and life "post"-COVID.

The lasting impacts of the pandemic have certainly not made teaching and learning any easier. For example, when schools started meeting in-person after more than a year of distance learning, behavioral challenges, such as defiance, threats, and fights soared. A survey conducted by the EdWeek Research Center from April of 2023 found that 70 percent of educators said "students in their schools are misbehaving more now compared with the fall of 2019" and 80 percent said that "the pandemic has made students less motivated to do their best in school" (Prothero 2023). Moreover, the mental health of students—from children, to adolescents, to adults in college—took a nosedive, where "rates of anxiety, depression, and substance use have increased since the beginning of the pandemic" (National Institutes of Health COVID-19 Research n.d.).

It may seem reasonable to some teachers to reign in students and double down on rules and punishment lest their classrooms become sites of chaos. But when students are not well emotionally and mentally, it is extraordinarily difficult, if not impossible, for them to learn and thrive. That is not to condone problematic behavior, but if student wellness and social-emotional learning are among our top priorities, then we must do better than simply institute blanket rules. Even when such rules "work" some or most of the time, if, at bottom, they create an *atmosphere* that rewards compliance and punishes resistance; if they motivate through fear; if they treat students as objects over which we have control, then we ultimately maintain a hierarchy that relegates students' autonomy beneath the desires and choices of us, the teachers.

To be clear, I am not advocating a relinquishing of one's authority or abandonment of classroom norms. As college-educated, credentialed, and salaried adults, we have enormous privilege and decision-making power, and it is important to be transparent with our young people about our responsibility as educators. Expectations matter and boundaries are crucial.

I'm not okay with a student disrespecting themself or someone else. I'm not okay with a student listening to music while we are sharing our writing together. I'm not okay with a student strolling into class forty-five minutes late because they wanted to go to Chick-Fil-A for lunch. But I *am* okay with and willing to dedicate time to talk through those moments with kids, hearing them out in order to support them in generating alternate strategies to meet their needs rather than defaulting to a knee-jerk reaction. What matters, in my view, is that we have control over establishing conditions that foster student learning *and* humanize our young people.

I don't view it as my job to manage young people; I see it as my duty to manage relationships so that we as a classroom community can recognize our interdependence by maintaining awareness about the impact of a given action, word, or decision on ourselves and each other. There is a fundamental difference between trying to control or coerce another human being to act in ways that privileges what *we* desire versus co-creating a space that honors students exactly as they are and still meets our needs as educators. What if we were to accept, even embrace, moments of disruption and resistance?

A Moment for Reflection

- What are some expectations, norms, or rules you set for your classroom? How do you enforce these?
- In what ways do you see negative peace in your teaching context?

ACTING OUT OR RISING UP?

In 1963, Mary Hamilton [Figure 3.2], a Black civil rights activist who participated in the Freedom Rides and helped register Black people in the South to vote, was arrested during a protest.

In the courtroom, the prosecutor questioning her repeatedly called her by her first name instead of using "Miss" or "Mrs."—honorifics that were frequently denied to Black people. Hamilton replied, "I won't respond until you call me *Miss* Hamilton" (Domonoske 2017).

Irascible at Hamilton's refusal to answer the prosecutor's questions, the judge "mutter[ed] lewd comments about what he'd like to do to her if she were in his kitchen" and "ordered her to answer the prosecutor and apologize" (Domonoske

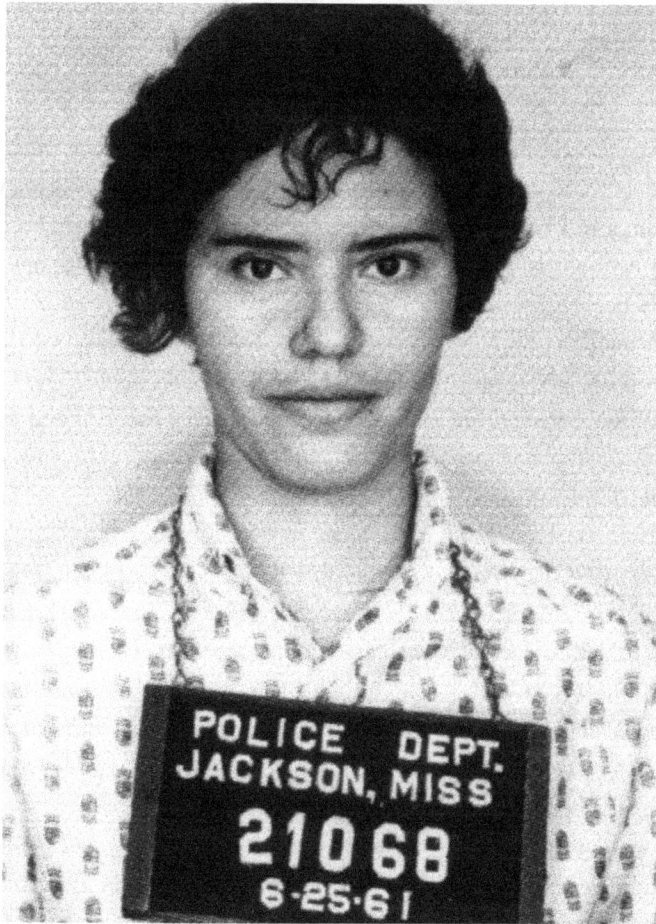

3.2

Mugshot of Mary Hamilton in Jackson, Mississippi in 1961 during the Freedom Rides.

2017). Hamilton refused to apologize; consequently, the judge threw her in jail for contempt of court and fined her $50.

With the help of the National Association for the Advancement of Colored People (NAACP), Hamilton's case was appealed, her lawyers arguing that her constitutional rights were violated by the prosecutor and judge. Her case went all the way up to the supreme court, and in *Hamilton v. Alabama (1964)*, the justices ruled in her favor, deciding "that everyone in court deserves titles of courtesy, regardless of race or ethnicity" (Yeager 2013).

Similarly, two years before, in 1961, after being arrested in Jackson, Mississippi for participating in the Freedom Rides, Hamilton refused to respond to an officer who was treating her disrespectfully. Initially, Hamilton, who sometimes passed as white, was asked, "Are you a Negro?" to which she responded "yes." When the officer followed up with, "What else are you?" Hamilton replied, "I'm Negro and nothing else that I know of" (*News & Letters* 1961, 4).

In a pamphlet titled *Freedom Riders Speak for Themselves* that was distributed around that time, Hamilton recounts the incident in detail:

> He [the officer] then took it upon himself to decide what other races I could be, and told the typist to put down that I am Negro, white, Mexican, and I believe that's all. This made me very angry because I felt he had no right to take it on himself to decide what race anyone could possibly be.
>
> After that, he began questioning me whether I had been in any other interracial demonstrations. Before I realized it, I said, "Yes."
>
> When he asked me, "Like what?" I realized I had decided I wasn't going to answer any questions, so I told him I wasn't going to answer any questions until I saw my lawyer.
>
> Then he began shooting questions at me very fast: "Are you a member of CORE? Are you a member of NAACP? Are you a member of the Communist Party?"
>
> I told him I refused to answer any question. He kept throwing these questions at me. I told him he was wasting his time. He said, "Did CORE tell you not to answer any questions?" I didn't say anything. I just sat there. He said, "Put down that she refuses to answer whether she belongs to the Communist Party."
>
> I said to him, and to the typist, "Listen, you put down that I refuse to answer any question whatsoever. CORE, NAACP, or anything else. But don't put down that I just refuse to answer whether I belonged to the Communist Party because that's misleading."
>
> He looked at me strangely, and then said, "All right. Put down that she refuses to answer any questions at all" (*News & Letters* 1961, 4–5).

Hamilton's willingness to remain steadfast in the midst of an oppressive, white power structure is incredibly admirable and courageous. What the judge, prosecutor, and police officer may have viewed as mere defiance were, really, powerful and unapologetic acts of resistance. Fueled by righteous indignation, Hamilton's staunch refusal to conform and acquiesce disrupted the negative peace that attempted to make her "stay in her lane."

Activists like Hamilton were often accused of—and charged with—"disturbing the peace." In reality, she made visible the tension that *already* existed, enabling others to learn about and sympathize with her struggle in order to achieve justice.

In his same sermon, "When Peace Becomes Obnoxious," King references a conversation he had with a man at a bus station who lamented "peace being destroyed in the community [and] the destroying of good race relations" that, in his mind, were a result of nonviolent protests (1956). King agreed that "there is more tension now" but argued that "peace is not merely the absence of some negative force—war, tensions, confusion but it is the presence of some positive force," namely justice and goodwill (1956).

Similarly, in his famous "Letter from Birmingham Jail" addressed to eight white clergyman who criticized the nature and timing of nonviolent demonstrations happening in Birmingham, King says of tension: "I must confess that I am not afraid of the word 'tension.' I have earnestly opposed violent tension, but there is a type of constructive, nonviolent tension which is necessary for growth" (2015a, 130).

That is, nonviolent direct action—be it sit-ins, boycotts, marches, etc.—raises to the surface "tension" by bringing into focus unjust conditions that must change. Such tension, King averred, is "necessary for growth" because it can garner sympathy from the masses, force conversations and negotiations with individuals in positions of institutional power, and ultimately lead to systemic change.

"And even if we didn't have this tension," King says, "we still wouldn't have *positive* peace [emphasis added]." Whereas negative peace is the mere absence of visible signs of violence and tension, positive peace works to eliminate structural, or institutional, violence such as unjust or inequitable laws, policies, and systems that harm one's well-being or quality of life (Orosco 2008, 73). For King, eradicating violence necessitates agitating the status quo and demanding change.

In the context of education, I am reminded of several moments in which courageous young people have exercised their agency to fight for positive peace, often by engaging in what the late John Lewis called "good trouble."

The youth of Birmingham who, in 1963, took to the streets and filled jails to demand an end to segregation.

The East LA students who, five years later, walked out of their classes en masse to protest unjust conditions in their schools.

Student leaders and organizers during the March for Our Lives rally in Washington, D.C. on March 24, 2018, calling for stricter gun control legislation.

The Parkland students who, fifty years later, inspired walkouts and marches across the country, galvanizing a nation to reckon with its epidemic of gun violence [Figure 3.3].

The Dream Defenders who, before Parkland, demanded change to gun legislation by occupying the Florida State Capitol for thirty-one days in protest of "Stand Your Ground"—the law that enabled the killer of Trayvon Martin to walk free.

The Tucson students who chained themselves to chairs at a school board meeting to prevent their successful and beloved ethnic studies program from being shut down.

The Bell Gardens fourth graders who pushed for—and succeeded in getting passed—legislation to include in California history textbooks the little-known, shameful history of forced repatriation of Mexicans and Mexican Americans during the Great Depression.

Students like Gavin Grimm, a transgender teenager in Virginia, who sued his school board over their discriminatory policy that denied him access to male-designated restrooms.

Students like Kaia Marbin and Lily Ellis who, in response to the thousands of migrant children caged and held in detention centers, led efforts to create and publicly display 15,000 handmade origami butterflies to visually represent the number of children being separated from their families.

When peoples' ability to meet their needs—such as safety, belonging, bodily autonomy, fairness, justice, etc.—is hindered, denied, or outright attacked, they *will* eventually resist in some fashion. Sometimes that resistance can come out in the form of "disruptive behavior"; sometimes it can appear more subtle and silent. Either way, people generally won't ask for permission to assert their needs.

But even in those instances when a young person is not necessarily motivated by righteous rage; when there is not an apparent unjust circumstance that would warrant a cry for positive peace; when they appear to just be "acting out"—there are unmet needs that that individual is attempting to meet.

And that begs a fundamental question for us educators: When it comes to our own classrooms, how do we tend to respond when a student challenges, questions, or resists us? Even if we have the best of intentions behind a particular lesson, activity, or interaction, how do we engage with students who are not on board with what we are offering? Do we respond defensively to protect our egos? Dismiss or deflect criticism to justify how right we are? Shut down the conversation to have the final word? Cast out "difficult" students so that we can more easily "manage" the classroom?

It can be uncomfortable to recognize these patterns and behaviors in ourselves, especially if they do not match our vision of who we want to be. But if we want to move toward something different for our classrooms and schools, it is important that we reflect on our responses to students amidst conflict and resistance.

A Moment for Reflection

- What student behaviors do you find most challenging to deal with?
- How do you generally respond to such behaviors?
- Does your response result in creating the kind of peace you desire for you and your students?

REMEMBERING

When I think back to my interaction with my student Xavier all those years ago, I wish I would have inquired about why he was resisting. It's possible that he was bored, as he sometimes completed his assignments without much difficulty. Maybe he did not feel challenged enough, or the topic didn't quite interest him.

Perhaps he was merely preoccupied with something that captivated his attention and he felt eager to share with someone. Maybe the topic of the narrative writing assignment struck a nerve and caused him discomfort, manifesting as disengagement and "misbehavior." I don't know *exactly* because I didn't ask.

But in all likelihood, I think Xavier was tired of being called out in class and was on edge. He had been more chatty and distracted lately, and as a result, I found myself increasingly trying to redirect his behavior. But repeatedly calling out his name, often in front of the class, took a toll: he likely felt embarrassed and annoyed and, thus, became less engaged while I felt frustrated and became less patient. Furthermore, in attempting to keep him in check, I lost sight of the importance of expressing gratitude and appreciation for what he *did* bring to our space: thought-provoking ideas and questions, laughter, vulnerability. I think his acting out was, really, his way of saying, *I'm not at my best right now. Can't you see?*

I also wish I would have responded to him differently in that moment. I could have had the rest of the class read in pairs or groups while I talked to him one-on-one, inquiring about what wasn't working for him. I could have acknowledged his apparent eagerness to talk to his friend and made a request for him to continue the conversation after I finished facilitating the lesson. That I was a rookie teacher is not an adequate excuse; yes, I can have compassion for being a less conscious, less effective teacher at that time, doing my best in the moment. And that is not to say that I'm okay with how he was acting, either. But as the adult in the room, it was my responsibility to respond more empathically and skillfully instead of engaging in a confrontational power struggle.

Thankfully, my relationship with Xavier got better. I apologized to him, worked to earn his trust and respect back, and he returned to his playful, funny self. At the end of the school year, my students wrote and shared Remember Me poems (shout out to educator Linda Christensen for the idea from her book *Rhythm and Resistance*). In some classes, students wrote about a classmate from that person's perspective. In other classes, students wrote about themselves.

Xavier wrote about wanting to be remembered "for being the best linebacker our school has ever seen." He wanted to be remembered for his dream to "get into UC Berkeley by any means necessary." He wanted us to remember that he "went from having problems with teachers to not taking anything too seriously." He wrapped up his poem by asking us:

Will you remember me?
I was the one who liked to kick it in class
The one that was chill but hyper
The one who was there if you needed a laugh
The one who was there if the class needed a volunteer

Will you remember me from
composition class taught by Mike Tinoco?
This went from being my worst class to my best one.

I am Xavier.

In the next chapter, we will take a look at the difference between being in control of others and command of ourselves. I will also share a more recent story from my classroom to support you in thinking through a conflict you are having or have had with a student of yours.

CHAPTER 4

Surrendering Control, Retaining Command

Several years ago, I joined a local dojo to learn and practice the martial art aikido. The word aikido is formed using three Japanese characters—ai, ki, and dō. Ai translates to harmony and is also read in the same way as the word love (Ueshiba 1996, 20). Ki refers to the "subtle energy that propels the universe, the vitality that pervades creation and holds things together" (Ueshiba 1992, 10). Dō means "way" or "path," and the concept is used in several martial arts (Ueshiba 1996, 14).

One of the tenets of aikido I learned early on is that when confronted with an opponent, the goal is not to defeat or injure that individual but to create flow and harmony in the midst of struggle [Figure 4.1]. If someone attacks with a strike, for instance, there are techniques to blend with the attack and redirect the energy, typically in a circular motion, in order to neutralize the imminent threat. Injuring the opponent is an absolute last resort.

I remember one evening in class, my sensei, a practitioner of the martial art for over fifty years, demonstrated an important distinction between *control* and *command*. To illustrate the former, he asked his opponent to grab his wrist firmly. Sensei wriggled his arm, somewhat exaggeratedly, attempting to bring the opponent toward himself while the opponent simultaneously pulled back. To be sure, either of them could have exerted more force to overpower and control the other person. But doing so would expend finite strength and ultimately prove futile in creating harmony, as their energy literally went in opposite directions.

Sensei then demonstrated the latter. With his feet slightly apart and firmly grounded, he sank into his center and turned his upper body slowly from left to right, guided by his core. His outstretched arms, slightly bent, flowed gracefully with his torso as he oscillated, like his palms were kissing the surface of water. A smile of pure contentment beamed across his face as if to say, "This is what returning home to oneself feels like." I couldn't help but smile back.

He then motioned to his opponent to once again grab his wrist. This time, however, instead of reflexively pulling back, Sensei stepped forward and turned inward, using his entire core in the manner he had just demonstrated. His opponent, still gripping sensei's wrist, moved in the same direction before the momentum swiftly propelled him into a roll on the mat. I was amazed at the deceptive simplicity, ease, and strength with which Sensei demonstrated the technique.

4.1

Two aikidokas (master-level practitioners) creating flow. Photo courtesy of Alexander Kolbasov.

By sinking into and moving from his center, having full command of *himself* rather than trying to dominate his opponent, he had more stability, grace, and agility. This enabled him to blend with the opposing force and initiate the emergence of a congruous flow. I have taken to heart the wisdom from this teaching, which has helped me during moments of conflict. In this chapter, we will explore the difference between being in control of others and command of ourselves and how empathy can support us through conflicts with our students.

BLENDING WITH

Tony was the kind of student who was not afraid to tell you what he thought of himself or anybody else. "I'm the smartest person in this room," he would often say with an air of smugness that invariably got eye rolls from his peers. "Y'all don't phase me!" This, in spite of the fact that he had a tendency to submit assignments, sometimes only partially completed, at the very last minute or late (if at all).

One day, toward the end of class, I was excited to introduce an activity I had dedicated substantial time to designing and planning. It was a literary restorative justice circle wherein students would take on the personas of characters from a text we were reading.

I was in the middle of explaining the activity when Tony blurted out, "Oh my God. This is so stupid. Why can't we just do a damn essay? Why do you have to make us do this dumb shit?"

Seriously, dude? I thought. *How are you going to complain about something you haven't even tried yet? Do you even know what you're talking about?*

I caught the judgmental thread starting to unspool in my mind, took a breath, and responded, "Sounds like you feel strongly about this, Tony. I wanna hear you out. Please stick around after class for a few minutes so we can talk."

"Damn, man," he moaned, followed by a loud *tsk*. He looked distressed, and I sensed there was something that genuinely bothered him.

The bell rang and after the room emptied, I pulled up a chair. "What's going on, Tony? I felt pretty thrown off by what you said."

"I told you, this shit is *dumb*!"

"I heard you. I just want to understand why you think that."

"Because," he protested, "other English classes don't have us do stuff like this."

I took a moment to take in his words. "Okay, so…the unfamiliarity of it— does that make you feel uneasy?"

He shrugged his shoulders.

"What else, Tony?" I asked.

"What do you mean?" he asked with a frown.

"I sense that you're still upset, maybe even angry. Is there something else bothering you?" I asked softly.

With his gaze downward, he said emphatically, "I hate this *stupid* school and just want to get the fuck *outta* here!"

I nodded my head, listening intently. "It sounds like it's really hard for you to be here. Can I ask why?"

He paused for a moment then said, "My brothers."

I nodded again, waiting a beat before responding. "I've heard you mention them before, but I don't know much about them. Did something happen that you'd be willing to share with me?"

"They live with our dad…and—" he paused momentarily, staring at his fore-finger pressing into the desk. "I barely get to see them."

"Thank you for sharing that, Tony. I'm hearing that you're pretty frustrated and sad about not getting to connect with them as much as you'd like. Am I more or less capturing what you're experiencing?"

His eyebrows raised slightly, as if he was surprised that someone had actually seen past his anger, and he said in a near whisper, "I guess…yeah."

"I appreciate you letting me know what's going on. Are you open to giving me a heads up the next time you're having a bad day? I don't need to know specific details if you'd prefer not to share, but it would help for me to at least know if you're not feeling whole so that I can better support you."

Tony nodded his head and said, "Alright."

By choosing to be in command of *myself*—meeting Tony where he was at, leaning into the conflict, and empathizing by attempting to discern his underlying needs, I was able to maintain and deepen my connection with him. Had I, instead, admonished him for the interruption and use of "inappropriate language," I am certain there would have been zero chance for sustaining connection.

While the activity I introduced may have stirred a reaction in him, clearly he was dealing with something much deeper. And truth be told, this was one of *many* challenging interactions I had with Tony. He had a tendency to get easily angry and irritable and made stinging remarks on more than one occasion.

But I was absolutely resolute in my commitment to show up for him and every other student, regardless of the circumstances. And by doing so, I have become a better listener. More patient. More compassionate. *That* kind of teacher I didn't know how to be when I first started.

On the last day of school that year, my students read aloud poems they had written to someone who had wronged them and whom they wanted to try to for-give. A few chose to write to someone they had hurt and wanted to ask forgiveness from. Tony, on his own accord, wrote the following to me:

Dear Mike,

For the times I upset you because of the choices I made, forgive me

For the times I cussed at you and said disrespectful things to you, forgive me

For the times I pushed you away when you were just trying to help, forgive me

For the times I tried to embarrass you and tried to make you feel dumb, forgive me

Now at the end of the year, you have helped me become a better and more open person

Thank you for not giving up on me

Sincerely,
Tony

What a gift Tony's words are. Despite its brevity, this poem came from the heart. No easy feat for a kid who loathed showing vulnerability in front of other people. His poem reminds me of something I once heard Kazu Haga say, which he said he heard from someone else: "'Conflict is the spirit of the relationship asking itself to deepen'" (2020, 80). Many of us tend to think of conflicts as negative and undesirable, when, in reality, they are opportunities for us to forge or deepen connection with those around us. And when we choose connection, doing all that we can to sustain it, we nurture peace.

NO "GOOD" OR "BAD" KIDS

One may wonder: *Why go through such lengths for the sake of connection, especially when a student is acting so blatantly disrespectful?* I suspect that students like Tony, who have had contentious relationships with teachers and other authority figures over the years, expect punishment, or at the very least, disapproval. Some of them have experienced trauma, and when they act out, it is a learned response, often to protect their safety or sense of dignity. At other times, resistant behavior may be a cry for help. But some students may lack the skills to articulate this in a way that isn't overshadowed by the behavior deemed disruptive. I have yet to meet a young person whose intention was solely to disrespect or cause trouble. Almost always, there is pain underneath.

In their book *What Happened to You?: Conversations on Trauma, Resilience, and Healing*, Psychiatrist Dr. Bruce Perry and Oprah Winfrey explore, through the sharing of stories and science, the impact of traumatic and adverse childhood experiences on our health and how we can heal from them. In discussing the impact of trauma, Perry says that "our body's core regulatory systems can be altered by traumatic experiences" (2021, 37).

Perry describes the scenario of a boy yelled at by his mother's new boyfriend. The event causes the child's stress response to become activated, resulting in a sped up heart rate, increased muscle tone, and preparation for fight or flight. As the child's brain is trying to process the experience, it is also storing it as a "trauma memory." When, as the child grows up, he is "exposed to a trigger or evocative cue that reminds his brain of that traumatic experience, his heart rate will go up. His body posture will change. The cocktail of hormones in his body will shift" (2021, 37).

Perry adds that "[e]ven in the absence of major traumatic events, unpredictable stress and the lack of control that goes with it are enough to make our stress-response systems sensitized—overactive and overly reactive—creating [an] internal storm" (2021, 61). Sometimes, a mere scent, sound, or image can trigger or evoke a traumatic memory and/or activate our stress-response system. This helps explain why some students can be triggered by stimuli that may appear harmless to others but feel threatening to the student who is experiencing stress.

This is in no way to suggest that all young people who experience trauma act out nor that resistant or oppositional behavior is necessarily a result of trauma. But having awareness of trauma's impact on the brain and body can better support us in responding with more patience, compassion, and understanding when students *do* act out. (Chapter 6 will explore the distinction between trauma-informed and healing-centered classrooms and ways we can support our students in healing.)

If we respond to wounded students with reprimands and punishment, the underlying wounds go unaddressed, and the individual is unlikely to shift their behavior in a positive direction. Moreover, such responses tend to feed into the false binary that there are categorically "good" and "bad" students. I've lost count of the number of times I've heard some kids say, in observing how I respond to someone in an agitated state, "you should have just kicked them out" and "you're too nice." My willingness to choose empathy over punishment is the real disruption—it dismantles this false binary, teaching everyone in the room an invaluable lesson: that no one is unworthy of unconditional love.

EMPATHIC PRESENCE

Merriam-Webster defines empathy as "the action of understanding, being aware of, being sensitive to, and vicariously experiencing the feelings, thoughts, and experience of another." It is one of the most powerful tools we have for connection and cultivating peace.

But there is a common trap many experience when trying to empathize. In our efforts to show up for someone in pain, we may feel compelled to give advice, relate their experience to our own, or commiserate with them. These well-intentioned attempts to show support may, indeed, help some of the time, but if we are doing so in an unsolicited manner, without first asking if that is what the person wants, then we leave it to chance. Furthermore, we may unwittingly contribute to worsening how they are feeling, thereby alienating them. If done frequently enough over time, our relationship with the other person may actually suffer without our realizing it, unless we are fortunate enough for it to be brought to our attention. Sometimes, all a person wants is to be heard and nothing else. This was certainly the case with my student Tony.

I once heard a mentor of mine, Edmundo Norte, say, "Empathy is not something that we *give*. It is something that we feel and experience inside of ourselves, which helps us to connect with others. This process creates empathic presence" (Norte 2018). By holding space with another person, listening with open-heartedness and trying as best we can to connect with what is alive in them, we give our full presence, which, as the late Thich Nhat Hanh observed, is "the most precious gift we can offer" to others (1995, 20).

Our young people yearn to be seen, heard, and understood for all of who they are, and this is especially so for the kids who wear hoodies over their heads, rarely attend class, barely complete assignments, exude a checked-out vibe, as well as those who "have grit" and display a veneer of high academic achievement that often masks woundedness. Empathy is an indispensable resource we can and should practice consistently to support these and the rest of our students, particularly during moments of struggle and conflict. And as every teacher knows, there is no shortage of opportunities for that.

In the following section, I invite you to think about a student you want to empathize and deepen connection with. Perhaps it's a student with whom you've butted heads. Maybe you've made a decision that you regret. Perhaps there's a situation that feels unresolved. Or maybe you're simply at a loss for how to engage in an effective way. Drawing from Nonviolent Communication (NVC), this process will guide you through empathically connecting with the student by identifying what they may have been experiencing. Ideally, you'd then have a follow-up conversation with them.

Step 1: Celebrate the Student

Think of a student with whom you have had (or are having) a struggle, conflict, or less-than-desirable interaction. Before we get to describing the actual situation, first name and share a little bit of who the student is, focusing on positive attributes. Doing so will, ideally, reduce the potential for negative judgments to arise which could cloud how you think about the student and situation.

Name of student:

Student's interests:

Academic strengths:

Non-academic strengths
(e.g., social-emotional skills, technological skills, creative talents, etc.):

Something I admire or appreciate about this student:

Step 2: Describe the Conflict

Now think of a specific conflict, struggle, or unresolved situation you have had with this student, one that, perhaps, has negatively impacted your connection with them or has made it difficult to establish much of one in the first place.

A word of caution here. In describing the situation in question, try to do so using observational language and avoid evaluations, interpretations, and generalizations to the extent that it is possible. Notice the difference:

> Example A: *Joelle is always coming late to class and obviously doesn't care about being here on time.*

> Example B: *Joelle came to class late today, yesterday, and twice last week, a pattern that concerns me.*

The word "always" in Example A is a generalization that carries a negative connotation and isn't even accurate. And stating that Joelle "doesn't care" about arriving to class on time makes an assumption about her motives. If one were to approach Joelle with this framing, undoubtedly, it would not go over well. Joelle would likely get defensive and disagree with this assessment, making it difficult or unlikely to establish any meaningful connection.

Example B, in contrast, is matter-of-fact and devoid of "reading into" what actually happened. This stance matters because if our intention is to sustain or build connection, then having shared understanding is absolutely critical. I am far more likely to get a student on board with me if I describe something unequivocal in observational language that isn't imbued with judgment. While there is no such thing as *absolute* objectivity, we can at least try as best we can to hold the intention of viewing the situation with an objective lens in the spirit of our end goal: to better connect with and support the student.

Additionally, trying to view a situation with some objectivity can help us teachers by not letting the emotional charge skew our understanding of what happened. This is especially important if we have students with whom we are struggling to connect and with whom we have had multiple challenging interactions. If we are not careful, it can be easy to conflate past patterns of behaviors with current ones and make generalized statements that might not accurately reflect what actually happened. How many of us are guilty of making an assumption about a student or have actually called them out for doing something "wrong" that they, in fact, were not even doing in the first place? We must be aware of our own biases and reflect regularly on how we interact with our "difficult" students.

▷ Describe the situation that happened (or is happening) with the student. What was said or done, by you and/or the student, that contributed to the situation?

Step 3: Discern Feelings

As we explored in Chapter 1, feelings represent our emotional state and bodily sensations, and they help us experience life in a meaningful way (Kashtan and Kashtan n.d.). They are especially important in that they signal whether needs of ours are met or unmet.

If a lesson I'm teaching is going exceptionally well and the room is alive with electric energy, I might feel *elated* because our community is strong and students are generating learning together. If I am running late in the morning, the copy machine is broken, and our Internet is down (not fun when we're reliant entirely on tech that day), I might feel *overwhelmed* and *irritable* because I don't have ease and spaciousness.

With regard to perceiving emotions in another person, we can't *know* for certain what they are feeling because we don't live in their head. A student might enter the classroom appearing to be depressed, when, in fact, they are simply exhausted because they just ran a mile for P.E. Or a student might giggle uncontrollably when presenting in front of the class, seemingly because they are amused by something, when, in actuality, they struggle with public speaking and feel very nervous.

Years ago, early in my teaching career, I had an introverted student named Angel, a skilled graffiti artist and emergent bilingual learner, who gave off a too-cool-for-school vibe. Often, when the class was writing, he would draw instead and decline my multiple attempts to help. I assumed he was bored or didn't like the class. One day, I pulled him aside and asked him what it was about writing that was difficult or unenjoyable for him.

"I dunno," he said with a shrug while looking off to the side.

I asked a few more questions, trying to glean what it was about writing that wasn't working for him, but he gave the same response.

I then switched my approach, asking, "Can you think of a time when you wrote something that felt special or important to you, Angel? Maybe something outside of school?"

He shifted his gaze, as if he had just remembered something.

I gave him a moment to let his thought marinate and then asked, "I'm wondering if there's something you're remembering that you'd like to share?"

I could sense that he was mulling it over, so I let the silence sit for a while in case he wanted to say something.

"It's okay if you're not ready to share that right now or don't want to share it at all. Do you want some time to think about it and we check back in later this week?"

He nodded his head.

The next day, Angel handed me a drawing with a person trying to climb out of what looked like a prison cell [Figure 4.2]. The drawing was accompanied with a caption that read, "Trap[ped] in a hole. Trap[ped] in a piece of paper when [it] comes to writing." On the reverse side, Angel wrote about a time when he and his uncle, who was in prison, wrote to each other. Angel said that doing so helped him feel closer to his uncle and he enjoyed being able to write in Spanish, his first language. When it came to school, however, as an emergent bilingual learner and migrant student, writing in English was extremely difficult and stressful for him. He said, "Writing is very hard for me. I was raise[d] without school, didn't have the opportunity to finish kinder or elementary school. That is why [it's] hard to keep on writing."

I didn't know that Angel hadn't completed elementary school; didn't know why writing was so hard for him; didn't know that he felt "trapped." And I wouldn't have known had I not asked. For the rest of the year, we worked together to try to make writing less stressful and more joyful. It wasn't easy, but his writing improved.

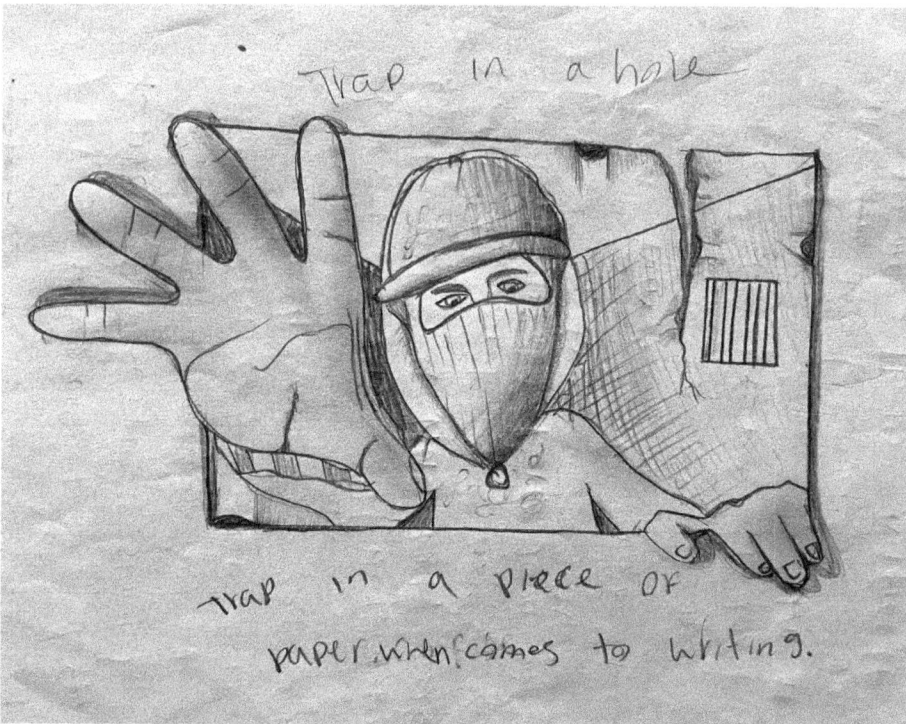

4.2

Angel's drawing and written piece describing how he feels when putting words on the page.

Often we won't fully understand someone else's feelings in the moment, but we can give space, listen, and release the desire to "fix." When attempting to discern other people's feelings during a conflict, the best we can do is guess and ask, based on the context, what we already know about the individual, and our relationship with them.

> ▷ Refer to the **Feelings Inventory** on page 26 to help you identify and list the feelings you think the student experienced during or as a result of the situation you described in Step 2. (The Feelings Inventory is also available in Appendix A.)

Step 4: Connect Feelings to Needs

Needs, as explained in the previous chapter, are universally shared and necessary for our survival. When we have the resources and capacity to consistently meet our needs, we are considerably more likely to feel whole and connected to ourselves and others. Conversely, when our needs remain unmet, especially over prolonged periods of time, our well-being suffers.

We educators are endowed with the remarkable gift of teaching, learning from, and building with young people every day. Despite the finite time we are afforded in a school year, we have myriad opportunities to help them meet various needs. Of course, not all students will have their needs met by the same lesson, activity, interaction, and that's okay. It is impossible for everyone's needs to be met 100 percent or even most of the time. But when we are intentional about designing an environment that is (w)holistic in nature—that is, when we teach to the heart, body, *and* head—students are far more likely to thrive and enjoy learning.

For our purposes here, in those instances when there is a rupture in connection, a conflict that arises, or a problem that appears intractable, continually being attuned to students' (un)met needs *will* make us more effective and responsive educators.

> ▷ Refer to the **Needs Inventory** on page 29 to help you identify and list the needs that you think underlay the feelings you identified in Step 3. (The Needs Inventory is also available in Appendix B.)

Step 5: Nonviolent Communication in Action

In preparation for engaging with the student you have in mind, review the observation, feelings, and needs you wrote down in the previous steps. The sentence frames that follow are meant to serve as merely a starting point for initiating dialogue with the student. The primary goal here, as stated earlier, should be to establish connection through empathic presence. The focus should not be to "fix" anything but to prioritize listening and reflecting back what you hear. Even if you don't get the feelings or needs right, that's okay; students will appreciate your effort, and you can try again.

> ▷ When you saw/heard/said _____ were you feeling _____?

> ▷ Were/are you feeling this way because you were/are needing _____?

Once you've had a chance to connect with the student and it seems that they feel heard, hopefully you'll have a clearer sense about how to move forward. There are a number of directions in which you might go, depending on the situation. Here are some possibilities:

Make a Request

Is there something you would like the student to do (or stop doing)? Why? Are you open to hearing a "no" and discerning what need(s) the student might be attempting to meet by responding in this way? When I asked my student Tony if he'd be willing to notify me the next time he was having a bad day, he could have said no, at which point I might've asked for elaboration and then determined whether a request would still be prudent. What I *don't* want to do, unless it is absolutely necessary—such as protecting one's safety or well-being—is make demands of students. Doing so perpetuates a coercive dynamic that upholds having power over others.

Examples:

- *Are you open to using an app to have your lunch delivered to school so that you can arrive to class on time?*
- *Would you be willing to use the restroom during independent practice time rather than the first or last ten minutes of class?*

Notice that the requests in these examples are phrased in affirmative language—that is, they name what it is I *do* want rather than what I *don't* want. The benefit of framing requests in this way is that they clearly state what it is we desire, and they provide concrete actions that the other person can choose or not choose to do. If I, instead, phrase my requests by stating what I *don't* want (e.g., "Will you stop goofing around?"), they may sound like veiled demands and leave the other person unclear as to *how* to meet my requests. Doing so may also increase the potential for resistance. That said, making requests using affirmative language takes practice, and as mentioned earlier, what's key is that we are creating an atmosphere that strives to honor and respect student choice.

Name the Impact on You

If you (or someone else) were negatively impacted by the initial conflict/interaction/situation with the student and you think they are willing and ready to hear it, it could be valuable for you to make this known. Students are not always immediately aware of the impact of what they say and do, especially in the heat of a charged moment. In naming the impact, though, we shouldn't try to elicit a forced apology or guilt-trip them. Simply naming from the heart how we were impacted will model vulnerability, an important way of showing our humanity.

> *Example: When you walked out of the room in the middle of our conversation yesterday, I felt frustrated and disappointed. I was trying to help but didn't experience openness from you. I really care about your well-being and want to collaborate with you on finding the kind of support that would best serve you. Would you be willing to try again at our conversation?*

Offer Strategies to Meet Needs

If it seems that the student would like additional help, you can, of course, ask them if they want advice, counseling, space, periodic check-ins, etc. If they seem unsure, it might be helpful to ask them which need(s) of theirs they would like to have met. From there, you can strategize with them about what kind of help might be best.

For example, I once had a student who witnessed domestic violence at home, which would cause her great distress while at school. During one encounter in which she came to me in tears, she said she did not want counseling in that moment, and Child Protective Services had already been called. Ultimately, the most helpful thing she wanted was a diary, separate from her class composition notebook, in which to write—a private space for her to *express* and *make sense of* her emotions. I bought her one after school and gave it to her the next day.

Examples:

- *Would it be helpful if you had…?*
- *Is there someone you would like to talk to about…?*
- *Have you considered…?*
- *I would like to get you in touch with….Are you okay with that?*

Reflect Inward

If there was something that *you* said or did that caused, or in some way contributed to, the initial conflict/interaction/situation, what, if anything, can you do differently moving forward? Was it something related to your instruction or lesson? Something tied to how you interacted with the student? A bias or misconception that you might not have even been aware of? This can be a difficult process, especially if we didn't intend to have a negative impact on someone else. But if our goal is to center positive relationships with our students, then we must have the humility to prioritize impact over intention. A simple practice that I use to help me with this is writing in a teaching journal at the end of each school day. It's a running document where I write down strengths and challenges or areas for growth. What follows is an example of the daily reflection template I use and an entry from this past year.

Class: English
Date: October 15

What went well +

- Gallery walk discussion went smoothly overall. Group discussions seemed rich and lively.
- I noticed Joyce and Ryan playfully disagreeing about their interpretations of one of the passages. Great to see them push each other in this way!

Challenges / areas for focus ▲

- Derrick, Jina, Aubrey, and Thinh's group barely spoke. I got frustrated with them and said they wouldn't earn participation credit if they didn't talk. This didn't help, and they seemed uncomfortable being pressured to talk
  - ▸ Next step: apologize to the group for my curt comment about participation credit
  - ▸ Try designating roles next time for more structure
  - ▸ Provide sentence starters to avoid lull in conversation

If I am struggling to identify how I might have contributed to a particular situation, I will confide in a trusted colleague to gain some perspective. Or, I'll ask the student directly what I said or did, if they're ready and willing to speak honestly. Sometimes, I'm not even aware that I said or did anything that had a negative impact.

Recently, a student of mine named Jazmine, who typically comes to class early and likes to chit-chat, was standoffish when she entered the room one day. At first I thought she was just having a rough morning, but she then asked to talk to me one-on-one. She said that the previous day, when I asked each group to select a member to share their writing, I had said something to the effect of, "Since Jazmine is done, how about she shares hers?" without first asking for her permission. She was the only person in the group who was finished and her piece was strong. But she was absolutely right—I didn't ask her first and assumed she would be up for it. She added, "I don't mind sharing, but it feels unfair when you pick me more than my group members."

The first thing I said after she told me that was, "Thank you, Jazmine, for your courage and vulnerability in disclosing how my actions negatively impacted you. I apologize for not having first asked for your consent to share your writing." I sensed immediate relief upon her hearing this. I then asked, "One of the needs that

I'm guessing wasn't met for you was shared contribution. Does that sound about right?" She nodded her head. I then said, "I will be more mindful about that in the future, and I will make sure to more effectively support your other group members in sharing more."

My conversation with Jazmine was a helpful reminder to not make assumptions about what students are or aren't willing to do. Acknowledging our missteps and apologizing to students is a powerful way of being in solidarity with them, and frankly, a lot of kids are *not* used to hearing adults do this.

NURTURING PEACE

If you are feeling skeptical about using this kind of approach in your own context, I get it. The idea of "giving up" any semblance of our power may seem scary. I've been told and asked the following by teachers:

> "That sounds nice and all, but it would *never* work with my kids."
> "Don't some kids take advantage of you?"
> "What does discipline look like in your classroom?"
> "How do you hold kids accountable?"
> "What do you do with the *really* tough kids?"

I am completely transparent with my students that I cannot control them, nor do I want to. To illustrate this point, I reference examples of student walkouts and tell them that, in theory, they, too, could simply walk out of the class en masse and there is absolutely nothing I could do to stop them. Without fail, I am met with looks of bewilderment and astonishment. Beyond my words, though, my actions attempt to dismantle the authoritarian teacher trope and bring to the forefront my humanity and humility.

My students notice the myriad ways in which I try to see and honor them: the check-ins during and outside of class; the unwavering patience I attempt to hold for each and every one of them, and owning up when I fall short; the respect I have for their thinking by regularly soliciting and using their feedback to inform my teaching; my refusal to give up on anyone. They know my care is deep and genuine because they *feel* it.

During my first year in the classroom, I equated being "in control" with good teaching because, well, that's what I experienced and was taught. Classroom management strategies from books like *Teach Like a Champion* (the first school

4.3

Shales and other students taking turns freestyling during a cypher in class as part of an impromptu community-building moment. Personal collection.

I taught at gave all new teachers a copy) were hailed as exemplary practice. But, thankfully, I learned early on that what really gave me power was humility, listening, and letting go of the idea that I can and should control other human beings. The shift literally transformed some of my most challenging classes into communities of amazing writers and poets who poured their hearts and souls onto the page. Sometimes, we would hold impromptu cyphers [Figure 4.3] during class wherein we'd push the tables and chairs off to the side and form a circle. I would then beatbox while students took turns stepping into the circle, freestyle rapping over the beat.

Shales, a gifted freestyle rapper and poet, shared a heartwarming poem at the end of the year where she celebrated the community we had built together. She took it upon herself to adapt the Remember Me assignment by writing about our class instead of herself. In her poem, "Bonded by English," she doesn't shy away from the fact that there were "class outbursts" and "attitudes," but she also acknowledges that working *through* our struggles made our class become "family" that would "go somewhere in this world" [Figure 4.4].

Bonded By english

A class no more like a family that's bonded
by a man who thinks we can Achieve
anything. From class outburst to attitudes
he's paid his dues we gave him a
hard time but we kept it pushing never
did we stop because we refuse to
be no where else but the top.
We do what we do never held our
tounge Steped down to none.
Now it's comming to an end And I'm
not Sad but Hurt that I won't meet
with this family again. We fought
hard and english was our goal to make
Snure that we go some where in this
World. Take our past and our backgrounds
We've all been considered less black &
brown. differnces occur but in the end
We all are crazy k196 & 1995 baybo's
so Pub 14 will go down As the
class that wouldn't stand down

Shales Steele
PerⅦ

4.4

Shales' end-of-year poem, "Bonded by English."

If you would like to watch a spirited performance of Shales reading "Bonded by English" from our last day of class, I highly recommend taking a look at this video, a strong companion piece to her written poem, which can be accessed using this QR code.

Father Gregory Boyle, Founder of Homeboy Industries, the largest gang rehabilitation program and re-entry program in the world, once said, "Nobody can take my advantage if I'm giving [away] my advantage" (Boyle 2018). I am not worried about students "using" me because I am choosing to use my power and privilege—my advantage—in service of their learning and humanity. The truth is, the vast majority of the time, things run smoothly, and it is extraordinarily rare for highly charged, overt conflicts to arise. That's not to say that conflicts *don't* happen. They do.

Some of my students struggle with excessive cell phone usage. Some take "extra long" bathroom breaks. Some push me away despite my earnest attempts to show up for them. But it's okay because they, and the rest of us, are continually learning how to be in relationship with one another, and learning necessitates making mistakes.

Creating opportunities for open-hearted dialogue—for connection—allows for reflection and growth, and as this becomes an integrated aspect of our practice, we generate a kind of peace that emanates from within and enters the hearts of our students.

"When I write and share my story, that story no longer lives alone in me but also lives in everyone who has heard it."

MT CHU, eleventh-grade student

Life as Text, Love as Ink

CHAPTER 5

Cultivating Self-love

I tugged at the hem of my red checkered polo shirt, heart racing, while scanning the packed bleachers and faces in front of me.

Oh, shit, I thought. *I'm actually doing this.*

The sweltering afternoon sun beamed down as I stood at the edge of the football field, gripping a microphone in my moist palm. A whiff of sweetly fragrant LA Looks hair gel met my nose as sweat dripped down my face.

It was our end-of-year rally, and I, a small-framed tenth grader who mostly blended in with the walls, was about to "battle" the one other known beatboxer at my school. He was a towering senior who, to me, epitomized cool, with his popular group of friends and sunglasses that seemed permanently affixed. We both knew of each other but hadn't actually met before; the battle was our official introduction, and it was about to go down in front of the *entire* school.

Beatboxing—the art of making percussive sounds with the mouth and popularized in the 1980s by hip hop artists Doug E. Fresh, the Fat Boys, and Biz Markie—was something I had stumbled upon just a couple of months prior. A classmate lent me a CD of a beatboxer named Rahzel, from the legendary hip hop group The Roots, performing live variations of original and popular songs and rapping over his own studio-recorded beatboxing. I thought the beatbox shtick was neat, if not a little strange, but I didn't fully appreciate it at first—not until I got to the hidden track at the end.

In front of a live audience, Rahzel performs a rendition of a song by the late R&B singer Aaliyah in which he beatboxes *and* sings simultaneously, "If your mother only knew." I had never heard anything like it before, and I was fascinated that a person could make realistic beats and sound effects using nothing but their mouth. It sounded so convincing that I initially thought it was fake. I was completely blown away, mesmerized, and inspired to learn. I could not recall having ever felt so enthralled in wanting to learn something; school had certainly never captivated my attention like that.

Self-taught

I spent the next several days and weeks teaching myself to beatbox and trying to figure out how in the world Rahzel performed that song. I listened to it over and over and over, along with my favorite hip hop albums, mimicking the rhythms and drum patterns. I sounded absolutely ridiculous in the process at first, getting spit everywhere and resembling farts more than drums, but I was steadfast in my desire to get better.

I practiced all of the time and nearly *everywhere*: my room; the bathroom; to and from the bus stop; on the bus itself; my first job at a pizzeria I had just started; and, of course, at school, much to the annoyance of teachers and the librarian, who once mistook my beatboxing for a real boom box (I won't lie—that was flattering).

Then, after a couple of weeks of nonstop practice, I deciphered the trick. In beatboxing, percussive sounds are generally produced by releasing pressure from the lips, e.g., "B" for kick drum and "Psh" for snare. But I discovered that by humming and making percussive sounds *without* pushing out pressurized air, I could sustain notes continuously. And that meant I could manipulate the formation of words, enabling me to talk (or sing, albeit badly) and beatbox at the same time, which, when amplified via microphone, sounds like an auditory illusion.

And, so, standing there on that football field, I knew what I had to do. I started off with a steady beat, threw in a few DJ scratches, and then transitioned into "If your mother only knew" [Figure 5.1]. In the world of battling, it is a major faux pas to copy, or bite, another artist's creative work, but I didn't know that at the time. It was my first time, ever, performing in front of a crowd. Maybe because of luck, skill, or both, they *loved* it. I had never received applause for anything as best as I could remember, and I certainly had not been seen nor heard by that many people at one time. It was exhilarating—and life-altering.

5.1

Me, pictured center, during my first-ever beatbox performance and battle in 2001.
Photo by Cherilyn Brown.

The Beat Within

Beatboxing entered my life at a time when I was at one of my lowest points. Now living again in California, my circumstances were, in many respects, much better than they were in Oregon in that my dad was able to provide me with the consistent attention and affectionate care I needed [Figure 5.2]. He made time for me and took genuine interest in things that mattered to me: skateboarding, hip hop, and my friends, to name a few. I was fairly happy those first few months after moving in with him, and there was no doubt in my mind that I was loved.

But this love, alone, did not inoculate me from the recurring racism I would once again endure and become scarred from, for I did not yet know how to envelop *myself* with love, did not yet know my own worth. Nor did I know how to process my trauma from Oregon. My dad had peripheral knowledge of what I went through, but he was unaware of the root causes and depth of my pain; it still felt too raw and shameful for me to ruminate on, much less talk about with anyone.

By the time I started high school, some of the wonderful friends I had made the preceding months, at the tail-end of eighth grade, ended up either attending different schools or grew apart; consequently, I struggled my fresh-man and sophomore years to establish friendships with the same quality of connection. Perhaps due to chance, or, more likely, because wounded kids

5.2

Me and my dad celebrating Christmas, 1999. Personal collection.

tend to gravitate toward each other, some of the people I associated with were, like me, deeply insecure and immature. Unlike me, however, these individuals were bound by whiteness and shared an understanding that I was not truly one of "them." I was frequently the target of their racist jokes, verbal assaults, and humiliating pranks, but I lacked the confidence to set boundaries for myself and to walk away.

After the tragic events of September 11, when racial hostility and violence toward Muslim communities and people of South Asian heritage swelled, I was cast even further as an enigmatic, ethnic Other. Racist nicknames and characterizations rooted in xenophobia and Islamophobia became familiar to me, which was flummoxing because I was neither Muslim nor South Asian. I felt unmoored in my own skin, immeasurably self-conscious about how I was perceived and vexed about where I belonged.

As I did in Oregon, I kept the shame a secret, but its looming presence refused to remain suppressed. I projected my insecurity onto those I thought were weaker than me, posturing in order to gain others' approval and to ameliorate my own compounding pain. I also started smoking again, wherever I could with whoever wanted to—be it at my pizzeria job or in the mornings before class, attempting to find comfort in a high that was always

STUDENT MICHAEL TINOCO						GRADE LEVEL 10	REPORT PERIOD	FROM 10/16/00 TO 12/21/00	
PRD	COURSE	TEACHER	MARK	CREDIT EARNED	CITZ	WH	CLASS ABS.	TEACHER COMMENTS	
1	P-WRLD HIST	LAFLEUR, M	D+				1	BENCHMARKS NOT MET FOR COURSE	
2	P-INTGR BIO	BECKSTEAD, T	F				1	BENCHMARKS NOT MET FOR COURSE ASSIGNMENTS NOT COMPLETED	
3	P-ENG 2	COCKSEDGE, M	B-				1		
4	P-ALG 1B 10-12	COLVARD, S	F				1	BENCHMARKS NOT MET FOR COURSE TEST SCORES ARE TOO LOW	
6	P-SPANISH 2	TOVAR, G	D				1	ASSIGNMENTS NOT COMPLETED TEST SCORES ARE TOO LOW	
*	REVISED MID-QUARTER PROGRESS REPORT AS OF 11/28/00								

5.3

A progress report from my sophomore year, two months before I discovered beatboxing.

fleeting. I cared not one iota about school and did the absolute bare minimum to avoid upsetting my dad about grades and attendance [Figure 5.3].

But the moment I started beatboxing, *everything* changed. Somehow, I was not afraid to go up in front of thousands of people and perform at that school rally, which, in hindsight, astounds me. I believe my deep yearning to be seen, for something positive, overrode any nerves I felt. After the battle, I continued to practice daily and improved exponentially. My ego was boosted by people telling me I was talented, and my drive was propelled by frequent requests for me to beatbox.

In my junior year, I discovered an online community of beatboxers from around the globe that I instantly clicked with. As these were the days before the proliferation of social media and YouTube, we used a message board to share with each other recorded audio clips of our beatbox routines and tutorials. Some of us went so far as to phonetically type out vocal drum patterns and DJ scratches to teach one another how to produce sounds and techniques. We literally spoke the same language and offered each other constructive feedback and unwavering encouragement. I had finally found my people.

And then, something magical happened: I slowly started to feel better about myself. I experienced profound joy in learning an endeavor that provided me and others entertainment and gratification. Having a creative outlet and supportive online community also met my needs for *expression*, *connection*, and *being heard*. As a result, my confidence steadily grew. By the time I was a senior, that confidence was channeled toward school, where, for the first time, I took genuine interest in all of my classes.

Maybe I am capable. Maybe I am smarter than I think, I remember pondering when I made the honor roll, an accomplishment previously unknown to me. Even if college was not yet on my horizon, I realized there was value in applying myself academically because, through beatboxing, I had experienced the satisfaction of dedicating time, effort, and struggle into learning something and enjoying the process.

In Rhythm

One of my favorite classes during this time was desktop publishing, where I learned how to type as well as design, create, and format text and graphics using word processing and publication software. I particularly found typing to be fun and loved the challenge of increasing my speed. My teacher, Ms. Johnson, noticed my aptitude for working with computers, and she acknowledged me in several ways: nominating me as student of the month for the Business and Technology Academy; setting up an interview for a possible internship with a national security and research facility; regularly asking how I was doing. Nothing novel nor extraordinary—she was simply showing genuine care.

The weeds of shame and self-loathing that had sprouted long before now began to wither, giving way to a budding sense of pride that entwined with a blossoming self-love. I stopped caring as much about how others perceived me, established healthier relationships, and reconnected with old friends. I also held nearly straight As during my senior year [Figure 5.4], although the grades were a mere byproduct, not the primary aim, of my academic effort. I was relatively unattached to the outcome and just enjoyed

5.4

A progress report from my senior year. Personal collection.

5.5

Me at my high school graduation moments after walking the stage. Photo from the local newspaper, *The Brentwood Press*.

learning; the biggest reward was in knowing that I was, first and foremost, doing it for me [Figure 5.5].

Then, shortly before I graduated, I connected with other Bay Area beatboxers who would soon become family, and we began performing regularly together in San Francisco and Berkeley. Being part of this amazingly diverse community that brought people together gave me a deep sense of belonging, and I felt part of something bigger than myself. This spawned a beatbox career that enabled me to travel overseas, be on television, and share the stage with musicians, singers, dancers, and hip hop legends, including Rahzel himself [Figure 5.6]. But most importantly, it paved a road that would, one day, lead me back to the classroom—to help young people, like I once was, discover and follow their own beat within.

What If?

Had I not found my *own* beat within, there is no question that my needs for *belonging*, *expression*, *creativity*, *purpose*, *achievement*, among others, would not have been met sufficiently, if at all, during that time. And had I not fulfilled those needs, had I not begun (re)writing my own story, I am not sure

5.6

Rahzel and me
after a show in San
Francisco (top).
Personal collection.
My beatbox crew
and me (in white
hat) after a show in
Berkeley (middle).
Personal collection.
Me performing at
Queen Elizabeth Hall
in London (bottom).
Photo credit: Adam
Parsons.

where I would be today. *Who* I would be. What is certain, though, is that I had to go outside of school—literally—in order to fulfill most of those core needs. But *why*?

Why, in all the years I was in school, did I not find my spark there? Why did it take venturing beyond the school walls to realize my potential and learn to love myself and others? To find *joy*? What about the students who aren't as "lucky" as I was and don't get to experience multitudes of needs being met? What about the ones who carry deeper traumas or endure more trying hardships? Or those who ostensibly have it put together and do well in school but minimize or supplant core needs in service of academics? What if school truly was and is that place where young people can tap into what makes them feel most alive?

As educators, our subject area, finite as it is within a single school year, can play a significant role in supporting or impeding the degree to which students are able to meet their needs. And when we are intentional about crafting learning opportunities that are grounded in needs and responsive to students' lives, we create the conditions that abolish violence and cultivate love.

In this chapter, we will look at why it's important to center love in our classrooms, followed by what it can look like to create a curriculum that helps students foster love for themselves.

when we are intentional about crafting learning opportunities that are grounded in needs and responsive to students' lives, we create the conditions that abolish violence and cultivate love

WHERE'S THE LOVE?

No human being—certainly no young person—wants to live without love; it is a universal need. Shared understanding of the concept, however, is far from universal, as it is rife with multiple, sometimes conflicting, definitions and interpretations.

In her book *all about love*, the late feminist writer, professor, and activist bell hooks writes, "Our confusion about what we mean when we use the word 'love' is the source of our difficulty in loving. If our society had a commonly held understanding of the meaning of love, the act of loving would not be so mystifying" (2001, 3). Love is often defined as a deep affection or romantic feeling, but these are just partial, incomplete aspects of love, says hooks. Instead, she offers a working understanding of love as defined by psychiatrist M. Scott Peck in his 1978 book *The Road Less Traveled*: "'the will to extend one's self for the purpose of nurturing one's own or another's spiritual growth'" (2001, 4).

In "extend[ing] one's self," this definition asserts that love is an *action* rather than merely a noun, something that must be *practiced* and not just felt. Love requires something of us in order to care for our "own or another's spiritual growth." But in schools, the topic of "the spiritual" tends to raise eyebrows or be conflated with religion; to this, hooks says:

> An individual does not need to be a believer in a religion to embrace the idea that there is an animating principle in the self—a life force (some of us call it a soul) that when nurtured enhances our capacity to be more fully self-actualized and able to engage in communion with the world around us (2001, 13).

Who wouldn't want their students to experience self-actualization, the pinnacle of Abraham Maslow's hierarchy of needs, and to "engage in communion" with those around them? Most of us would be hard-pressed to think of a single person. And yet, such talk of love in schools, especially as a necessary component to teaching and learning, is scant.

I recently perused the California Common Core Standards for English and was struck by the absence of the word love. I did not see it *anywhere* in the nearly one-hundred-page document. Nor did I see the words heart and empathy (the word emotion appears a total of four times, once in the introduction and three times in standards for grades K–8).

Similarly, the word love does not appear in the California Common Core Standards for History, Mathematics, Physical Education, Art, nor Science. Probably not a huge surprise to most of us. The English Language Arts CCSS document *does* acknowledge its limited scope and states the following in its introduction:

> While the Standards focus on what is most essential, they do not describe all that can or should be taught. A great deal is left to the discretion of teachers and curriculum developers. The aim of the Standards is to articulate the fundamentals, not to set out an exhaustive list or a set of restrictions that limits what can be taught beyond what is specified herein....Students require a wide-ranging, rigorous academic preparation and, particularly in the early grades, attention to such matters as social, emotional, and physical development and approaches to learning (California Department of Education 2013, 4–5).

I appreciate the recognition of the need for students' "social, emotional, and physical development" and the importance of teacher autonomy, as well as the disclaimer that the standards are not intended to be prescriptive. For all intents and purposes, the standards are not masquerading as something they are not, and there is nothing wrong with standards in principle; they are a helpful roadmap that lays out a set of valuable skills students should learn, with, in theory, consistent learning across schools.

However, a "focus on what is *most* essential" (emphasis added) may lead one to conclude that skills and qualities not contained within the standards are ancillary to and, therefore, not *as* essential nor fundamental as the standards themselves. For some teachers and administrators, content standards are sacrosanct, and to question them is akin to blasphemy.

I once heard a teacher, well-regarded by many, say, "If it's not in the standards, I won't teach it." There is a strong degree of legitimacy, of "clout," automatically conferred to content standards and, by proxy, textbooks and district-created curriculum resources. But when such materials focus exclusively on traditional academic skills (e.g., analyzing, inferring, rationalizing, reasoning, etc.)—which, to be clear, are necessary—we attend to enriching only *part* of our humanity, leaving the development of other, equally important capacities and ways of being to chance.

That said, in recent years, an increasing number of schools across the United States have been recognizing the vital importance of attending to students' emotional well-being and mental health through social-emotional learning (SEL), restorative justice circles, and trauma-informed and healing-centered teaching practices. Social workers and wellness centers are becoming commonplace, and some schools even have specialized restorative justice coordinators and support specialists who assist teachers in building inclusive, equitable learning environments. These resources and approaches exist for a reason—many young people

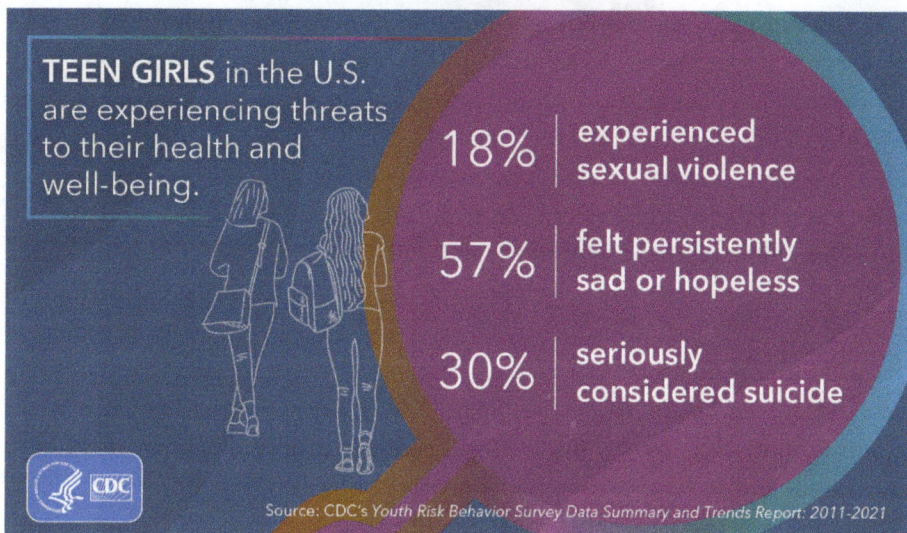

TEEN GIRLS in the U.S. are experiencing threats to their health and well-being.

18% experienced sexual violence

57% felt persistently sad or hopeless

30% seriously considered suicide

Source: CDC's Youth Risk Behavior Survey Data Summary and Trends Report: 2011-2021

5.7
———
An infographic from the Center for Disease Control and Prevention illustrating mental health risks for teen girls.

are hurting, especially as we continue adapting to life amidst the COVID-19 pandemic.

In February of 2023, the CDC released alarming data [Figure 5.7] from their Youth Risk Behavior Survey that found that between 2011–2021, "While all teens reported increasing mental health challenges, experiences of violence, and suicidal thoughts and behaviors, girls fared worse than boys across nearly all measures" (2023). The report adds that girls have been experiencing "record high levels of violence, sadness, and suicide risk" and LGBTQIA+ youth "continue to face extremely high levels of violence and mental health challenges" and "extreme distress" (2023). And much of what this data illuminates *preceded* the COVID-19 pandemic.

To their credit, many schools are taking important and necessary steps to address the dire mental health crisis facing our youth. However, implementation of the aforementioned approaches varies significantly across schools and districts. In some schools, these efforts to support students' mental health are limited to optional workshops or inconsistent professional development that don't neces-sarily require the ideas be put into practice. Instructional coaches, for example, are often paired with new teachers, but, depending on the school and district, veteran teachers can opt out. Sometimes, the intervention work happens *outside* the classroom, without teacher participation, such as when administrators or advi-sors facilitate student mediations or healing circles that, ideally, would include the actual teacher.

In other cases, there is outright resistance, where some view SEL as a "vehicle for critical race theory, an effort to divide students from their parents, [and] emotional manipulation"—a kind of boogeyman designed to brainwash students (Meckler 2022). While certain SEL programs focus exclusively on managing and mitigating stress, expressing emotions, and mindfulness, others integrate issues of race, racism, identity, and gender because there is a need to do so.

Dena Simmons, educator and founder of LiberatED, says, "educators often teach SEL absent of the larger sociopolitical context, which is fraught with injustice and inequity and affects our students' lives" (2019). Without attending to issues of inequity, injustice, racism, etc., SEL and related areas run the risk of being band-aid approaches to deeper problems. "Why teach relationship skills if the lessons do not reflect on the interpersonal conflicts that result from racism? Why discuss self- and social awareness without considering power and privilege, even if that means examining controversial topics like white supremacy?" Simmons asks. But some parents, teachers, and politicians, particularly in conservative regions, have taken umbrage with this kind of approach to SEL, successfully removing such programs from their schools and districts or working to pass legislation that limits the teaching of SEL.

Even if such programs and approaches do exist, they have little impact without all stakeholders on board. A couple of weeks ago, I visited a friend at their school. While walking to their classroom, I heard two teachers scoff at a meeting that invited vulnerability among its staff as a way to model community building. The first asked, in a mocking voice, "Were you ready for those 'hugs and feelings' today?" to which the other responded, "Man, I *hate* that stuff. I don't know why we waste our time on it." It's possible that these teachers did not feel safe being vulnerable with their colleagues. Or, perhaps it seemed like an agenda item to check off a box that, rather than offering richness and depth, felt shallow and forced. Whatever the reason, without buy-in and a concerted, systematic implementation of the aforementioned practices and approaches, they will, at best, carry minimal effectiveness, and, at worst, maintain or exacerbate existing conditions, leaving myriad student needs unmet.

Where does this leave love in our classrooms and schools? If love is viewed as unacademic, secondary to content standards, or solely the responsibility of families to teach and foster, then what does that say about the purpose of schools in a society rife with violence and hatred, especially toward people of color and queer folks? How are schools to teach students to value and love themselves and each other—unapologetically and unconditionally—if the institution that promulgates preparation for "the real world" fails to treat love with the same importance and urgency as standardized testing, "learning loss," and college and career readiness?

MEETING NEEDS AS AN ACT OF LOVE

When schools neglect love, they also undermine needs and enact violence toward those entrusted to its care, especially Black and Brown students. Dr. Bettina Love, professor, abolitionist educator, and author, writes about the violence of love-lessness toward Black and Brown children. She cites several incidents in which teachers and administrators verbally assaulted, physically hurt, or psychologically harmed Black and Brown students through racist behavior and policy that crimi-nalizes, degrades, and dehumanizes.

Oftentimes, Love says, when such stories hit the news, school districts "por-tray [them] as isolated events, the work of a few overzealous, culturally insensitive but 'good' teachers" (2019). However, such instances illuminate "more than just racist acts by misguided school educators" or a few bad apples—they exemplify "spirit murdering" (2019). Coined by legal scholar Patricia Williams, "spirit mur-dering," according to Love, occurs when schools deny young people "inclusion, protection, safety, nurturance, and acceptance" (2016), the result of which is "a slow death, a death of the spirit, a death built on racism and intended to reduce, humiliate, and destroy people of color" (2019).

But even if one has the best of intentions and considers themself "not racist," if, at the end of the day, their words, actions, curriculum, or policies result in denying or impeding opportunities for students to feel safe, accepted, valued, and loved—to meet core needs and be fully human—then students' humanity is also denied.

In October of 2021, a video of a white math teacher in Riverside, California went viral. In the video, she is wearing a faux headdress and performing offensive stereotypes of Native Americans by stomping, gesturing a "tomahawk chop," and chanting in a supposed attempt to help kids remember a mathematical concept. Shortly thereafter, several Twitter users posted a yearbook photo of the teacher wearing a similar headdress and posing with an imaginary "tomahawk"—from ten years prior—accompanied with a caption: "I find that if I tell them a story using math along the way, it's like a memory device! It just may stick with them forever" (Tiel 2021). *Ten years* of students having to endure that.

If I had to guess based on the teacher's words and video, she probably wanted the lesson to be entertaining and engaging and "didn't intend" to insult anyone. She might even say that she loved her students. But good intentions and positive sentiment mean very little when the *impact* causes great harm. According to Native American activist Akalei Brown, a spokesperson for the family of the student who recorded the footage and who is also Native American, the student "'felt that violence was being committed against him'" (Cohen 2021). Spirit murder.

Without cultural competence and rich understanding of and respect for students' identities and lives, how can one truly *know* their students and expect to provide "protection, safety, nurturance, and acceptance—all things children *need* [emphasis added] to enter school and learn" (Love 2019)? If students endure violence to the mind, body, heart, and spirit, then, as Love asks, "Where does the soul go to heal when school is a place of trauma" (2019)?

Like me, you are probably thinking, *I would never do anything like that.* And I'm with you. It is easy to distance ourselves from egregious, reprehensible behavior. But it doesn't take overt violence in order for students to be harmed. What about the moments that don't hit the headlines? The everyday decisions that determine what is taught, including whose perspectives are represented and whose aren't? Decisions that influence how safe students feel being vulnerable or honest? Decisions that support or impede the degree to which students are able to have their needs met? The absence of opportunities for love and healing—be it within or beyond school—can cause or perpetuate harm, especially for those who carry deep wounds and have little self-worth.

For some young people, the wounds run so deep that they'll externalize their pain (e.g., fighting, bullying). For others, the pain becomes internalized (e.g., cutting, substance abuse, etc.) or a combination of both. Schools' increasing focus on student wellness and mental health is significant and a clear indication that our young people are, by and large, not feeling *whole*. Students like me. Students like some of yours. The "average" ones, the "high-achievers," the "unmotivated" kids, and everybody in between. And this is not to suggest that youth are deficient or weak and simply need "grit." They *are* resilient already. But resilience, alone, cannot engender love nor provide sufficient healing if, as Love says, "school is a place of trauma" or a place that privileges the head but not also the heart nor spirit, especially when one is carrying wounds.

We may have little control over what happens beyond our classroom and school walls, but given that our students share a great deal of time with us, day in, day out, we have immense opportunity to dream and build anew when we place love and needs at the center of what we do. Every effort toward helping our young people develop self-worth, building communities of care, and replacing a culture of violence with one of peace absolutely makes a difference. Even the actions of a single teacher matter and can create ripple effects.

My mentor and friend Dr. Roxy Manning says that "attending to needs is how we show love, and love for self validates our needs" (2023). This idea aligns with my philosophy because I believe that when we craft learning opportunities that *attend to* students' holistic needs and are responsive to their lives, we create the conditions that abolish violence and cultivate love. And what better place to do this than with what we already know very well—our own content area? Let's now explore what it can look like to help students foster a love for self in our curriculum and classroom.

A Moment for Reflection

- What does love look like in your own teaching/classroom?

PRACTICING SELF-LOVE

A core tenet of my teaching philosophy and practice is that students' lives are an intrinsic part of the curriculum. Not occasionally tied-in but *embedded* in. Writing and sharing about oneself are powerful means through which self-love and self-knowledge can be stimulated. After all, to be oneself authentically requires knowing and embracing oneself. But that can't happen if students aren't provided with opportunities to do so.

Not too long ago, I came across a district-created pacing guide that outlined, in sequential order, writing genres for high school students to practice. Each grade level consisted of six marking periods, and only *one*—the first marking period of freshman year—listed narrative writing; all other marking periods focused on either informational, analytical, or argumentative writing. A student whose English classes strictly adhered to this pacing guide would have had, in theory, a single opportunity to write a formal, narrative essay about themselves throughout their entire high school experience (presuming their other classes didn't provide such opportunities).

Although one could argue that the student could still write about their interests and experience through the other genres, there is still a tacit idea that narrative is somehow not as important or "academic." Why else would it be on the pacing guide only once? What else does that communicate? Hard to imagine how a student would adequately be able to know and "extend one's self for the purpose of nurturing" their own growth without having ample space to do so.

The following are some of the ways I strive to help my students enrich understanding of and love for who they are. These are not one-offs, but rather, part of an array of learning opportunities that I consistently weave in throughout the school year in companionship with other skills, standards, writing genres, and unit foci. Additionally, I am intentional about designing learning opportunities that honor both joy and struggle to account for the range of human experience, but also to ensure that there is balance when we are in a unit with heavy topics (e.g., oppression and resistance).

The individual and collective needs I strive to help my students meet through these include but are not limited to: *inclusion, trust, belonging, mattering, being seen/heard, companionship, connection, healing, creativity,* and *safety.*

As you'll see, some of the learning opportunities offered in this chapter and the following one ask students to explicitly identify and describe needs and associated feelings (using the lists presented in Chapter 1 and located in Appendices A and B). Other learning opportunities attempt to meet the aforementioned needs *through* the writing and sharing processes themselves. I hope that you might be able to adapt some of these learning opportunities into your own classes, whatever subject matter you teach.

Annotated Life Maps

Annotated Life Maps, great at the beginning of the school year, allow for students to visually represent impactful moments from their lives with drawings or pictures and a brief description of each [Figure 5.8]. Sometimes, I'll ask students to identify the underlying needs that were met or unmet during their experiences to help them understand *why* those moments were particularly significant.

5.8a

Brandon's Life Map.

Brandon writes about the positive effect of the role-playing video game Genshin Impact: "Through this game, I could find *companionship* with the characters! All the story writing ties in with the playable cast who come from all walks of life. By projecting myself into the fictional world, I find *inspiration*." On another part of his Life Map, Brandon expressed fear of being targeted amidst violence directed toward Asian American, Native Hawaiian, and Pacific Islander (AANHPI) communities: "Since the start of the COVID-19 pandemic, there's been a surge in xenophobic/racially motivated hate crimes. I feel paranoid that my family or I could experience a lack of *justice* or *peace* because of racism."

5.8b

Angie's Life Map.

Angie writes of the evolution in her relationship with her mother: "My mom and I used to have a very tumultuous relationship. Car rides alone with her were awkward, as we rarely ever saw eye to eye on our values. Since I started high school, our relationship has become one of *trust* and *respect* for one another….Now, car rides are a place of *comfort* and *solace*."

Alondra's LIFE MAP

Home

Growing up I was either hearing my parents arguing or them working being left home alone. in order to survive I had to learn new things on my own with no support, also I learned that no life was perfect.

Parents

Being left alone wasn't their best choice, but was needed to make since we had no family. They needed to work and didn't always make the best decisions, but still tried to love and care for me. As I grow, they noticed I wanted a voice in the family. Finally being heard and seen.

Friends

Having different friendships like being used, disrespected, bullied by your "friends" was hard, but when real friendships came in my life; the one that you want to keep forever and showed me that kindness and respect still existed, especially trust made me feel part of a community or like having a second family.

Stanford

Summer 2022 I went to a highschool internship program at Stanford University where I was taught many things. Also the experience of meeting new people was fun but I wasn't just socializing but also contributing to Stanford's community as I volunteered.

Moving

When I was 7, I moved to Nevada starting all over, being difficult and especially felt alone, lost, and unheard, not wanting to move away from home. I struggled, didn't trust anyone. I needed the presence of my parents, one year later I moved back meaning I needed to start from zero again.

Brother

Being 12 and finding out that I was going to be a sister gave me relief. Knowing that someone was going to protect me and I will protect them back. Giving me the purpose to take care of him. I'd be the big sibling I wish I had.

Party

Being a female hispanic meant having quinceanera due to could I had a sweet 16, but in that day all attention was on me, I felt loved and cared for. It made me feel thankful and appreciative of every special person and moments in my life because you only live once.

Job

Being 17 I wanted to make money on my own and be responsible. Having a job meant I was given power and trust. I learned how to be more social and speak up. I felt needed. Working gave me hope that one day I'll be making money in the career I love.

5.8c

Alondra's Life Map.

Alondra writes that through her first job at age seventeen, she was "given *power* and *trust*." She "learned how to be more social and speak up" through this job, which, she says, also helped her feel "needed." She adds that "working gave me *hope* that one day I'll be making money in the career I love."

While Annotated Life Maps are a wonderful avenue for reflection and creative expression, they are also a useful launching point into more developed writing. In my journalism class, for instance, I'll have students partner up and exchange their maps. After some icebreaker activities, they will then develop questions based on their partner's map with the purpose of interviewing them and writing a published profile story. (I pass out large sticky notes for anyone who would prefer to conceal moments they do not want to be asked about.)

For my English classes, sometimes I'll ask students to write a Life Trajectory essay about pivotal experiences and people that have shaped their lives. They first brainstorm key moments using a graphic organizer [Figure 5.9], also available in Appendix C, that "chunks" their lives into different time periods—elementary school, middle school, high school to present, and future for goals and aspirations. Having students brainstorm impactful moments like this can be done in addition to or instead of Life Maps.

Prompt: What experiences in life and school have shaped your trajectory? What do you envision for your future?		
Elementary School	Middle School	High school (9th grade–current)
		My future
	My metaphor (thesis statement)	

5.9

Graphic organizer for the Life Trajectory essay.

Students then write about the most significant moments from their brainstorm, weaving a metaphor throughout their essay to symbolize their life's trajectory. Students are not always aware of how certain experiences and forces beyond their control have impacted them and shaped how they show up in the world. So I ask them to reflect on needs that were met and/or unmet to gain insight as to *why* they felt or acted the way they did. Their lives are literally treated as the text to analyze and learn from.

For example, tenth-grade student Ever wrote about his elementary school years, with football as his metaphor. He includes met and unmet needs and associated feelings from this time. Here is an excerpt from his essay, the first he said he completed for an English class in years:

> In elementary school I was a rookie football player who got tackled right away. This messed me up and made me want to quit the game. I'd always make fumbles and never be able to catch the ball. My sister joined a gang and got into a lot of trouble. She skipped classes and eventually dropped out of high school. Sometimes, she wouldn't come home at night and when she did, there'd be arguments between her and my mom. Cops would come to my house and bring my sister home after she'd done something really bad. I remember like it was yesterday seeing her in handcuffs which made me so sad.
>
> Growing up seeing that would be scary, and there wasn't always *stability* at home. During this time, I'd hang out with people that weren't a good influence but I was looking for *friendship*. We would smoke and tag up walls and roofs which was fun but also got me into trouble. I was getting tackled hard and fumbling the ball a lot. 4th through 6th grade my grades dropped and I'd rarely turn in my work because I lacked *motivation*. My report cards were mostly Fs but as 6th grade started coming to an end, I decided I wanted to graduate. I got it together, dashed toward the end zone and walked the stage. I was proud of myself for this *accomplishment* and felt happy. After all that, my sister found her way out of that gang stuff.

If you would like to read a student's Life Trajectory in its entirety, Freedom's is located in Appendix D.

Variation

- **Literacy Maps:** Literacy Maps invite students to represent experiences relating to the subject matter of the class. For example, if I am a music teacher, I could ask kids to represent a favorite song lyric or album cover, an important memory involving music, and what songs their personal soundtrack might include and why. From there, students can move into some writing. My friend and colleague Rachel deLahunta asks her students to tell their "math story" by reflecting on experiences that have shaped how they feel about and understand math. Literacy Maps can be done with any subject and are a great way to build community, validate students' experiences with the content, and ease them into the space.

Living Moments

I like to think of Living Moments as the memories that live in students' hearts and minds. Sometimes, I will pose a question and ask students to do a short brainstorm in their composition notebooks by listing or drawing ideas, as Carolina does in Figure 5.10. Afterward, students will pick one of the items from their brainstorm

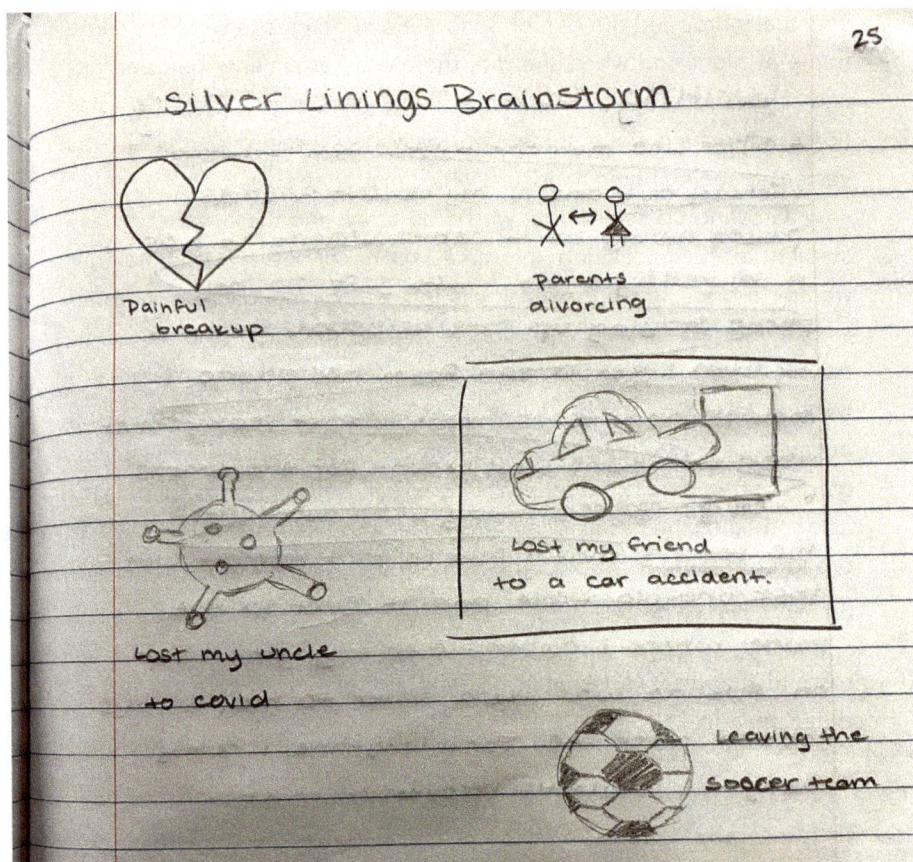

5.10

Carolina's Silver Linings Brainstorm.

and generate a "writing sketch"—a short, informal piece of writing wherein they jot down key details they remember. In Figure 5.11, Jizel writes about teaching herself how to play the guitar.

Depending on the unit and time of year, these might be turned into a formal narrative essay with sensory details and figurative language; if so, I try to make sure students have two or more writing sketches to choose from. But the writing

5.11

Jizel's Precious Moments Brainstorm and Writing Sketch.

sketches don't have to become full-on essays for them to be worthwhile; simply giving students some space to reflect, write, and share with a peer or group goes a long way in building community. Sometimes, we do the writing sketches at the beginning of a unit, sometimes in the middle, at the end, or in between. Here are just a few of students' favorite prompts:

- **Precious Moments:** What are some of your favorite memories? Moments that live in your heart (or your camera roll)? These could include achievements, moments of joy, pride, etc.
- **Silver Linings:** What are some disappointments, challenges, failures, and/or hard decisions you've faced? Was there anything good that possibly emerged? *(Note to reader: An important caveat is that I tell students that not all difficult experiences necessarily have a silver lining nor is it always helpful to "look on the bright side." Otherwise, we may perpetuate toxic positivity.)*
- **Teachable Moments:** What are memorable learning experiences of yours? These can include learning *how* to do something, learning *about* something, or learning *from* an experience, such as a life lesson.
- **Everyday Heroes:** Who in your life do you admire, respect, and/or appreciate? Who are the people whose efforts, contributions, or way of being you want to lift up?

If you would like to read a student's narrative in its entirety, Jenae's Precious Moment is located in Appendix E.

Variation

- **Great Little Stories**: If you are looking for writing ideas more specific to your content area, the micro-documentary series Great Big Story is a fantastic resource. They have tons of engaging videos about artists, scientists, musicians, mathematicians, historians, athletes, writers, and more who have unusual, inspiring, or remarkable stories. Many of the videos are under four minutes, and they are a fun way to connect content to everyday people. Perfect for quick-writes/warm-ups/do nows, especially if you feel constrained by time, content standards, scripted curriculum, or something else. Their YouTube channel can be found at @GreatBigStory.

Snapshot Stories

Inspired by KQED News' Perspectives radio series and PBS NewsHour's "Brief But Spectacular" videos, Snapshot Stories are short pieces that offer a small glimpse, a "snapshot," into an aspect of students' lives. What makes the Snapshot Stories really come to life is when students record audio, include photos, and share them. For example, my journalism class has a website where students post their stories, with audio linked to SoundCloud, so that people can listen and read along [Figure 5.12]. Here are some of my students' favorite prompts:

- What is an aspect(s) of yourself that you want to be known for (especially if people wrongly assume or misunderstand something about you)?
- What are you passionate about? What could you not live without?
- What's an experience you're trying to get through or make sense of?
- What's a current issue/event that is impacting your life in a significant way?
- What issue(s) do you have a unique perspective on that you'd like others to consider?
- What makes you feel alive?

5.12

Descriptions of a few Snapshot Stories as displayed on our class website; the images and story titles link to students' stories.

Depending on the time of year and what's happening in the world, I'll adjust the prompts accordingly. For example, when we returned to in-person learning following nearly eighteen months of school campus closure, one of the prompts asked, "What has it been like returning to school in-person? How does it compare to distance learning?" I continue to be in awe and admiration of students' introspection and the wisdom they glean from their experiences.

For instance, in her Snapshot Story, "Impermanence," Shannon shared the value of being fully present with her father—something that took her time to fully appreciate. Here is an excerpt:

> My deepest regret is that I had listened to him with my head but not my heart. Every conversation we had ever had—around the dinner table, on long drives in the car, in my room on calm nights—I had understood his advice about cherishing those moments, and yet I failed to be truly present. I'd nod whenever he'd remind me that time is short, yet I wouldn't give it a second thought when it came to the time we had together. One of the things he's always emphasized most is "the only permanence is impermanence." Everything is temporary, for good or bad. That's why, he says, we cherish the positives in life and let go of the negative.
>
> And so, that's what we'll do. I've made grave mistakes, and I may only get to my dad once or twice a month, but we'll make those times count. I know I'm extremely lucky to still have these chances. I also know that less time with family is an inevitable part of growing up. The importance of our time together is not in its quantity, but rather, its quality. And what he passes down to me, I will uphold whether he's present or not. He will still be there as the harbor to my ship, no matter the distance or time.

If you would like to read and hear Shannon's story in its entirety, you can find it using this QR code.

Variation

- **Historical or Character Perspectives**: Students can take on the perspective of an historical figure, literary character, famous artist or musician and write (or artistically express) from their point of view. This could be great for looking at character motivations, internal conflict, impact of major events, or underrepresented perspectives.

Special Voices

Special Voices are recorded audio conversations students have with important people in their lives. Inspired by StoryCorps, whose vast collection of audio conversations seek "to help us believe in each other by illuminating the humanity and possibility in us all," my students get to know people more intimately (StoryCorps n.d.). We first listen to some examples from StoryCorps, followed by examples from former students of mine. (StoryCorps' YouTube channel is @storycorps.)

I then have students brainstorm people in their lives with whom they want to talk. Oftentimes they will choose a family member or friend they are close to, but some students will jot down someone they feel estranged from or don't know much about. Next, I have my students brainstorm what they already know about the person and develop interview questions about what they want to know. They then schedule a date and time for their interview. I encourage them to hold it in-person, if possible, and to aim for at least fifteen–thirty minutes. (Many go beyond that.)

For my journalism classes in recent years, I've had students use audio editing software to trim the raw conversation down to its best three–five minutes. They then create an audiogram—a video with a static background image overlaid with captions and optional media elements like moving waveforms, progress bars, etc. [Figure 5.13]. Some students have gone so far as to create their own animation. These are uploaded to YouTube and posted to our class website for others to enjoy.

If you would like to listen to an example of a student's Special Voices conversation, this QR code links to Delilah's conversation with her dad.

5.13

David's Special Voices (top) and Shannon's Special Voices (bottom).

For my English classes, depending on the unit, I'll adapt the assignment and have students write from the perspective of the person they interviewed. For example, our Family Legacy Story project asks students to identify someone in their family (biological or chosen family) whom they want to lift up and to tell that person's story. The idea is for students to shine light on a meaningful or impactful experience that they and the rest of the class can learn from—to guide us all in thinking about the legacy we want to actualize and leave behind.

Family Legacy Stories are a kind of oral history project that my students do as part of our Counterstories Unit, which includes first-person accounts from individuals in our communities whose experiences and perspectives have historically not been represented in mainstream media. Our project specifically amplifies the voices of people of color, migrant families, single and working class parents, the LGBTQIA+ community, and other individuals whose stories have not been widely told. Family Legacy Stories celebrate students' familial and cultural wealth, embedding their people's histories and stories in the curriculum (Yosso 2005).

If you would like to read an example of a student's Family Legacy Story, you can find Jesse's in Appendix F.

Variation

- **Historical or Literary Dialogues:** Students take on the perspective of historical or literary characters and pair up with each other to hold a conversation. This can be particularly useful for helping students understand diverging points of view or conflict. A note of caution: sometimes teachers ask students to role-play with little to no regard for cultural appropriation or how reenactment of certain moments from history, such as slavery, causes immense harm. The following QR code links to a great article about the benefits and potential pitfalls of role-play from the Zinn Education Project.

> ### Centering Love in the Curriculum
>
> ▷ What opportunities do you currently provide for students to write about themselves?
>
> ▷ How often do you provide such opportunities?
>
> ▷ Thinking of the examples offered in this chapter, what idea(s) might you want to try out or adapt for your own context? What variations might benefit your students?

Providing students with ongoing opportunities to write about their lives in meaningful ways can help them develop both skills as a writer and joy for writing. Doing so also helps students see their lives and the lives of their classmates as an intrinsic part of the curriculum that celebrates and reflects back to them who they are. When students are reminded of their own self-worth, they are more likely to see and affirm the worth of others.

The learning opportunities offered in this chapter and the following one almost always culminate with some form of sharing. Sometimes that sharing is just with a partner or in groups; other times it's with the entire class and beyond. Providing an authentic audience lets students know that their stories matter and deserve time to be heard. But in addition, our sharing is also where students experience individual and collective healing.

In the next chapter, we will explore ways we can help our students cultivate love for each other—for humanity—by centering collective healing and justice.

CHAPTER 6

Cultivating Love for Humanity

A few years ago, I came across an important distinction between trauma-informed care and healing-centered practices. Professor of Africana Studies and author Dr. Shawn Ginwright contends that "[w]hile trauma-informed care offers an important lens to support young people who have been harmed and emotionally injured, it also has its limitations" (2018).

One of those limitations, says Ginwright, is that trauma-informed care tends to treat trauma as "an individual experience, rather than a collective one." But doing so fails to address how systemic and environmental factors contribute to *collective* trauma. "By only treating the individual we only address part of the equation[,] leaving the toxic systems, policies and practices neatly intact," he writes (2018).

Another limitation of trauma-informed care is that it may focus on the *impact* of the trauma—"anxiety, anger, fear, sadness, distrust, triggers"—but not necessarily on fostering *wellness*: "hope, happiness, imagination, aspirations, trust." A healing-centered approach, according to Ginwright, is "holistic" and involves "culture, spirituality, civic action and collective healing" (2018). While not dismissing some of the value of trauma-informed care, Ginwright does argue that schools must move toward a healing-centered approach if we are to fundamentally address root causes of trauma and bolster student wellness.

As teachers, it is important that we be intentional about creating learning opportunities that center joy because celebrating students' interests, passions, and precious memories nourishes and strengthens the spirit, heart, and mind. It is equally important that we intentionally provide consistent opportunities that invite students to write about vulnerable and difficult moments because this, too, honors their lived experience and lets them know they are not alone in their struggles. However, doing so requires a strong degree of mutual trust to be established in the writing community; students must trust that the classroom is a supportive space where they can compost pain into healing.

Having said that, inviting students to write about their difficult, even painful, experiences should never be treated or perceived as an exercise in "trauma dumping." We don't want students to go to a place that triggers or re-traumatizes them. I am not a therapist nor social worker, and I am transparent about the limitations of my skills and role as a teacher (including as a mandated reporter). Having a healing-centered approach, however, does necessitate acknowledging causes of harm and trauma, which helps us foster wellness. And when we foster wellness as a *community*, taking care of and holding space for one another, we practice love for humanity—what Dr. Martin Luther King Jr. called agape love.

In this chapter, we will look at ways we can help our students cultivate agape love—that is, love for humanity and for each other—by centering collective healing and justice.

COLLECTIVE HEALING THROUGH WRITING

King characterized the Greek word agape, in part, as "love in action"—love that is *practiced* and not merely felt—by "seeking to preserve and create community" (1958, 105). Agape is a love that builds, brings forth, and holds together. It kindles vulnerability, empathy, and understanding which breathes life into community. When I trust that my students are emotionally ready, I invite them to write pieces that help us put agape love into practice. Here are two such examples.

A Letter to My Shadow

A Letter to My Shadow invites students to write to an internal struggle, a "shadow," they carry, as if it were a person. When introducing the assignment, I tell students that we all carry shadows, and they are not entirely of our own making since we live in an interdependent world. This idea is important, as I want students to understand that their pain is not a sign of some inherent flaw or character deficit, and while it may be part of them, it does not define them.

First, we read a few examples from former students of mine. Sometimes, I will have students do a Silent Conversation reading jigsaw that allows for quiet engagement with the text and each other [Figure 6.1]. In a Silent Conversation, each student, in pairs or small groups, has a different passage from the same text. They each read and write a response to or question about their text; then, after a few minutes, they'll swap with a group member. In addition to writing about the text, they also write to each other. Without exception, students find that they relate to each other; this experience fortifies the safe container we are building that encourages students to tell their own stories.

Second, I ask students to generate a brainstorm in their composition notebooks in response to the following question: "What internal 'shadows' do you carry that affect how you think or feel?" On a sticky note, I then ask each student to write down, anonymously, the shadow they plan to write to, which I collect. Using the whiteboard or a digital slide, I'll display the collective shadows and consolidate duplicates [Figure 6.2].

Next, I'll have them do a writing sketch in their notebook, describing how the shadow manifests in their lives. Finally, I'll ask them to write a fully developed letter, personifying their shadow, with the following guiding questions in mind:

- What does your shadow say? What does it look like? Feel like?
- What's a concrete memory where your shadow had a strong presence?
- What do you hope to do/think/feel differently going forward?

Passage C

> I hate when you appear when I am with my friends and family, especially when I am with my mother—the woman who gave me life, who I respect and love with my whole heart. You make her sad. She doesn't understand why I'm so angry all the time and neither do I. I guess only you know.
>
> The time she threatened to send me to anger management therapy, we laughed at her. You didn't care what she did because the more she tried to help the more you grew, the more powerful you became. It was as if when people tried to help, they were only feeding into your darkness. It's like you are a deep black hole. No light. No stairs. No rope. Just me, at the very bottom.

I can relate to the way you feel, can't control my emotions and I don't understand why, and finish hurting others

I respect how the writer's feeling because when you have a hard time with your emotion, it's hard to control it.

I agree, I get too mad or too upset sometimes & it causes me to say or do things that I don't mean to do.

I admire how the writer describes the "darkness" and the "hole" with no escape

6.1

Silent Conversation between students.

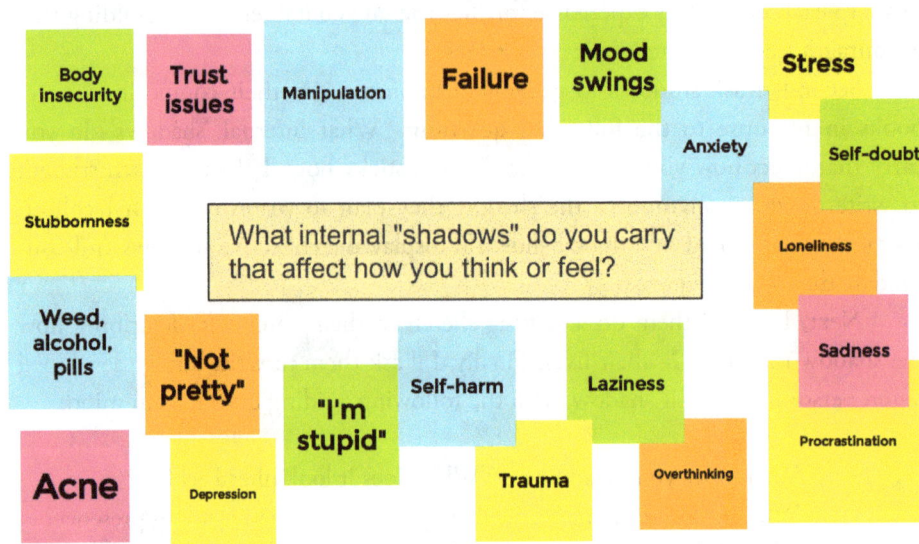

6.2

Collective brainstorm of students' shadows.

In "Dear Body Insecurity," Anthony expresses regret for pressuring himself to lose weight. Here is an excerpt from his letter:

> I'm sorry I have been mistreating you, but ever since last year when I realized I had gained so much weight, I couldn't help but completely immerse myself into 'self-improvement'. I'm afraid of looking weak by giving in to everyone's pleas to gain weight. I have this screwed up idea that weight gain equals weakness or lack of self-control. If anyone were to look hard enough, they would see that my healthy eating is scarce and my exercising is obsessive and excessive.

I find it courageous of Anthony, especially as a young man, to write about the effect of his internalized body insecurity. He does not sugarcoat his struggle or conclude with a superfluously optimistic ending. But he does hold himself with compassion, writing, "It's a battle I'm waging with my mind and the mirror." He ends by saying, "I know you deserve better" and that he is hopeful "to find that balance."

In "Dear Anger," Josee writes about the anger issues she developed as a result of losing her mother. "When you make me angry, I tend to break, rip, punch things, and hurt myself," she writes. She compares her anger to a "pot of boiling water sitting on the stove" and to a "hot breeze in the air that never goes away during the summer." But, like Anthony, she also holds her anger with tenderness and reminds herself of what she *can* do during heated moments: "close my eyes and breathe in and out and tell myself it's going to be ok." She reminds herself that, while her anger may feel all-consuming at times, it does not render her powerless. I admire Josee's strength in choosing to write about this experience and how she wraps herself with care.

When students share these letters, time and again, many express how much more they learn about themselves—and each other. In a reflection, one student wrote:

> I was scared to share my story at first, but then it felt good because my peers shared too. I always thought that I was the only one who was going through hell due to the fact that I've been bullied my whole life. But hearing other people's stories let me know I'm not alone. I have respect for them because they were brave to open up.

Another student wrote: "I learned new sides of certain people I didn't think I'd see before. I see people's humanity, their emotions. It's like I'm peering into a window into their lives. I see so much, yet the curtain is only barely cracked open." When

I asked the student to elaborate on what they meant by the curtain being "only barely cracked open," they told me: "I don't mean that in a negative way. I mean that when we share parts of ourselves with each other, we let others in and show that there is so much more to who we are than what a person might assume based on what they see."

If you would like to read and hear a student's Letter to My Shadow in its entirety, you can find Ashley's using this QR code.

Empathy Letter

Whereas the Letter to My Shadow asks students to write to themselves, the Empathy Letter asks students to write to a person(s) who has harmed them in some way. The letter, first and foremost, gives students space to practice self-empathy by understanding how they were impacted. It also invites students to empathize with the other person by attempting to understand why they acted in the way that they did. This is not at all to excuse or minimize the source of the pain or center the other person at the expense of students' own experience, but rather, to reinforce the idea that all human behaviors are attempts to meet needs. Sometimes, people resort to harmful or destructive strategies to meet their needs because they themselves are wounded.

My friend Kazu Haga does nonviolence training and restorative work in jails with individuals who have caused great harm. In his book *Healing Resistance: A Radically Different Response to Harm*, he writes:

> We cannot cause harm to another human being without harming ourselves in some way. Degrading life does something to degrade our own sense of dignity and humanity. Seeing ourselves as somehow separate from the person you are harming, seeing ourselves as being outside of the web of interdependence takes away from who we truly are. Enacting violence on another person hurts that person, but it is also an act of internal violence that we are doing to ourselves....It is very common for a person to be buried under so many layers of trauma that they cannot even connect or feel their pain for causing harm on someone else. It may feel like we can harm someone without it having any negative impact on ourselves (2020, 151).

I frame the assignment along these lines as we read mentor texts and examples from former students. I highly recommend the anthology *Reclaiming Our Stories*, edited by Mona Alsoraimi-Espiritu, Roberta Alexander, and Manuel Paul López, which contains moving pieces that many students find very relatable.

Next, students brainstorm in their notebooks a list of people who have said or done things that left them feeling distressed, upset, or wounded [Figure 6.3]. I tell students that it doesn't necessarily have to be something that was done on purpose or out of malice; sometimes, people say or do things out of lack of mindfulness or even with seemingly good intentions that nonetheless result in our being impacted negatively.

Before asking students to pick someone on their list, I remind them: "Please don't go to a place that's too painful, re-traumatizing, or that you are not ready to talk about. The invitation, here, is to write about something that still feels alive within you, something that has some intensity or feels incomplete that you think writing about would offer some relief or support. You are the author of your own story and have choice about what goes on the page."

6.3

Aleena and Richard writing in their composition notebooks.

Once students know whom they want to address, they fill out a graphic organizer [Figure 6.4], also available in Appendix G, where they discuss:

- what happened (to the extent that they are comfortable disclosing),
- what they felt in relation to their needs that went unmet (impact),
- the other person's perspective, attempting to understand what needs they might have been trying to fulfill and how they might have felt.

Audience Who will you be writing to?	
Description of issue What happened? (For now just write down key points; you'll go in more detail in your letter)	
Impact: your feelings What did you feel during / after this experience? Please explain. (Refer to feelings list)	
Impact: your needs Which of your needs went unmet or were violated from this experience? Please explain. (Refer to needs list)	
Their perspective • Why do you think the person said/did the thing that caused you harm? • What might they have been feeling? • Which needs might they have been trying to meet?	

6.4
Graphic organizer for Empathy Letter.

After they complete their organizer, students then write their fully developed letter. In "Dear Parents," Cheyanne writes to her mother and father, who both struggled to be emotionally and physically present for her and her siblings. She describes frequently being "woken up to the sound of screaming and things in the home being thrown around and broken." After her father was "taken to court" and gone "for a long time," her mother became more absent, which wreaked havoc on Cheyanne's life:

It got so bad that when you couldn't find a babysitter, you would bring us along to be with other guys as we sat in these strangers' homes eating tuna out of a can. Sometimes it was our only meal.

I felt hopeless, lonely, and frustrated all the time, with no food to fill me. At times I had to sleep on neighbors' couches when you would be gone for nights. No one to talk to about how I felt, what I was going through, feeling as though no one truly cared about me.

I never blamed you guys for it. Instead I would blame myself.

I would wonder, "Is it my fault? Is it me that deserves this?"

I often felt stressed because my need for safety wasn't met and I never knew who to trust, or when my next real meal would be.

Cheyanne writes that while she is not ready to forgive her parents for the pain they inflicted, she understands that they acted from a place of hurt:

I'm guessing you were feeling *broken-hearted* and *hopeless* because maybe you needed support. At this point, you were a single mother raising us three young kids. I could understand that you never asked to be a single mother and have arguments daily.

I also understand the emotional generational trauma my dad has gone through, that he's passing down. You never asked to be born in a society surrounded by bad influences. You were young, and everyone makes mistakes.

Many students related to Cheyanne's experience of having an adult, fathers in particular, as the source of their pain. In "Dear Dad," Thien writes about the confusion of growing up knowing that his father cheated on his mother and being told to keep it a secret from her. "I remember you teaching me to lie," he writes. "I was confused. You told me that 'a white lie is okay sometimes.' That's something a kid my age shouldn't have heard from a role model."

Thien's father eventually became unhoused and Thien never saw him again. In the closing of his letter, Thien allows for multiple truths to coexist by naming the devastating impact of his father's actions and still loving the person he remembers fondly:

One of the biggest lessons I've learned from being alive on this earth is that life isn't fair. The world constantly throws us in bad situations and difficult choices. Your absence is why I am the person I am today. The weight of your actions didn't matter until I was old enough to understand and was strong enough to carry it. I'm still working on who

I am and who I want to be, but I think I'm heading towards the correct path. At the end of the day you tried your best to be a father. I will always remember your kind smile, and the smell of clothes stained with the strong aroma of cigarettes will always remind me of you.

Once students crack the curtain open, they are able to see how some of their collective shadows and external sources of pain share similar patterns and root causes. They recognize, for example, how patriarchy is taught and can be unlearned; how eating disorders can arise from manufactured beauty standards; how racism is not inevitable and can be disrupted.

Invariably, when students share their letters, there are tears. But there is also laughter, hope, and love—love for self and love for one another. The vast majority of students say they enjoy sharing these letters in community, as it allows them to celebrate their resilience and see one another's humanity. As some of my students wrote in the reflection for their Empathy Letter:

- "It was hard but it made me realize how much I'm truly worth."
- "This helped me so much. I wanna thank you because I needed that. I honestly didn't know what to do, but after writing the letter I feel like I'm moving on."
- "I could take some weight off my back after writing my letter. I feel much better and I can breathe a little more."
- "It was better than I thought, not going to lie. It's sad how we all have something that left a scar/wound in our hearts, but at least I don't feel alone anymore because there are people I relate to."
- "I wanna give my classmates the biggest hug."

If you would like to read a student's Empathy Letter in its entirety, you can find Remy's in Appendix H.

FORGING A BRAVE SPACE

It takes immense courage to read and share one's story—especially for young people who have *never* or seldom done so before. Sometimes, students aren't ready to share with the entire class, and that's okay; they can do so privately with me or with their tablemates, if that would meet their needs (e.g., safety, support). Time and again, though, I find that the more opportunities students have to share with each other, the more willing they are to lean into vulnerability, forging a brave space.

We do not always know how others will react to what we say, and there is a degree of risk in putting oneself out there. This is why I prefer the term brave space over safe space. A fellow educator and good friend of mine, Ray Ramirez, once told me that "vulnerability leads to authenticity, which is a conduit for human connection." When students are willing to show up vulnerably, placing trust in the community to receive each other as they are, with care, there is no need to put up a front.

Any time the entire class is sharing writing, I first frame the process with some expectations [Figure 6.5], which are grounded in our Warrior Scholar Principles discussed in Chapter 2.

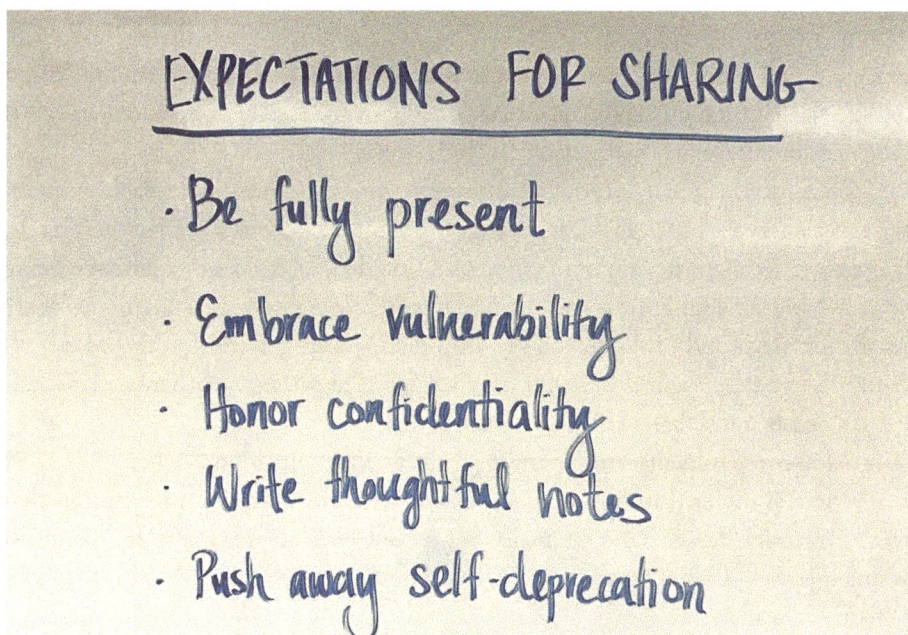

EXPECTATIONS FOR SHARING

- Be fully present
- Embrace vulnerability
- Honor confidentiality
- Write thoughtful notes
- Push away self-deprecation

6.5

Expectations for sharing that I use with my students, adapted by my good friend and colleague Emily La. She added "Push away self-deprecation," which, in turn, I now use. I took this picture of her white board on a day when students were sharing their stories.

Positive Notes

- A strength of your piece is...
- I admire how you...
- I feel moved by...
- My favorite part is...
- I can relate to...

6.6

Sentence Starters for Positive Notes. Sometimes I write these on the board; at other times, I share a digital slide for students to pull up on their own devices.

I remind my students that being seen and heard are human needs, and offering our presence to each other by bearing witness to our collective stories is one of the greatest gifts we can offer. One way I have students practice presence is by writing a Positive Note for each student who shares (Emily calls them Thoughtful Notes). Using colored 8.5" x 11" printer paper, I cut out a bunch of squares ahead of time so that each table has a giant stack ready to go. I always offer some optional sentence starters, which many students find helpful [Figure 6.6].

Doubtless, students do not *have* to delve into their most vulnerable or painful experiences in order to find healing. Students have told me that they rarely, if ever, get to share in community in some of their classes, to experience being affirmed and affirming others. Creating consistent openings for students to share what they are proud of, happy about, inspired by, and grateful for also *matters*—especially for those who do not yet see themselves as writers, mathematicians, scientists, artists, musicians, historians, etc.

Moreover, students are far more likely to invest in school when they trust that school is invested in honoring all of who they are. And in an institution that has historically denied, and in many ways continues to deny, the humanity of young people—BIPOC and LGBTQIA+ youth in particular—bringing people together *is* healing.

A Moment for Reflection

- What opportunities do you currently provide for students to share authentically and deeply with each other?
- What openings are there (or could there be) for students to share more of themselves?

Connection and healing emerge when students are able to authentically be, *and* when they extend themselves for the purpose of nurturing their own and each other's growth. Moreover, a natural outgrowth of this process is hope—hope for more healing, love, and change in the world. But healing from and eradicating violence requires engaging with violence and injustice as they currently exist—and have historically existed. If we want to move *toward* building a fundamentally different world, we must reckon with what it is we want to transform and move away *from*.

Nonviolence is as much about creating as it is about resisting. Martin Luther King Jr. said of agape love: "When I am commanded to love, I am commanded to restore community, to resist injustice, and to meet the needs of my [people]" (1958, 106). Restoration. Resistance. Meeting needs. That is, as teachers, love *requires* us to take a stand for the sake of our immediate and broader communities and not pretend that we can be neutral in the face of injustice. To do otherwise is to abdicate the call to love and neglect the need for justice. Let us take a look at a freedom fighter whose work bridged literacy and liberation and then explore some of the ways that justice can be a core part of our curriculum.

LITERACY FOR LIBERATION

Septima Poinsette Clark was a lifelong educator and human rights activist who was integral to the civil rights movement. Born to a Haitian mother and a father who was formerly enslaved, Clark was instilled with the importance of education early on. At a young age, she began a decades-long career as a public school teacher in South Carolina.

During her tenure as a teacher, she confronted and helped change unjust conditions that she and other Black educators faced. With the help of the NAACP, she was instrumental in helping change a discriminatory policy that barred Black educators from teaching in public schools in Charleston, SC (SNCC Digital Gateway n.d.a). She also partook in a class-action lawsuit that helped establish pay parity between Black and white teachers (The Martin Luther King, Jr. Research and Education Institute. n.d.b).

An educator-activist who was unapologetic about her staunch commitment to racial and social justice, Clark refused to renounce her membership with the NAACP after South Carolina instituted a statute that barred educators, among other employees of the city and state, from affiliating with or belonging to civil rights organizations (The Martin Luther King, Jr. Research and Education Institute. n.d.b). Consequently, after a forty-year teaching career, her teaching contract was not renewed. But she did not waver in her determination to continue helping others learn. She subsequently directed her energy toward working with adults who could not read nor write, at Highlander Folk School in Tennessee, where she had already begun working during previous summers.

Highlander was a racially integrated grassroots educational institution that focused on social justice, desegregation, and other topical issues—rare for such an institution in the South at that time. Participants included Rosa Parks, who attended one of Clark's workshops shortly before the Montgomery Bus Boycott and subsequently returned to Highlander, becoming a mentee and friend of Clark's [Figure 6.7]. Highlander utilized a democratic model of teaching and learning "that was rooted in the lives and problems of its students. The school used small group discussions and workshops to enable students to delve into their own issues and use their collective knowledge to find solutions" (SNCC Digital Gateway. n.d.b).

Clark was renowned for leading workshops on citizenship education and community empowerment, where participants learned about voting rights, housing issues, traffic laws, sewing, and other areas that Clark believed participants "would have to know in order to start on their way to becoming first-class citizens" (Clark and Blythe 1962, 150). But, for Clark and other Highlander teachers and students, acquiring the skills to participate as civic members of society was part of

6.7

A gathering at the Highlander Folk School in Monteagle, Tennessee in 1957. Septima Clark (center), civil rights activist Rosa Parks (third from left), labor organizer Ralph Helstein (far left), educator Myles Horton (second from left), educator and activist Charles Gomillion (second from right), activist Bernice Robinson (far right), and others.

a more pressing goal. She and others believed that having the power and agency to transform unjust conditions in one's own community *through* economic, political, academic literacies was paramount. In her 1962 memoir, *Echo in My Soul*, she wrote:

> People came to Highlander to seek enlightenment on issues whose proper solution, followed up by adequate social action, would promote the advancement of all....[O]ur workshops seek always to gear themselves to the times and are concerned primarily with current issues and problems and practical methods of solving these problems, so that when the workshop student returns from Highlander to [their] home community [they are] better equipped to lead the homefolk in attacking and disposing of them (Clark and Blythe 1962, 178, 193).

Of particular interest to Clark was the problem of adult illiteracy. Some of her students did not know how to read nor write, not even their own name. If people could not read nor write, they could not fill out voter registration forms, and if they could not fill out voter registration forms, they could not vote on, let alone read about, material issues affecting their lives.

Rather than using traditional children's primers to teach reading, however, Clark focused on teaching words within a political context. "We were teaching words, but the words were words of an adult world and they were words of an informed citizen," she wrote (Clark and Blythe 1962, 193). For example, she would write down the word "government" on the chalkboard and help her students "make smaller words from it, and then use these words to make sentences." She would then do the same with "senatorial" and similar words that would appear in voting forms and the like (Clark and Blythe 1962, 204). That is, she ensured that what students read and wrote, and the skills they practiced, were relevant to their lives and sociopolitical contexts [Figure 6.8].

"Literacy means liberation," Clark wrote several times in a 1964 essay featured in *Freedomways Magazine*. In her piece, she exalts the efforts of everyday folks whose development of political, financial, social, and reading and writing literacies empowered them and their communities to effect material change in their lives. Whether it was forming a credit union, running voter registration drives, fighting for quality education and adequate resources, creating a community center, or

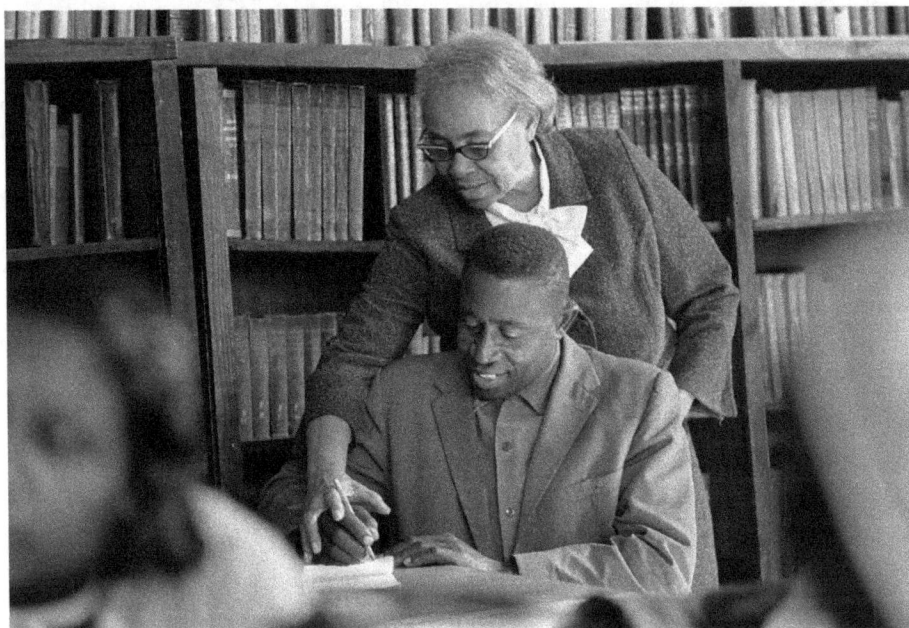

6.8

Septima Clark helps a man write during a citizenship education workshop, 1966.

organizing and mobilizing people to take political action, Clark saw an inextricable link between literacy and social justice (1964). She was resolute in helping her students develop the tools and skills to become more *free* in the world—and to do the same for others.

Clark's approach exemplified Brazilian educator Paulo Freire's notion that "[r]eading the word and learning how to write the word so one can later read it are preceded by learning how to write the world, that is, having the experience of changing the world and touching the world" (Freire and Macedo 1987, 49). Such liberation, Clark believed, could only be achieved through nonviolence. In a speech she once gave on the importance of nonviolent resistance, she said: "[W]e must struggle passionately and unrelentingly for the goal of justice, but we must be sure that our hands are clean in the struggle….Freedom is a costly[,] precious thing. It has never been given. It has always been won" (Clark n.d.).

Clark's example of bridging literacy and liberation can help us be mindful about designing learning opportunities that are both responsive to students' lived experiences and don't shy away from uncomfortable truths.

Reflecting on this Historical Moment

- In what ways does Septima Clark's approach to literacy align with or differ from yours?
- What connections do you make between literacy and liberation?

NEUTRALIZING NEUTRALITY

In my own classroom, I am deliberate about addressing sociopolitical issues that directly and indirectly affect students, their families, and broader society. I am not interested in indoctrinating them because doing so would require that students "accept a set of beliefs uncritically"—the very antithesis of what I and many other teachers want for our kids (*New Oxford American Dictionary* n.d.). That said, I want my students to work through their own ideas, and I am clear with them that they don't have to agree with me.

As mentioned earlier, if our goal is to eradicate violence, then we must acknowledge the presence of violence. Needless to say, discussing violence is not easy and can be taxing on the mind, heart, and spirit. But when we keep hope and love at the center, we minimize the chance of becoming consumed by despair. Moreover, centering hope and love helps our students move through difficult, even uncomfortable, emotions for the sake of their growth and a more just world.

For example, one of the texts I teach is the graphic novel *March: Book One* by John Lewis, Andrew Aydin, and Nate Powell. The first book of a trilogy, *Book One* focuses on the story of the late civil rights icon and congressman John Lewis' childhood, journey toward nonviolence, and activism during the lunch counter sit-in movement in Nashville. It is an absolute favorite for many of my students, who are inspired by Lewis' unwavering commitment to nonviolence and how he and scores of other young people dreamed of and helped create a better society.

One student shared in a post-reading reflection:

> In the beginning, I didn't know much of nonviolence except that it refrained from harming others. I didn't think that nonviolence could influence others and raise awareness. My current view is that it's more than avoiding violence; you're trying to spread awareness without causing harm onto others and instead attacking systems and the status quo.

Another student wrote, "I have the utmost respect for those who practiced nonviolence, fighting for equal rights. It looks so hard, and the mentality they had must have been made of steel."

Disrupting Comfort

Last year, after students had wrapped up an essay about *March: Book One*, Taylor, one of my few white students, wrote a letter to me, of her own volition [Figure 6.9].

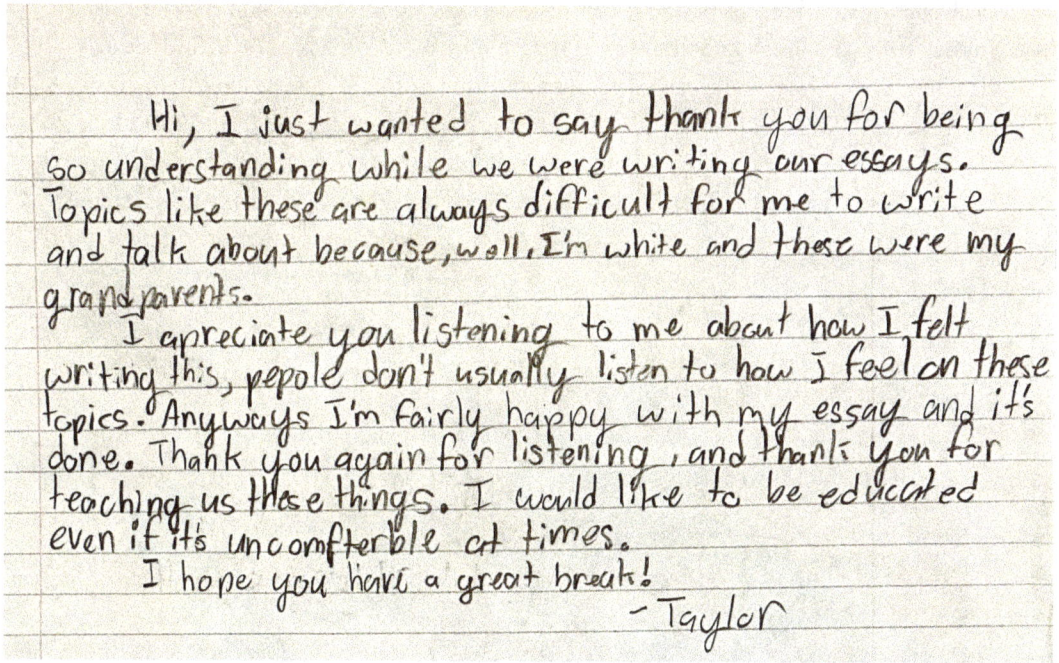

Hi, I just wanted to say thank you for being so understanding while we were writing our essays. Topics like these are always difficult for me to write and talk about because, well, I'm white and these were my grandparents.

I appreciate you listening to me about how I felt writing this, pepole don't usually listen to how I feel on these topics. Anyways I'm fairly happy with my essay and it's done. Thank you again for listening, and thank you for teaching us these things. I would like to be educated even if it's uncomfterble at times.

I hope you have a great break!

-Taylor

6.9

A handwritten note from my student Taylor, following our reading of John Lewis' graphic novel *March: Book One*.

"These were my grandparents." Wow. I can only imagine how hard it was for Taylor to reckon with this hard truth. It *was* uncomfortable for her, indeed. And yet, it was this discomfort—in conjunction with space held to process it—that allowed for both a fuller, more compassionate understanding of those who maintained, either actively or passively, the status quo *and* a deepened appreciation for those who actively resisted it.

If all human behaviors are attempts to meet needs, then it stands to reason that acts of malice, indifference, and violence are attempts, albeit tragic and catastrophic ones, to have needs met. Taylor was able to recognize that people of her grandparents' generation had wounds and flaws of their own and were not static caricatures. She was still angry and hurt about the violent, untarnished truth of segregation and white supremacy, but in wanting to continue "to be educated even if it's uncomfortable at times," she allowed for discomfort to be a constructive and illuminative conduit for learning and growth rather than something to fear and avoid.

Such enlightenment cannot happen, however, if students are denied opportunities to grapple with discomfort. I am gravely disturbed by the so-called "war on wokeness," epitomized by many states' efforts to restrict or outright ban teachings of vital topics that some misguidedly believe are intended to indoctrinate kids.

In January of 2022, for instance, as part of a manufactured backlash to critical race theory, Florida passed a bill prohibiting public schools and private businesses from teachings and trainings on race and racism that result in individuals feeling "discomfort, guilt, anguish, or any other form of psychological distress" (Simonson 2022). Ostensibly for the purpose of "protecting" kids. And Florida is far from an outlier. According to an analysis conducted by Education Week [Figure 6.10], "Since January 2021, 44 states have introduced bills or taken other steps

■ Bill was signed into law or a similar state-level action was approved
■ Bill has been vetoed, overturned, or stalled indefinitely
■ No state-level action or bill introduced
■ Bill has been proposed or is moving through state legislature

SOURCE: Education Week reporting

EdW

6.10

⬢ A Flourish map

A map from Education Week showing, as of February of 2023, states that have proposed, vetoed, or passed legislation targeting critical race theory.

that would restrict teaching critical race theory or limit how teachers can discuss racism and sexism" (Schwartz 2023).

The blistering, growing assaults against the LGBTQIA+ community, trans people in particular, from healthcare to education to sports to library books, are just as swift and fierce. The ACLU has found, as of February of 2024, that over **400** anti-LGBTQIA+ bills have been introduced. The ACLU notes that "[w]hile not all of these bills will become law, they all cause harm for LGBTQ people" (ACLU 2024). How in the world are LGBTQIA+ youth to feel affirmed, safe, seen—*loved*—when their very humanity is denied? What is the point of school if it does not enable human beings to *be* their fullest, truest selves and to learn about issues affecting their identities and lives?

It seems that a kind of neutral education is what some proponents of the "war on wokeness" desire. Arizona's current superintendent of instruction, who also served in that role from 2003 to 2011, supported a 2010 law that banned Tuscon Unified's highly successful Mexican American Studies program, which ill-informed critics falsely derided as "anti-American." Shortly before winning reelection to his role as superintendent in 2022, he said, "We need to teach kids that we're all individuals. We're all brothers and sisters and we need to treat each other as individuals and that race is completely irrelevant" (Sievers 2023). He also said that his priority as superintendent of instruction would be to "get rid of the distractions, to focus on academics again, and get the kids' learning up and their test scores up" (Stanford 2022). If the goal is to create a seemingly apolitical, ahistorical, colorblind, and ruggedly individualistic society, then this kind of education would be apt. But most of us know better than to promote such a myopic, misguided education for our kids.

I feel for the teachers, librarians, parents, caregivers, and, of course, young people in regions directly impacted by the sweeping "anti-woke" laws. And as a teacher with a relatively strong degree of autonomy in a state without such laws (currently, anyway), I do not believe it is my place to cast judgment on educators who, for fear of losing their jobs and livelihood, are tiptoeing carefully around issues of race, racism, gender, sex, etc.

I also believe that we cannot afford to be neutral if we are to create the Beloved Community and achieve collective liberation from all forms of oppression. For those of us who have the leeway, support, or capacity to explicitly teach the messy, painful, beautiful, hopeful, and contradictory truths of this country, we *must* do so—even if that means there's discomfort in the process.

John Lewis said of the sit-in movement, "We wanted to change America—to make it something different, something better" (Lewis, Aydin, and Powell 2013, 103). He and many others recognized that the project of American democracy is not guaranteed nor ever finished, and it requires ongoing fighting for. Lewis' belief that America was capable of realizing its potential and promise of freedom and justice was fueled by an unshakable ethic of agape love that *demanded* confronting and transforming the oppressive reality of segregation.

Moreover, Lewis and others knew that such a fight would stir discomfort for many people who were complacent with the existing order of things. But such discomfort was recognized as a necessary part of changing ideas, beliefs, and systems; it was not something to weaponize and use against their opponents.

And while Lewis and countless others faced extraordinary risk, sacrifice, and pushback, their efforts garnered support and involvement from people sympathetic to their cause. Such a noble embodiment of courage, love, and hope for the sake of a "different" and "better" America was, perhaps, the *most* American thing to do. Similarly, it is important for us teachers to decide what discomforts we are willing to endure as we work for change and co-create the kinds of learning spaces we dream of for our precious young people and for ourselves.

Projecting Hope

Creating opportunities for students to engage with the world *as it is* allows them to move toward the world as they *want it to be*. In so doing, we practice teaching and learning that are *just* because they are responsive to current and historical realities.

One example of this in my own practice is The Coloring Book of Freedom Fighters, a class project my students have taken beyond the walls of our classroom [Figure 6.11]. The coloring book consists of historical and contemporary individuals and groups, many seldom taught about in schools, who have led or played important roles in justice and liberation movements and struggles.

Introduced midway through the second semester, this project follows curricular units on oppression, resistance, and feminism in order for students to have a solid understanding of key terms and concepts. The timing also allows for them to *apply* their knowledge.

After introducing the project, my students, either individually or in pairs, sign up for a freedom fighter (I provide a list of suggestions, and students are welcome to add to it). They then conduct research on that person, group, or movement and are guided by three central questions and sub questions:

- **What is the background of your freedom fighter?** What experiences led to their activism?
- **How did (or does) your person, group, or movement fight for justice?** In what ways do they resist injustice?
- **What legacy has this freedom fighter left behind?** How have they influenced your thinking about _____? What problem(s) are we confronted with today that their efforts can help us address?

6.11

A coloring page of Angela Davis (top left). A coloring page of the People Power Revolution in the Philippines (top right). Students reading and coloring a page about Malala Yousafzai (bottom left). Students reading and coloring a page about Amanda Nguyen (bottom right).

After conducting research, students write up a one-page description of their freedom fighter with cited sources. They then create an original drawing or stencil image of their person, group, or movement. Finally, I collate the descriptions and drawings and have the booklets printed at a print shop. The finished product is a beautiful coloring book that every student across my English classes contributes to.

The most exciting part is the walking field trip wherein my classes visit an elementary school in our community and share the coloring book with younger students. Enough copies are printed for each of my students as well as the kids we visit. It is thrilling to see students color, read, and talk together, teaching and learning from each other. Building intergenerational connections and knowledge. Engaging with the world as it is in order to imagine the world as they want it to be.

Here are but a few examples of other amazing projects and learning opportunities that classroom teachers have done with their students.

Middle school art teacher Ben Stanton partnered with a nonprofit organization that constructs schools and skate parks in Honduras. He and the organization created the Compton Plywood Project, where students, using donated skateboard decks, created custom artwork pieces. Students then contacted skate and surf shops, who exhibited and sold students' art-adorned skateboards, the proceeds of which went to charities of students' choice (Posnick-Goodwin 2018, 14).

Fourth-grade teacher Ryan Brazil and her students created a children's book, *Anti-bias ABC's*, as a way to inspire "love, empathy, and compassion." Their book "features anti-bias–related words for each letter of the alphabet, along with descriptions and illustrations penned by Brazil's students" (Peeples 2022, 38).

Fourth- and fifth-grade teacher Aba Ngissah partnered with foundations and organizations with the aim of "increas[ing] representation in entertainment, gaming, media, and tech for women and underrepresented people." For example, at Girls Make Beats, students learn about "sound engineering, podcasting, and careers as music producers." Through the smartphone filmmakers project that Ngissah created with funding support from her district, students learned "writing and filming skills while collaborating with industry experts" in film (Posnick-Goodwin 2021, 18–19).

High school history and ethnic studies teacher Alexander Nguyễn created anthologies of his students' writing at the end of the school year. *History in Our Hands: The Power of Letters to Preserve our Past, Present, and Future* is a collection of student letters in the form of narratives and essays wherein students explore their identities, passions, culture, and history. In a similar anthology for a different class of his, *East Side San Jose Food Stories: How Food Connects to Our Past, Present, and Future* contains students' memories, recipes, and narratives about the intersections of food, identity, and love.

These teachers helped their students create projects that address important issues in their lives and communities. An education that honors students as they are, inspires them to create positive change, and excites them in the learning process is an education that is just.

If you are interested in learning more about culminating projects and learning opportunities that extend beyond the classroom, there is a plethora of resources on project-based learning online (Edutopia.org has some great materials). In addition, youth participatory action research (YPAR), which draws from social justice principles and frameworks, is an especially powerful way of helping students engage with issues impacting their lives and communities. UC Berkeley's YPAR Hub offers some excellent resources and materials: yparhub.berkeley.edu.

LIFE AS PRIMARY TEXT

James Kass, founder of the renowned poetry organization Youth Speaks, says that we must treat "life as primary text" if we want students to see themselves reflected in and shape their learning. "Literacy is a need, not a want," he writes on Youth Speaks' website. "Having knowledge, practice, and confidence in the written and spoken language is essential to the self-empowerment of an individual," and when one feels empowered, they are better able to "deconstruct current dominant narratives by creating a more inclusive and active culture" (Kass n.d.).

I spoke with Kass and asked him to elucidate the philosophy of "life as primary text" in the context of the classroom. At its core, he said:

> It aims to support young people in being in real deep conversation, deep learning, and deep listening about any given topic. Life as primary text doesn't mean you can *only* write from a first-person perspective. The conversation starts with where students are already, and as educators, we move that conversation onward, to help expand their frame of reference and knowledge base (Kass 2023).

That is, "life as primary text" taps into the existing funds of knowledge (Moll et al. 1992) of students—where they "are already"—and helps them deepen knowledge of self, enrich understanding of each other, and expand political consciousness. Students' lives are an inextricable part of the curriculum in that their interests, experiences, and perspectives help guide what is taught and discussed.

Clearly, this approach might vary depending on the subject area, but the spirit of "life as primary text" can be extended and applied regardless of what one teaches. Kass offered some questions, which I have adapted and added to, that can be particularly helpful when thinking of an issue or problem that students (or we) want to focus on.

Similar to the K-W-L process in which students assess what they *already* know prior to a lesson or unit, determine what they *want* to know, and reflect on what they have *learned* following the lesson or unit, these questions can be useful whether students are thinking about a real-world issue, mathematical problem, scientific hypothesis, or historical moment, among other things. The more that students practice inquiry-type thinking, the more familiar with and accustomed to it they become.

Furthermore, what's great about the Life as Primary Text framework is that it is something we can integrate into our daily lessons, regardless of the subject we teach. We do not have to wait until doing grand or lengthy projects; treating students' lives as primary text is something we can—and should—do regularly.

For example, in an interview with *Rethinking Schools* magazine, educator and writer Dr. Christopher Emdin discusses how he embeds justice into his teaching. Drawing from practices he shares in his book *STEM, STEAM, Make, Dream: Reimagining the Culture of Science, Technology, Engineering, and Mathematics,* Emdin says, "One of my favorite activities with young people is to have them identify an issue in their community that they are viscerally dissatisfied with" (2023, 29).

Emdin describes an example of a student feeling upset about how their neighborhood park is in poor condition while a park in a wealthier neighborhood is clean and nicer. Emdin then tells the student, "'That's a phenomenal written piece. Now, I want you to find math facts to support your assertion. Your park was mad dirty? Word. How many pieces of garbage were there per square foot in that area? Calculate that. Your emotions are valid. Now use mathematical observations to support your arguments.'" After his students "begin with an emotional articulation through writing," Emdin then shows them "how, when you add science and math, no one can be unconvinced about your pain. So, math and science become tools for us to achieve justice" (2023, 29).

Emdin adds, "My vision for science is that young folks have it as a piece of their identity: *I write, I dance, I'm a scientist, I'm a mathematician*. I want it to pour out of young folks fluidly and with ease. I want them to see themselves through these disciplines. And I see science and math as tools for achieving justice" (2023, 30). Regardless of our content area, when we center students' lives in the curriculum, the skills and concepts within our subject area(s) carry much more meaning and purpose.

We can help students see that the teaching and learning are not *just* for college and career but also for helping them see themselves and each other as active agents of positive change in the world.

Applying Life as Primary Text to Your Classroom

▷ Is there an issue or problem currently facing your students or school that you could address through your content? What form might this take?

▷ Is there a lesson or unit that would lend itself to an inquiry approach, driven by student interest and need? If so, what might this look like?

In "Love as the Practice of Freedom" from her book *Outlaw Culture: Resisting Representations*, bell hooks writes, "The moment we choose to love we begin to move against domination, against oppression. The moment we choose to love we begin to move towards freedom, to act in ways that liberate ourselves and others. That action is the testimony of love as the practice of freedom" (2006, 298). hooks reminds us that love is a *practice* grounded in action that liberates. A love that moves away from violence and toward peace. A love that creates. A love that connects. In this way, love fulfills a deep spiritual need to belong and to be in community. Every effort we make to forge a community rooted in and motivated by love is a practice that frees us from the forces that breed violence: disconnection, domination, lovelessness.

Similarly, aikido creator Morihei Ueshiba says in *The Art of Peace: Teachings of the Founder of Aikido* that through ongoing practice and discipline, we strengthen who we are: "[e]veryone has a spirit that can be refined, a body that can be trained in some manner, a suitable path to follow. You are here…to realize your inner divinity and manifest your innate enlightenment" (Ueshiba 1992, 13). That is, we are unfinished beings with abundant capacity to grow in heart, body, mind, and spirit.

Ueshiba himself experienced enlightenment when he secluded himself in the mountains and engaged in intense physical, spiritual, and mental training to strengthen his body, heart, mind, and spirit. After fighting against a high-ranking swordsman who had challenged Ueshiba to a duel, Ueshiba subsequently recounted:

> Suddenly the earth trembled. Golden valor welled up from the ground and engulfed me. I felt transformed into a golden image, and my body seemed as light as a feather. All at once I understood the nature of creation: the way of the warrior is to manifest divine love, a spirit that embraces and nurtures all things. Tears of gratitude and joy streamed down my cheeks. I saw the entire earth as my home, and the sun, moon, and stars as my intimate friends. All attachment to material things vanished (Stevens and Krenner 2004, xv).

For Ueshiba, to feel intimately connected with life was to embody and promote love in the world, in the universe. And to embrace and nurture all things was to disrupt all that inhibits love and life. But this love didn't and doesn't just appear by happenstance; it is a result of ongoing cultivation and practice.

If we treat our classrooms as spaces that attend to meeting students' holistic needs, then we can support them in realizing their "inner divinity" and "innate enlightenment." Loving themselves, each other, humanity. And if we think of our students' lives, as well as our own, as texts written by *how* we show up in the world, with love as our ink, then the words we live and breathe will reflect the beauty and depth of who we are—and can be—as a people.

"I slip gradually into the arms of a rest that demands nothing, gives all that is needed, then comes back around again....May all beings know love and the source of all love. May all beings know rest. May all beings rest."

NAKACHI CLARK-KASIMU, poet and educator

SECTION IV

Slow Urgency

CHAPTER 7

At the Speed of Breath

It was the middle of the night when the sounds of slow, deep breathing punctuated the quiet air and roused me from my slumber.

In.

Out.

In.

Out.

Before my disoriented, sleep-deprived brain had even reached its fully awakened state, I instinctively already knew: *It's time*.

I rolled over and saw my partner, Rachelle, in a near fetal position, caressing her swollen belly while she continued to breathe. *In. Out. In. Out.*

"Are you okay, Love?" I asked, gently rubbing her back.

She slowly nodded her head while breathing loudly, eyes closed and brows furrowed slightly, before mumbling in a near whisper, "I think I'm in labor."

I called the nurse, who advised me to do as we had practiced in a new parenting class a few weeks before: count the number of contractions per hour, and when they start occurring every few minutes and last for approximately sixty seconds, then it's time to go to the hospital.

"Okay, that was, um, every five to seven minutes, you said, right?" I asked, the nervousness in my voice an obvious signal that I was new to this.

"You got it, sir," the nurse responded with a smile that was audible on the other end of the line. "Everything is going to be just fine. Just do your best to count those contractions using the app I mentioned, and pay attention to when her water breaks."

"Okay, thank you, ma'am," I said, feeling a small boost of confidence from her reassurance.

"You have your hospital bag ready to go?"

Shit.

I stood frozen and stared at a fold in the comforter as the realization hit me that we had not yet packed it, as our child had decided to make her entrance to the world early.

"I'm going to handle that right now," I said before thanking her again and hanging up the call. The next interval of time stretched into what felt like infinity as I fumbled my way through counting contractions and simultaneously packing our hospital bag, trying earnestly not to forget any of the essentials—medical information, snacks, blankets, change of clothes, diapers, Pillow Pet.

Thankfully, we had decided to stay at my in-laws' place that evening. Rachelle's mother was extremely helpful with checking in on us, assisting me in preparing the hospital bag, and bringing us snacks and water. The hours blended into each other like ocean waves greeting and receding from the shore while my partner's breathing intensified and contractions became more recurrent. When her water broke around 6:00 AM, we knew it was time to leave.

As eager as I was to get us to the hospital, however, walking from the bedroom, down the stairs, and to the front door was a Herculean effort for Rachelle, as her growing discomfort required us to stop every few steps—and wait. And wait.

In.

Out.

In.

Out.

Her body was following the rhythm of its own ancient wisdom, which seemed to render the construct of time obsolete to her in her dazed state.

We finally made it to the car, where my mother-in-law and I helped Rachelle inside and loaded our belongings. When I started up the engine and adjusted my rearview mirror, I paused for a moment. Reflected back to me was an empty car seat that I knew would soon have our baby sitting in it, joining us in life, companioning the world. I smiled and felt my heart flutter. I looked over to Rachelle and placed my hand in hers, massaging it with my thumb, feeling awed by her strength and ability to grow a human being inside of her. We then made our way to the hospital, toward the morning horizon, where the birth of a new day, a new life was greeted by a rising sun awakening the sky.

Arrival

Our baby, Tala, made her arrival to the world on a glorious, sunny morning in early August [Figure 7.1]. Thankfully, Rachelle's labor went smoothly and our child was born healthy and strong. We felt enormous elation and gratitude for the miracle that was this bundle of joy, of beauty, of life in our hands and hearts. To hold her for the first time, feeling her warm, tiny body pressed against mine, was love incarnate. Those first days and nights of gentle intimacy, figuring out nursing, and little sleep will forever live in my mind and heart.

Originally, Tala wasn't due until mid-August—which, as my luck would have it, also happened to be the *first day* of school. The timing could not have been worse for someone who suffers from anxiety that runs in the family and is debilitating at times. As we educators well know, the foundational first few days and weeks of school can make or break one's year.

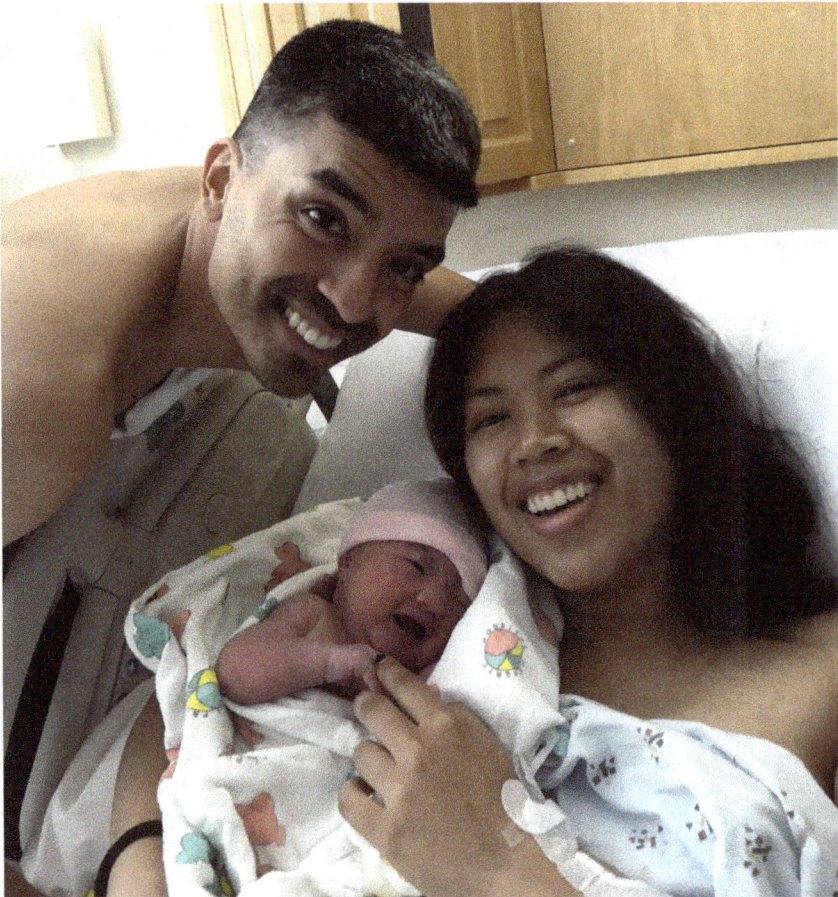

7.1

Two new overjoyed (and tired) parents with their baby shortly after birth. Personal collection.

Prior to Tala's arrival, I was prepared to take some time off, although I was worried about worst-case scenarios: *What if the sub starts things off poorly and I inherit a mess? What if the sub leaves and students are left with a revolving door of fill-ins? What if I can't recover and am stuck in survival mode the rest of the year? What if I'm super stressed all the time? What if...what if...what if?*

Maybe I was catastrophizing. But one of the hallmarks of generalized anxiety disorder is that when we feel a lack of control or are in situations whose outcomes seem uncertain or unpredictable, it can cause excessive and persistent worrying. This can lead to physiological problems including insomnia, digestive issues, restlessness, and muscle tension, all of which I was well familiar with. I did not want to be in a situation that would cause me undue stress as a new parent. I did not want to bring that kind of energy home.

And so, shortly after Tala was born, I started wondering whether it might ease my anxiety and help me be more present if I started off the school year with my students and took family leave at a later date. I figured that once relationships, classroom culture, and flow had been established, it wouldn't feel as consequential if I weren't there. I would not have entertained this thought, however, were it not for family nearby we could stay with and who were available and willing to assist us. There is no way I would have left my partner on her own, anxiety be damned.

I talked it over with Rachelle, who, bless her, understood my dilemma and did not pressure me either way. No doubt, she would have loved for me to have more than just a couple of weeks at home before starting work. But she also trusted my capacity to be fully present once the school day was done because she knew how much I had grown in reaching a healthier work–life balance.

When we first started dating, early in my teaching career, I would frequently work late into the night and dedicate hours of my weekends for lesson planning and grading, which felt impossible to finish within my measly prep period and contractual hours. Occasionally, I would take a personal or sick day just to *catch up* on grading a stack of essays. Thinking about that now, I wince.

But by the time Tala came along, I was no longer burning the midnight oil every week nor banking on playing catch-up during weekends. It wasn't that I had decided to no longer take *any* aspect of work home; I still did and still do, including occasions that call for a late night or weekend session. Frankly, I was a more experienced and effective educator who had developed more efficient processes for creating curriculum and assessing student learning. And, fortunately for me, that school year I was given the same courses I had taught the previous year, so I had material ready to go to help start things off.

Also influencing my decision was the addition of a fall break, a first for me, that stakeholders in my school district had previously voted in favor of. Having a full week off in early October, followed by several days in November, and two weeks in December-January seemed like well-timed breaks for any teacher during the first semester, but especially for a teacher in my shoes. After some deliberation, I decided: I would start off the school year with my students and revisit taking family leave.

The first few months went without a hitch. Sure, I was plenty exhausted from the demands of being a new parent and teaching, but I was proud of myself for ensuring that once I got home, I was *present* with my family and treated our time as sacred because it was. If I was behind in grading, so be it. If a lesson flopped, I would swiftly make some changes for the following day and try to be at peace with any imperfections. I had become more adept as a teacher at knowing where to invest more of my energy and where I could afford to scale back.

But before I knew it, caught up in the hustle and bustle of the school year, the end of the first semester was nearly over and I had not yet planned family leave. I remember thinking: *Maybe I could take off time at the end of the year and have an extended summer? I still have time to figure it out.*

And then COVID-19 struck.

Bringing the world to a screeching halt.

Arresting the literal breath.

Suspending the ebb and flow of life in a kind of purgatory of precarity, where those of us who could, held our breath, containing swelling uncertainty and fear, waiting for the moment when we could collectively *exhale*.

Multiple Truths

Amidst the devastating loss the world witnessed as the pandemic swept across the planet, for me and my family, it was an unintended blessing of sorts. When my school closed, we were not yet doing synchronous online learning. I continued to check in with my students and post optional learning opportunities for anyone who chose to do them, but doing so asynchronously enabled me to have an abundance of time with my child. Time we needed. Time we deserved.

I will, for the rest of my days, cherish our daily strolls at Cataldi Park. Our trips to the library. Our hikes at Alum Rock Park. Our laughter and play with Mama, Lola, Nanay Bebot, Ate Wen, Lolo, Grandpa Tony, and other loved ones who were there for us as we trepidatiously navigated the early days of the pandemic. It was the closest thing to family leave that I would get to experience.

In retrospect, it is difficult to say unequivocally what the "right" choice was, knowing what I now know about myself and the world. My anxiety was and is real. I had not yet sought therapy about it. Starting the year off strong at school *did* allow me to be more present at home. The pandemic was a catalyst that helped me significantly slow down and *be*—not just *do* all of the damn time [Figure 7.2].

7.2

Me with Tala, at three months old. Personal collection.

But I also grieve the fact that taking family leave was even a question in the first place. That I work in a profession that could trigger and exacerbate my anxiety so intensely. That I did not fully trust in my ability to rebound from hypothetical worst-case scenarios, despite the fact that I excel at building strong, positive relationships with students.

I am holding that multiple truths can coexist. My decision to start off the school year with my students did not come at the expense of my family. It was, first and foremost, for the sake of my health and wellness, and, by extension, that of my partner and child. *And*, it would have been wonderful to have had time replete with rest and leisure, unadulterated by anything related to teaching. Both truths are real.

The other night, I was talking to my partner about when we became new parents, and she said, "It's not just the first few weeks and months that matter; every successive moment of our child's life is just as important."

As teachers with an extraordinarily demanding and taxing number of responsibilities, how can we ensure that we take care of ourselves and each other so that we can treat each moment as sacred? To not get lost in the trap of scarcity mentality?

In this chapter, we will explore ways to practice slowness amidst the nonstop, fast pace of school and ever-growing demands placed on educators. By slowing down, both in our classrooms as well as our personal lives, we can attend to our holistic needs, sustaining that which sustains us: the breath. Through every single moment of life.

In. Out. In. Out.

by slowing down, both in our classrooms as well as our personal lives, we can attend to our holistic needs, sustaining that which sustains us: the breath

WHAT'S THE RUSH?

It is an incontrovertible fact that teachers have an astronomical number of things to track, respond to, follow up with, create, and decide. An oft-referenced study from the 1990s, when teaching was already hard, estimates at least 1,500 decisions each day (Klein 2021). That is likely a very conservative number today, if we take into account our increasing usage of and reliance on superfast technologies that have developed in the time since, pressing and overlapping social issues including mental health, gun violence, racism, LGBTQIA+ phobia, cyberbullying, and life "post"-COVID.

It is almost trite to name that teaching is an exceptionally complex, multi-faceted craft with a seemingly endless list of responsibilities and duties that extend far beyond "just" teaching content and standards. We mentor, counsel, hold, inter-vene, problem-solve, adapt, build, repair—repeatedly, often on the fly, and in the midst of constant interruptions and crises. The whopping amount of energy and stamina required to attend to such demands while trying to design and teach crea-tive, engaging, and relevant lessons each day is truly staggering. The workload and challenges are undeniably immense, especially in schools and communities sur-viving through poverty, violence, racism, and other oppressive conditions and in regions where teachings of certain topics are controversial or banned.

And yet, the fast pace of modern life and multitudinous societal crises not-withstanding, the afforded time we have to get it all done has largely remained unchanged over the decades. Most of us still have the same number of instruc-tional days. With the same number of students (sometimes more). With the same number of school hours in a day. Time—as it is conceived in many Western socie-ties, anyway—is finite, as is our capacity to direct our energy toward all that pulls at our attention, often in divergent directions. There are, of course, physiological limits to what we are able to do, yet most of us are not encouraged nor shown how to slow down. Consequently, many teachers feel as though they are invariably run-ning on empty, regularly crossing into the threshold of emotional, mental, physi-cal, and spiritual exhaustion and depletion.

That it is universally assumed that first-year teachers will be in survival mode starting out—often losing sleep, sacrificing personal time, and feeling perpetu-ally stressed and fatigued—underscores unsustainable aspects of our profession. Certainly, years of experience do make the workload more manageable, but even veteran teachers, particularly those who continue to learn, improve, and inno-vate, struggle to balance the myriad demands of teaching. As my good friend Ray Ramirez once told me, "It gets easier, but it's never easy." Like anything worth doing well, time, effort, and struggle are necessary for growth. But if or when teaching well becomes easier, it happens, for many of us, *in spite* of our navigating often inhumane, unsustainable conditions—not because the conditions themselves actually change.

I remember being told by an administrator during my first year in the classroom, when I was drowning in grading, lesson planning, and everything else that comes with being a new teacher, to "work smarter, not harder." I am sure nearly all of us have heard or said these well-intentioned words at some point. There is absolutely wisdom and value in finding shortcuts to ease the weight of our workload, especially when one feels isolated and unsupported.

However, when the idea of working "smarter, not harder" is a kind of guiding philosophy from administrators and people in leadership positions who aren't necessarily tackling systemic conditions in a materially substantive or transformative way, it places the onus on *individuals* to make their work more sustainable. Such words also run the danger of feeding into the capitalist idea that one can be just as, or more, productive by "streamlining" their labor. Time is still treated as a limited, fixed entity to operate within in order to "produce" results.

Many of us feel unrelenting pressure to go! go! go! and teach as much as we can in the allotted time that is a school day, marking period, semester, year. The frenetic pace of school itself often seems unyielding because the system itself was not designed to be anything different. But, as we know, it was not that long ago when the arrival of COVID-19 upended nearly all aspects of life, calling such design into question.

During the early days of the pandemic, when the fragility of the breath was becoming increasingly stark, efforts to minimize spread of the coronavirus and care for our young people and families were done with a collective zeal that was singularly swift in schools. Campuses across the United States and world closed, and many schools switched to distance learning. Teachers, administrators, and school staff scrambled to improvise, literally overnight in many cases, finding ways for students and families to access technology, food, learning, and other material resources. Federal school funding quickly materialized when Congress passed the Coronavirus Aid, Relief, and Economic Security (CARES) Act to support schools' soaring "emergency costs for remote learning and personal protective equipment" (Baker and Education Week Staff 2022).

Many educators also hoped that, perhaps, we could transform public education in a collectively seismic, unprecedented way. Standardized tests, both for public schools and colleges, were put on pause. The glaring faultiness of conventional letter grades were grappled with through automatic As, grading floors, pass/no pass options, among other approaches. Most important, many administrators and district leaders rightfully encouraged educators to prioritize holding space with and for students—to connect and provide some semblance of stability and emotional safety in a horrifying and uncertain new reality unfolding before us, even if that meant teaching "less" material. There was a collective will to meet the moment and try to do things differently, with money, technology, personal protective equipment, and other resources being made readily available.

It felt like a time of innovation, reimagining, rebuilding. Each day, there seemed to be a growing number of people who cast doubt on the efficacy and functioning of the modus operandi of the education system—who believed that we didn't *have* to do things as they had been done before. Many of us hoped that maybe, *just maybe*, we could usher in a radically different epoch of teaching and learning. I remember seeing friends post a quote on Facebook by writer and activist Arundhati Roy, who said:

> Historically, pandemics have forced humans to break with the past and imagine their world anew. This one is no different. It is a portal, a gateway between one world and the next.
>
> We can choose to walk through it, dragging the carcasses of our prejudice and hatred, our avarice, our data banks and dead ideas, our dead rivers and smoky skies behind us. Or we can walk through lightly, with little luggage, ready to imagine another world. And ready to fight for it (2020, 47).

Maybe this is our portal as educators? I thought. *How will we emerge on the other side?*

BRAKING THE MACHINE

There is no question that remote learning was unforgettably and remarkably difficult for everyone involved. It left veteran and novice educators alike proclaiming, with shared commiseration and helplessness, "I feel like a first-year teacher all over again!" I felt it, too.

It was *so damn hard* teaching through a screen, physically removed from my kids, nearly all of whom had their cameras off most of the time. Eyes strained and body tired from hours of sitting and screen time. Heart heavy from attending to weekly emotional breakdowns and mental health crises. Mind awash with frustration and disappointment at all of the unseen, unacknowledged, unappreciated labor that I and so many other educators put in. Spirit weary from moments of despair at the vast chasm between all that my kids needed and the limits of what I and we could actually offer. Moments when I questioned my efficacy, my impact, and my willingness to do another year (or more) of teaching from afar. I felt for the educators who had to care for their own children, parents, or other loved ones while teaching, and it's hard to fathom how much harder it all would have been had my partner and I not had family to help watch our child.

The seemingly Sisyphean task of remote learning during that time was not in vain, however. Despite the many challenges—laggy Internet, unresponsiveness, chronic absenteeism, hand-delivering materials to students who couldn't access them online, and more—some of my best teaching emerged that year. My students and I were still able to have rich and lively discussions, forge strong connections, and co-create a brave space for sharing our stories, hopes, and fears through laughter, joy, and tears. Not every class of every day, but, like the undulant current of a gentle river whose wide channel helps determine its unhurried velocity, the predominant flow and depth of our space were consistent and formed largely by the general speed with which we moved: *slowly*.

Starting every class period with a check-in question or interactive activity grounded us in connection. Teaching less content relative to a "normal" year allowed for more depth over breadth and learning that was enriched, engaged, and sustainable. Prioritizing wellness checks—through feedback slips, private breakout rooms, text messages, emails, and phone calls—allowed me to be as attuned as best I could to how students were doing and feeling.

These practices weren't new to me, as I had already been doing them to varying degrees before the pandemic. During distance learning, though, I doubled down on slowing down; that is, I concerned myself less with outcome and trying to teach it all and, instead, prioritized process and moving at a tempo that honored capacity, afforded spaciousness, and minimized stress. There were, of course, days when we moved more swiftly depending on the unit, time of year, or what was happening in the news, but generally, I strived for our pacing to be unrushed.

Slowing down in the face of a system defined by achievement, standardization, production, competition, speed, and stratification felt radical—especially when cries of "learning loss" began to roar and mounting calls to reopen schools morphed into a politicized pressure cooker bulging with acrimony. And I could empathize with such concerns on the one hand.

The consequences of students—BIPOC youth, in particular—missing out on a year-plus of typical academic and social learning while enduring a mental health crisis are not trivial. At the very least, those who fall "behind" may be subjected to remedial courses, credit recovery, delayed graduation, dropping out/being pushed out of school, and more. In the extreme, such a domino effect could shape an individual's academic path and life trajectory, and some research shows that educational attainment is commensurate with health outcomes and life expectancy (Case and Deaton 2021; Hathaway 2020; Zajacova and Lawrence 2018).

On the other hand, I was troubled by the vociferous exhortations to quickly get students back into classrooms to "catch up" despite safety concerns held by many educators and families. Moreover, it seemed to me that the thunderous insistence to return to "normal" was drowning out the collective fervor at the onset of the pandemic to question and rethink public education. That is not to say I didn't want to be at school with my kids—I did, badly—but I did not want us to simply revert back to the old way of doing things and discount or ignore what we may have gained during that time. Which is exactly what happened, in my view.

A NEW NORMAL?

As we transitioned into the 2021–2022 academic year, traditional grading systems, standardized testing, and virtually all other aspects of school pre-pandemic came back into full swing. Except now there was also "lost" learning to account for, rendering an already challenging year even *more* hurried, frenetic, and fraught for everyone. And where did that get us? The stress for both students and educators went through the roof, exacerbating a teacher shortage and mental health crisis for both students and educators.

So much for the notion that schools would be "forever changed" as news headlines promulgated early in the pandemic. The supposed idea that there would be no going back to the way things were pre-pandemic seems all but moot now, a not-so-distant memory that some might dismiss as wishful thinking. But even in the face of enormous pressure and seemingly unstoppable momentum, when nearly everyone and everything else around us appears to be moving at breakneck speed, we can *still* slow down.

Doubtless, there are times when we may feel as though we are just tiny, replaceable cogs in a wheel, who, beyond affecting the lives of our students, ultimately have no perceptible or sizable impact on the school system itself. I understand this feeling full well. I also believe that the intentional choice to slow down and hit the proverbial brakes on the juggernaut of school, even if on a small scale, matters immensely because how we show up and orient ourselves to time can influence how we and our students *feel*. Collective behavior can influence collective action and collective action can lead to systemic change.

Moreover, slowing down in a society that epitomizes grind culture is a powerful act of resistance and survival. It allows us and our students to function, teach, and learn at a pace more aligned to the rhythm of life, the rhythm of breath. That is, slowing down affords everyone in the room time to integrate learning more deeply and interact with each other at a pace that feels natural, healthy, and sustainable.

A Moment for Reflection

- Where do you tend to dedicate most of your time and energy as a teacher?
- What do you find difficult to prioritize in your practice?

FROM SCARCITY TO ABUNDANCE: PRACTICES FOR SLOWING DOWN AT SCHOOL

One of the most important and biggest shifts I have made as an educator is consciously and continuously unlearning a scarcity mindset—the idea that there is never enough time (or money, resources, etc.). Admittedly, our time with students is limited, and putting energy toward one thing means that something else will not receive our attention in that moment. Limits are real and resources are finite.

What I am suggesting here is that even within the constraints of a school year; even if or when we don't get to teach all that we want or "have" to; even when the amazing activity, lesson, or unit we so diligently and arduously planned out has totally crumbled; grounding ourselves in the present moment can keep us attuned to the reality of what *is* and minimize our attachment to immediate, desired results. This is not to suggest that learning outcomes don't matter and we should just be laissez faire about things, but by having some flexibility with time, we can teach in a way that is more abundant and less scarcity-driven.

Certainly, there are weeks that are fuller than others, moments when we'll feel in a hurry, days when a multitude of crises warrant immediate attention. Shifting away from scarcity and gravitating toward abundance is not an all-or-nothing approach. The speed with which we move will shift from moment to moment, depending on our internal resources and circumstances. Although we may not have much, if any, control over the external forces we are confronted with, we do have choice about how we engage with time.

If our words, choices, and actions are principally influenced by a perceived lack of time, as if the clock is an adversary to constantly race against, then we ourselves risk unconsciously harboring and emitting energy from a place of lack. If, instead, we strive to remain tethered to the present moment, maintaining ongoing awareness of our (un)met needs while not losing sight of very real goals and time constraints, we are better able to teach—and live—from a place of centeredness and mindfulness.

Some of the following strategies and practices may seem simplistic in nature and in their application, which they may very well be; they are not necessarily groundbreaking in and of themselves. But when taken in their totality, the accumulative and positive effect of these practices on our own and students' well-being—in a system not designed for people who are Black, indigenous, of color, or part of the LGBTQIA+ community to thrive—is significant, and, in my view, radical. Following this section, we will explore how to slow down and take care of ourselves outside of school.

Micro Moves: Daily and Weekly Practices

The following practices are great for doing each day or week, and they are simple and repeatable in nature, making them accessible for us and our students.

Kissing the Earth

Who among us hasn't rushed to and from the copier in the morning? Ignored a colleague as we hurriedly walked right by them? Worked through lunch glued to the computer, too distracted to hold a sustained conversation with our full presence? We've all been there, and sometimes we're just in a rush. But for those of us who find ourselves *constantly* on the go, how well are we served by an endlessly restless body and busy mind?

The late and revered Vietnamese Buddhist monk and peace activist Thich Nhat Hanh, endearingly known as Thay, writes in his beautiful book *Peace Is Every Step: The Path of Mindfulness in Everyday Life*, "Although we walk all the time, our walking is usually more like running. When we walk like that, we print anxiety and sorrow on the Earth" (1992, 28). I know this to be true for myself. For years, I unconsciously moved about, seldom noticing how my fast pace was a reflection of my internal, anxious state. But when I learned how to walk mindfully, "not in order to arrive, but just to walk," I found myself feeling *so much better*—in body and mind. Thay invites us to practice what he calls "walking meditation" by simply aligning our breath with our steps, enjoying slow breaths in and out as if our feet are kissing the earth. When I practice "kissing the earth," I like to draw a slow inhale while taking four or five slow, gentle steps; then, I'll exhale while taking a similar number of slow and soft steps.

Even if it's just for a few minutes during lunch or before or after school, I

7.3
An outdoor area on my school's campus. Personal collection.

find that moving in this way—away from the computer and off my phone—brings me so much joy and relaxation. Fortunately, my school has a sprawling campus with outdoor hallways populated with lovely green trees, plants, and bushes that are particularly resplendent during springtime [Figure 7.3]. It is a bonus when soundscapes of chirping birds, honking geese, and rustling leaves fill the air, allowing my senses to become awash in the beauty and vibrancy of life that is already there. This practice isn't just for those who teach at schools surrounded by conventional beauty or warm weather, though. Whether it's a loop around the parking lot or a lap around the school building itself, taking a quick walk has tremendous benefits for us as well as our students.

Since I teach on a 95-minute block schedule, most days my classes go on a brief walk near the middle of the period (barring rain or very cold weather). Typically, we'll circle around an adjacent building, and if it's a day of heavier lifting, we might take a longer route. The goal isn't to "get anywhere" but to simply be, and many students tell me they look forward to it. The practice also normalizes caring for ourselves beyond the bounds of "official" break times and lunch.

When I allow myself to gently and slowly kiss the earth with my feet, eyes, and ears, I feel more connected to other living things and to myself. In touch with my needs and more likely to foster inner serenity. "When we are able to take one step peacefully and happily," Thay adds, "we are working for the cause of peace and happiness for the whole of humankind" (1992, 28).

Words Beyond Measure

Some time ago, I came across a post on Instagram by educator Terry Kawi (@ms_kawi) that asked, "What message does our language send students about 'work'? Our students are more than the work they produce and they are not workers, so why does our language reflect that?" (Kawi 2020). Her post challenged educators to reflect on the pervasive tendency of using phrases like "good work" and "[So-and-so] is a hard worker," which, she argues, "center the work and act of working rather than the humanity of the learner and their growth." It helped me notice just how ubiquitous and embedded economic metaphors are in our everyday language, as well as the idea that time is something that can be commodified. For years I used the following words and phrases without thinking twice: work on, homework, class work, hard worker, work habits, pay attention, good job, spend time, kill time, take time, steal time, waste time, lose time, produce, productive, volume, maximize, etc.

So, what's the big deal? Well, words represent ideas, and ideas shape how we think, behave, and create policy. Language entrenched in ideas of depletion and production reinforce a capitalist mentality and can create a toxic environment, even more so if the teaching and learning are unendingly hyper-productive and fast-paced. Students and teachers are already immensely stressed; why not find alternate ways of framing what we are doing and asking our students to do? Students are not workers, nor should their learning be viewed as an outgrowth of work. I am well aware that one of the definitions of work is to engage with a task that is not necessarily related to a job, but even this definition is grounded in succeeding or producing a desired result or outcome. *Process*—being, moving through—is not included in the definition and is sometimes more important than outcome.

In my own lexicon, I have tried hard to stop using the aforementioned words and phrases in most instances in the classroom, and, instead, have shifted to using language that is not associated with measuring time and productivity.

Instead of...	You might consider...
"Today we'll be working on..."	"Today, I would like for us to engage with..."
"Let's take some time to share out."	"Let's surface our ideas by sharing out."
"What are you working on?"	"What are you attending to at the moment?"
"Your homework for tonight is..."	"If you are able, please ___ outside of class."
"Great/good job!"	"I appreciate the thought/effort you dedicated to..."
"Stop wasting/you're wasting time."	"I see that you are ____, though my request was for everyone to ____. How can I help?"
"We're running out of/running short on time."	"I want to ensure that we are able to ___, so I would like for us to transition to..."
"We don't have (enough) time to..."	"I would love for us to ___, but because I am choosing to prioritize ____, we won't ____ at the moment."
"You are a hard worker."	"It seems that you devoted a lot of energy/time to..."
"[Student's name] is a hard worker."	"[Student's name] did very well on ____ as a result of..."

What are some words/phrases you use that tend to reinforce a scarcity or economic mindset?	What are alternate ways to communicate what you want to say?

Eliminating economic and time metaphors is not mere semantic play; the words we use profoundly shape the learning environment and provide students an alternate model for what and how learning can be.

Rethinking Schools magazine curriculum editor, writer, and veteran educator Bill Bigelow writes in his article "Let's Stop Using Metaphors that Celebrate Extraction, Colonialism, and Violence" that metaphorical language, if we are not careful, can "confine our imaginations to what exists." He adds that "[b]ecoming more conscious of the metaphors we use to describe the world can help us to picture a different one" (2022, 56). We may slip up at times, and that's okay—I know I do. If our goal is to eschew and disrupt hustle culture and language steeped in capitalism, then what matters most is that we go in that direction.

Loving Breath

Each day, the average person breathes between 17,000 and 23,000 times (Harvard Health 2019). Through every moment of life, the breath is there to accompany us like a loyal friend, yet it is so automatic, so habitual that many of us don't even notice when we do it. However, practicing slow, deep, mindful breathing—that is, inhaling and exhaling with awareness of the breath itself—can strengthen our ability to be present, which is a gift to ourselves and to the world.

Again, to invoke the wisdom of Thich Nhat Hanh, mindful breathing (what he sometimes called "conscious" breathing) "is the link between our body and our mind. Sometimes our mind is thinking of one thing and our body is doing another, and mind and body are not unified" (1992, 9). In order to bridge the body and mind, Thay offers a simple and accessible exercise that I love and have been practicing for years:

As you breathe in, you say to yourself, "Breathing in, I know that I am breathing in." And as you breathe out, say, "Breathing out, I know that I am breathing out." Just that. You recognize your in-breath as an in-breath and your out-breath as an out-breath. You don't even need to recite the whole sentence; you can use just two words: "In" and "Out" (1992, 8).

In. Out. In. Out. Nothing fancy. Already within us. We can breathe in such a way after waking up in the morning, during meals, in the car, and, of course, throughout our day at school. Given the taxing nature of our profession, being able to reground, recenter, and reconnect through conscious breathing is *critical* for our health and wellness. Even just a few seconds of it can induce calmness, reduce stress, and slow our heart rate (not to mention that it feels wholly wonderful).

This delightful exercise is also something we can practice with our students. I have experimented with different breathing exercises with my classes over the years and have found that guiding them through the process is most helpful. First, at the beginning of class, I'll turn off the lights and then invite students to close their eyes, keep their feet flat on the ground, and straighten their backs to comfortably and fully inhale and exhale [Figure 7.4]. Then, I will guide them through a series of in-breaths and out-breaths, saying something like, "soft, gentle, loving breath in," followed by a pause, then "soft, gentle, loving breath out," followed by a pause.

7.4

Kimberly, Savio, Phung, and Angie breathing together.

Sometimes, all I say is "in" and "out" as Thay offers. Other times, I may say more such as, "As we breathe in, may we cultivate ease and slowness for this moment, for this day." Pause. "As we breathe out, may we try releasing any stress we might be holding onto." Pause.

It is worth noting that I do not force my students to participate. As much as I'd love for everyone to practice and benefit from conscious breathing, not everyone is ready nor wants to. I invite those who'd prefer to opt out to maybe put their head down or close their eyes. That said, I will periodically check in and gauge if or when they might be willing to try. I tell my students that such breathing is not "Mike's thing" but rather is a practice that has spanned centuries, cultures, and religions—Buddhism and Hinduism in particular—and been passed down from our ancestors.

As Thay reminds us, "Life is only available in the present moment. We need to return to *this* moment to be in touch with life as it really is" (1993, 16). When we draw attention to our breath, "dwelling in the present moment, we put an end to attachments to the past and anxieties about the future" (1993, 16). In this way, bridging the body and mind through our breath is a loving act because being present keeps us connected to ourselves, right here, right now.

Opening the Week

As mentioned in Chapter 2, my students and I start off every class reciting the Warrior Scholar Principles. On Mondays and Tuesdays (I see each period every other day), we also have a check-in question that everyone, myself included, responds to. It's not a quick-write but rather a question that students verbally discuss in their groups before we share out together.

Sometimes the question is, "What's a rose or thorn from your week(end)"? A rose refers to a highlight or something sweet; a thorn refers to a difficulty or something unpleasant. Occasionally, the questions are light, even silly, such as: "If you could be any video game or cartoon character for a day, who would you be and why?" Other times, they are more substantive and lend themselves to "next day" discussions that follow significant, tumultuous, or unfolding events (e.g., celebrations, tragedies, etc.). For example, after the U.S. Capitol was breached by insurrectionists on January 6, the following day I asked students, "What are you left thinking, feeling, or wondering in response to what happened at the U.S. Capitol yesterday?"

Depending on the time of year, unit, and group dynamics, we might start off with a group connector, e.g., getting-to-know-you questions, ice breakers, riddles, rebus puzzles, guess the picture, etc. These are particularly great for helping students get to know and interact with each other earlier in the year, but they are still fun and useful to carry throughout to build and sustain community.

Following the class share-out, I'll ask for a volunteer to read the Thought of the Week I've written on the board [Figure 7.5]. These include quotes, song lyrics, questions, proverbs, etc., and I try to align them to traditions, diversity-themed months (e.g., AANHPI, African American, LGBTQIA+, etc.) as well as curricular units. At the beginning of the year, I ask students to share some of their favorite quotes and I'll try to incorporate strong ones.

7.5

A Thought of the Week written on one of the whiteboards in my classroom.

Macro Moves: Periodic and Ongoing Practices

The following practices and approaches, like the micro moves, are ongoing in nature. And while they can also be done each day or week, they are more "macro" in that they can shape the overall movement of the class and our teaching.

Wellness Checks

When students enter my classroom each day, I greet them at the door. It is important for me to acknowledge their presence; doing so is also a quick wellness check that helps me get a sense of how students are doing, depending on body language, tone, and mood. I do my best to identify and track who might need extra support or space that day, but sometimes it is not always visibly apparent whether a student is having a difficult time.

For this and other reasons, I frequently ask my students to complete Feedback Slips. Similar to Exit Tickets, Feedback Slips are a quick formative assessment but they double as wellness checks. Generally, I will pose questions about their week, understanding of the concepts or skills, suggestions for me, and any other questions, comments, or concerns. If I am asking three or fewer questions, I'll usually have students respond on a scrap of paper. I try to read them immediately so I can follow up the next time I see them. Typically, I'll circle the room and check in as students are engaging with the lesson. Depending on what the student has written, I may ask them to step outside to check in privately or try to connect with them during my prep period.

If I have multiple questions to ask and want to easily look for patterns in students' responses, I will have them do the Feedback Slip on a Google Form. I am always intentional about asking students about what's happening in their lives and how they are doing mentally and emotionally. Sometimes the question will ask how they've been feeling lately with a list of applicable feelings they can checkmark [Figure 7.6], or they can review their Feelings Inventory and write them in. From time to time, I also ask them to identify needs of theirs that are being met and unmet in our class [Figure 7.7].

How've you been feeling lately? (check the ones that apply)

Copy

28 responses

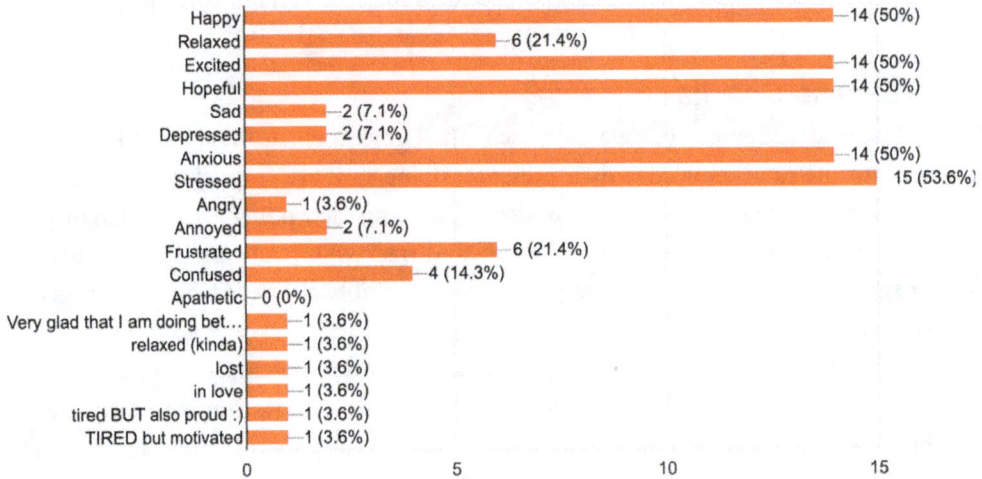

- Happy — 14 (50%)
- Relaxed — 6 (21.4%)
- Excited — 14 (50%)
- Hopeful — 14 (50%)
- Sad — 2 (7.1%)
- Depressed — 2 (7.1%)
- Anxious — 14 (50%)
- Stressed — 15 (53.6%)
- Angry — 1 (3.6%)
- Annoyed — 2 (7.1%)
- Frustrated — 6 (21.4%)
- Confused — 4 (14.3%)
- Apathetic — 0 (0%)
- Very glad that I am doing bet… — 1 (3.6%)
- relaxed (kinda) — 1 (3.6%)
- lost — 1 (3.6%)
- in love — 1 (3.6%)
- tired BUT also proud :) — 1 (3.6%)
- TIRED but motivated — 1 (3.6%)

(x-axis: 0, 5, 10, 15)

7.6

Students' responses when asked to indicate how they were feeling. One of the checkboxes on the form was "other" so that students could write in how they were doing (indicated by the responses at the bottom).

What need(s) of yours is our English class helping fulfill? (Check the ones that apply) *

☐ Stability and consistency

☐ Safety and security (emotional or physical)

☐ Support (emotional, academic, personal, etc.)

☐ Deepened awareness (of self, others, and/or the world)

☐ Connection, belonging, or relating to others

☐ Self-expression

☐ Writing skills (e.g., organizing ideas, analyzing texts, etc.)

☐ Other...

7.7

A list of needs that students check off to indicate how they are doing in class.

If students are willing, I include optional questions where they can elaborate on how they are doing [Figure 7.8]. Administering Feedback Slips regularly (such as following a lesson or at the end of a week and term) is a helpful tool to inform and refine instruction. If, for instance, a number of students share that they feel stressed, I might have us start off the following class with a quick-write asking them to share strategies for how they take care of themselves (or would like to do so) when they have a lot on their plate. Or, if a number of students share that our class is meeting needs for safety and security, that tells me that we might be able to go a little deeper into some vulnerable writing during the next unit.

Anything you'd like to elaborate on from the previous question?

22 responses

School hasnt been the best for me lately

not really ive just been in an amazing mood recently ive been extreamly happy.

Last year was our first year back from quarantine so pretty much everything was new to me and so I tried my best so good on some of my classes but it didn't end up happening, I told myself that I better change now before it's too late and thankfully it is paying off and my grades are good now.

Finals have been stressful especially with the pile of work my teachers assigned right before the deadline of the semesters work.

im a little sad that im leaving high school soon

PE final is making me stressed, I have to run three laps without stopping 😭😭😭

7.8

Some responses from students elaborating on their response to the question, "How've you been feeling lately?"

Feedback Slips also allow for staying in regular dialogue with students and provide critical information that might otherwise be missed. Just last week, a student of mine, who is generally very quiet but has increasingly opened up to me over the year, handed me a page-long letter on their way out after class. They shared the torment of suffering through insomnia, having dark and suicidal thoughts, and said they didn't know what to do or whom else to talk to. It was an obvious cry for help, but given that they had already gone to their next class by the time I read the letter, I contacted our social worker immediately who was able to meet with the student promptly.

Given the rapport I had been building with the student, I trusted that they would understand my reason for contacting the social worker. Indeed, when I checked in with them the next day, they told me that they appreciated the support. Had I not made it a point to consistently check in with them and take genuine interest in their and all my other students' well-being and lives, I'm not so sure the student would have handed me that letter. We don't always know when our students are dealing with difficult feelings and thoughts. The information we glean when we dedicate time to check in is always valuable, and we never know when it might be the difference between life and death for some kids.

Wellness checks also enable us to know when to slow down and where to best direct our energy. Like many teachers, I use a backward design approach to unit and lesson planning, but I keep things flexible, knowing that plans may shift depending on how my students are doing and what they need in the truest sense of the word. Our classes may not be able to always help students meet their needs, and that's okay; just asking, though, and attempting to meet our core, shared needs goes a long way in sustaining a community enveloped in genuine care.

Community Circles

One of the ways that my students and I reflect on and tend our classroom community is via Community Circles. Different from restorative circles and discussion activities specific to academic content (e.g., Socratic seminars, Fishbowls, etc.), Community Circles bring us together in celebrating our classroom space and who we are. It is one of my favorite things to do with my students, and we hold them several times a year. As a member of the classroom community, I, too, participate in the circles, sitting next to the kids. No one sits outside the circle [Figure 7.9].

Usually, a circle consists of a few "rounds," each of which are facilitated with a different prompt. A round is completed after each person has spoken; if a student is not ready when it's their turn, we'll skip and come back to them. Depending on the time of the year, I'll adjust the prompts to support where we are at as a community.

If it's early in the year, for example, I'll start off by asking how their first few days of school are going, followed by inviting them to share a little about themselves. I find it helpful to have students introduce themselves by sharing something tangible and visual they have already created in class, such as a Name Plate [Figure 7.10]. Students don't have to share anything grand, especially at the beginning of the year, when nerves are strong and some might feel reluctant to speak into a big group. That is why low-stakes opportunities that allow students to share a little bit of who they are—their name, passions or interests, goals or hopes, and pronouns (if they choose to share them)—can be very helpful. I then might ask them to think of and say a few words about someone or something they can lean on when times get difficult.

7.9

Students sharing out during a Community Circle.

7.10

Ngoc's Name Plate (top) and Delilah's Name Plate (bottom). These Name Plates, as individual "bricks," form a community wall in the back of my classroom to represent strength, solidarity, and students. Shout out to educator Jill Acompañado-Guevarra for originally inspiring the idea.

If it's midway through or at the end of the school year, once we've been together for several months, the focus will be more on our class. I'll first pose a light prompt to warm up the circle (e.g., "What was a highlight from your break" or "What's something beautiful you've seen/heard/felt lately?"). I then might ask them to revisit and talk about the goal or hope they set at the beginning of the year; sometimes it's a "skin" they want to shed, that is, a habit or behavior not serving them well. Then we'll talk about our classroom space itself, and I always provide optional sentence starters for this purpose [Figure 7.11]. When asking students to talk about our community, I typically frame the request with: "My ask is for us to speak from the heart, as our words and presence are a gift. That might be about someone or something from our space that means a lot to you. Remember, the sentence starters are optional; please say what feels right to you however you want to say it."

Community Circle Sentence Starters

- Something I appreciate about our space is ... because ...
- Something I value about our space is ... because ...
- Someone in our space who I appreciate is ... because ...
- Something I've enjoyed learning this year is ... because ...
- Something that's pushed me /my thinking is ... because ...
- One way I've grown/evolved since the school year started is ...
- Something I've learned that I'll continue thinking about is ... because ...
- Something I'll remember from our class is ... because ...
- A struggle of mine that our space has helped me with is ...

7.11

Optional sentence starters for our Community Circle at the end of the year.

To support students in speaking vulnerably from the heart, we use a bright red heart plush as our talking piece. This gives them something tangible and comforting to hold, which can be particularly helpful for anyone who might cry, feels nervous, dislikes public speaking, or is easily distracted. For our closing circle at the end of this past school year, my students and I responded to the following questions:

- Round 1: What are you most excited for this summer? What will bring you joy?
- Round 2: Who or what from our space would you like to lift up and celebrate? Why?
- Round 3: As we wrap up this school year and transition, what is something about yourself you would like to focus on?
- Round 4: Is there anything else anyone would like to say into the circle?

Better Late than Never

A confession: there is no such thing as "late work" in my class. Sure, many of my assignments have requested due dates, and I ask that students do their best to honor them. But they are not penalized for turning in something "late." Lest one think that it is a free-for-all in my classes and students wait until the very end of a marking period to submit their assignments, that is not the case.

Asking students to complete an assignment within a specific window is just that—a request. If they are struggling with understanding or completing the material, then it's on me to find out what they need and support them accordingly. Sometimes, that means more time. I find that most teachers are flexible, especially when students advocate for themselves. But as we all know, not all students do so; some willingly resist or disengage. What then? Should such behavior be grounds to preclude them from learning?

I know hardliners who won't budge when it comes to late assignments because they want students to be successful in the "real world": *How to be responsible. Actions come with consequences. Bosses won't tolerate lateness. It's a choice whether we pass or fail. Life isn't always fair.* I understand where these sentiments come from and imagine that those who hold such views are attempting to meet needs for contributing to students' well-being and showing care and support. I imagine, too, that many teachers desire to have shared reality with their students about how the world works so that students can be prepared to deal effectively with challenging situations in life.

I think it is important that, as teachers, our needs are taken into account. However, I take issue with hardliners who center *only* their own needs and preferred time frame, which often comes at the expense of students' actual needs and despite the realities of life that don't adhere to a clock. I want to co-create a different paradigm with my students, an alternate world that is not as rigidly time-bound.

To be clear, I am not suggesting that we bend over backward and unquestionably cater to our students, either. It is completely reasonable to ask students to honor due dates and deadlines so we can provide timely feedback and not get inundated with things to assess or leave feedback on. Timely feedback, in particular, can only happen, of course, if there is something for us to actually assess and provide feedback on.

One of the ways I try to approach due dates with flexibility is when my students are writing essays. They will first practice in their notebooks the one or two skills I'll primarily be assessing (e.g., textual analysis, inferences, claims and counterclaims, sensory details, etc.). We do modeling, guided practice, group practice, and solo practice so that when the actual essay writing comes, students will have had multiple opportunities to practice the core skills; they also have exemplars with notes and optional sentence starters housed in their notebooks for reference.

I try to provide as much feedback as possible *while* students are in the drafting process rather than waiting until they have completed a draft. When I'm reading through essays and see that a student has not written much relative to the dedicated writing time, I'll provide feedback based on what they do have, then review their outline the next time I see them. If it's clear they understand the skill(s), I can offer quick feedback based on their notes and ask what, if any, support they need from me to further their progress. If they're at a loss for where to go, I'll review their outline, assess what they currently know and can do, then provide one-on-one help (or hold a small group conference or reteach a mini lesson depending on trends and numbers). When it comes to something as complex and difficult as writing, I try to keep the process malleable to balance the needs of my students with my own as the teacher.

Some students who struggle the most with meeting deadlines are those with myriad responsibilities outside of school. They care for family members, act as translators, juggle work and school, help pay rent and other bills, among other things, yet school seldom values these responsibilities. Other students have challenges with executive function and might need support in chunking segments of assignments, setting reminders, asking for assistance, etc. And, yes, some students might be straight-up unmotivated and checked out, which is incredibly frustrating when we feel as though we've gotten nowhere despite earnest, repeated attempts to support them.

If we are serious about teaching with an equitable approach, however, and want to disrupt the futile tendency to control time, then being flexible and staying in ongoing dialogue with students matters. This includes letting students know the impact on us of their completing assignments past our requested due dates, especially if it's habitual. Depending on our own capacity and limitations, how much time has elapsed since the learning opportunity was first assigned, or where we are at in the marking period, we may very well decide that drawing boundaries is necessary in order to maintain sustainability and meet certain needs. Here are some questions I ask myself when it comes to students and late assignments:

- If considerable time has elapsed since the initial due date, what needs are met by (not) allowing the student to submit the assignment at this point?
- Does it make sense for the assignment to still be done in its original form, or is there an alternate way for the student to access and demonstrate their learning? (e.g., voice recording, video, slide show, etc.)
- What pattern(s) am I noticing with this student and late assignments? What interventions have I already tried? What might I try differently?

I know this can be a hot-button issue, and I don't claim to have all the answers. But I do know that this approach, imperfect as it is, works for me and my students. If you'd like to explore this topic more, educator Jennifer Gonzalez, who runs the excellent podcast and website Cult of Pedagogy, offers some great questions, suggestions, and tips when it comes to late assignments: cultofpedagogy.com/late-work

---

Slowness and Our Practice

▷ How do you currently practice slowness as a teacher?

▷ In what area(s) of your teaching would you like to slow down more?

▷ Which of the micro and macro strategies offered in this chapter might you try or adapt for your own context?

▷ What needs would this meet for you/your students?

SLOW AND SELF-CARE BEYOND SCHOOL

The micro and macro moves I have shared for slowing down have, without question, afforded me more spaciousness within myself and throughout my day. They constitute an orientation to time and speed that is less bell-to-bell and more breath-to-breath. Like anyone else, I have my share of stress, busyness, and exhaustion from all that teaching entails. But I find it much easier to manage those things when I remind myself that slowness is not a classroom strategy but an embodied way of being and living that can greatly improve the quality of our lives.

An increasing number of school districts, including mine, are recognizing the importance of teachers' mental health in addition to that of students; some offer mindfulness classes and discounted or free subscriptions to programs that provide guided meditation and conscious breathing exercises to improve sleep, mood, and overall wellness. I know that for some people, these resources can go a long way, and I appreciate the accessibility and benefits provided to those who find them worthwhile. Something is better than nothing.

That said, no amount of individual practices can entirely mitigate the impact of nor fix unsustainable, inequitable aspects of the schooling system. That is yearslong, collective labor that requires ardent advocacy, resistance, and policy change. The fact that such resources even exist is a clear indication that teachers are wiped out and the work is not sustainable. And the increasing toll it's been taking in recent years is alarming.

In a study conducted by Pennsylvania State University and the Robert Wood Johnson Foundation from 2016, researchers found that 46 percent of teachers reported "high daily stress" *on par* with that of nurses and doctors (Pennsylvania State University and Robert Wood Johnson Foundation 2016). A more recent study, published in *Educational Researcher* and conducted between September of 2020 and March of 2021, found that as a result of the pandemic, "teachers showed a significantly higher prevalence of negative mental health outcomes during the pandemic when compared to healthcare and office workers," in addition to high rates of isolation and depression (Kush et al. 2022).

Additionally, according to the National Center for Education Statistics, 44 percent of public schools reported teacher vacancies for part- and full-time positions at the start of the 2022–2023 academic year. Resignations were, according to the report, "the leading cause" of more than half of those vacancies (NCES 2022). There is no denying that many educators feel exceedingly stressed, spiritually crushed, and blatantly undervalued and disrespected—especially as schools have gone "back to normal" in the "post"-pandemic era rife with culture wars.

I felt such sentiments acutely during the wave of COVID-19 infections in January of 2022, when the Omicron variant surged. Teachers and students were out sick left and right, and I was regularly called to sub during my planning prep period. I obviously knew it was nobody's fault, but I was still upset at how the problem fell on individual teachers to "fix." Even if there was nothing that could have been done in that moment to alleviate the weight of all that we were holding, just thoughtful acknowledgement of *how hard* it all was in the face of unceasing momentum would have met needs for being seen and understood [Figure 7.12].

I, like many others, was hanging on by a thread. Somehow, I made it through the initial COVID-19 waves and January Omicron surge unscathed, but that April, my family and I finally caught it. It was the first time in my *entire* teaching career that I had taken off more than a few days consecutively. And while it was initially hard to be away from my students, who were going to have to finish off a

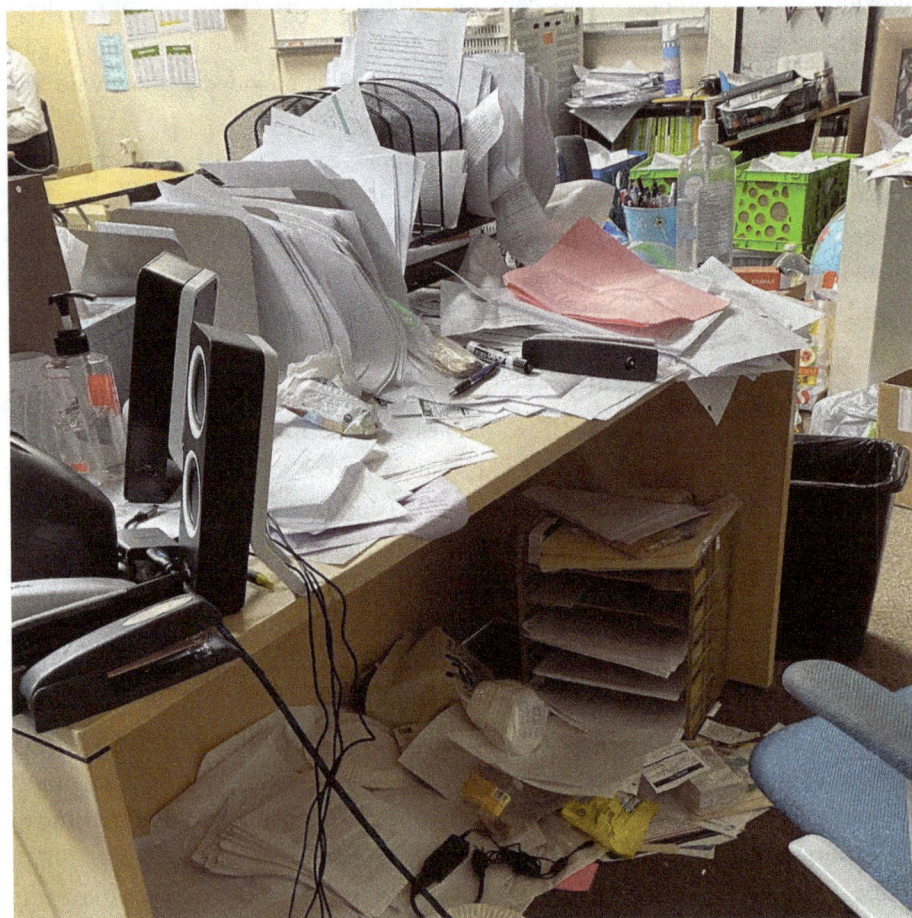

7.12

The desk area of a colleague—symbolic of what many teachers felt internally during a massive COVID spike in January of 2022—on a day when my students and I had to borrow their classroom due to a power outage. The colleague gave their permission for this photo to be shared.

fun and engaging unit by themselves, I gave myself permission to let go of feeling attached to the outcome of the unit. I trusted that my kids would be okay without my being there and that even if things didn't go according to plan, I could wait to figure it out upon returning to school. Most important, I did not check email nor do anything beyond what was necessary for my students to access assignments. I prioritized rest, recovery, and leisure.

In her book *How to Do Nothing: Resisting the Attention Economy*, artist, writer, and educator Jenny Odell argues that in an age of toxic grind culture that permeates the American workforce, "[H]aving recourse to periods of and spaces for 'doing nothing' is of utmost importance, because without them we have no way to think, reflect, heal, and sustain ourselves—individually or collectively" (2019, 22). Sometimes, we can do nothing in the most literal sense, such as resting, sitting, and breathing. But doing nothing is not limited to the absence of activity; Odell invites us to consider engaging in activities that are not always tied to productivity, measurables, and unchecked growth. These can include going for walks, bird watching, visiting a museum, listening to music, among other things, if for no reason other than enjoyment, exploration, and being.

For myself, shortly after recovering from my nasty bout with COVID-19, I tried something, somewhat on a whim, I had only dabbled in years prior: rock climbing. I enjoyed (and still enjoy) running, biking, and working out at the gym, but I was drained from a particularly grueling year of teaching three preps and was yearning for a rejuvenating activity that involved both body and mind. For the first few weeks after I started, my muscles were sore and I tired quickly, but I enjoyed the humbling experience of being a beginner again and stretching my own zone of proximal development. It was also an incredibly satisfying full-body workout that relied on concentration, hand-foot coordination, nearly all muscle groups, strength, stamina, and, most important for me, *presence*.

As teachers, it can be easy to get stuck in our heads, consumed with thoughts and worries about all we are mentally tracking and emotionally holding. Sometimes, even when I am doing something I enjoy such as jogging or lifting weights, my mind can wander. When I climb, though, I am able to practice what my aikido sensei called "body-feel."

"Don't *think* about the technique so much," Sensei would say. "*Feel* it in your body first. Flow with it." He once had us practice this teaching using a bokken (wooden sword). With our feet slightly apart and planted firmly in the ground, we would inhale while raising the sword up with both hands. On our exhale, we would swiftly yet gently bring the sword down, sinking into our center. Too much exertion, and it would look like a chop. Too little force and the bokken would lack stability. Like aikido, rock climbing helps me get unstuck from my head. It allows me to practice techniques *while* staying connected to my body without my thoughts becoming adrift. The more integrated my mind and body are, the more present I am. Body-feel.

What began as a pastime has now become an invigorating form of self-care I do multiple times a week. It meets my needs for *movement*, *accomplishment*, *community*, *joy*, among others, and I absolutely love it. Additionally, it helps me manage my anxiety in that whatever stress might be harbored in my body, I am able to release it on the wall or rock [Figure 7.13]. My partner, Rachelle, recently started climbing regularly, making it an even more joyful experience that we can share and learn through together.

No matter how hard a school day it's been or how busy I might be, unless I am ill, injured, or fatigued, climbing is a non-negotiable for myself. Granted, I recognize my privilege in being able to say that and to enjoy such a hobby, as my partner and I are both employed and can afford memberships and child care. We are also able to take turns climbing when we're unable to do so together, a luxury not easily afforded to single parents or caregivers.

7.13

Me bouldering at Castle Rock Park. Photo by Alan Pham.

Still, I so want all teachers—and everyone else—to be able to do what brings them joy and makes them feel alive because caring for ourselves should be seen and treated as a need, not a privilege or luxury. (Chapter 10 will explore the importance and role of community care in our work as educators.)

It goes without saying that not everyone's form of self-care will be the same. Some people enjoy sitting meditation while others prefer moving their bodies. Some like to draw or paint; others read. Many find great pleasure in watching movies and shows or playing video games (I know I enjoy my occasional weekend fix of platform games like *Celeste*, *Inside*, and *Super Mario* on my Nintendo Switch). People should do whatever helps them meet needs and reset.

That said, at times it's not activity we need but simply rest. I love those moments when I am sitting in my recliner and looking out the window. No scrolling on my phone. No fidgeting. Sometimes a book in hand but other times just resting and sinking into relaxation. For some of us, the thought of having nothing to do can seem unbearable because we might feel guilty for not taking care of chores nor doing something "productive." But rest is a basic need we deserve and owe to ourselves to make time for.

For single parents or caregivers, if there are friends, family, or community whom you can lean on in order for you to rest, please consider making requests for support. Your need for rest is not a burden. If someone has offered to avail themselves to assist you, that is a beautiful gesture of love that we can receive full-heartedly.

Whether we are prioritizing rest or choosing activities that rejuvenate or preserve our heart, body, spirit, and mind, when we mindfully engage in pastimes and ways of being that allow us to, as Odell says, "think, reflect, heal, and sustain ourselves," we live in such a way that slowness becomes an embedded part of our lives. And having sufficient internal space to choose *how* to meet our needs, rather than running on autopilot, is paramount for our wellness and efficacy as educators.

Caring for Ourselves

▷ What's one way you currently take care of yourself outside of school? Or one way you would like to take care of yourself (differently)?

▷ Refer to the list of needs (see page 29 or Appendix B). What need(s) does/would this form of self-care meet for you?

▷ How often would you ideally like to practice this form of self-care and during what part of your day? What's a back-up plan for when you feel too short on time or energy to do this self-care activity?

▷ If necessary, is there someone you could reach out to for support?

Optional sentence starter: Hi _____, I am really wanting to [type of activity] in order to ensure that I am taking care of myself. It would meet my need(s) for _____. Would you be available and willing to support me by _____?

It is commonly said that we cannot effectively show up for our students if we do not fully show up for ourselves. So true. When we prioritize our health and wellness, slowing down enough to be attuned to how we are meeting our needs and recovering ourselves, we are more likely to thrive and experience joy in our teaching. Symbiotically, when we embed slowness in our pedagogy and fundamentally reorient ourselves to time, we reduce the likelihood of feeling perpetually stressed and fatigued, thereby increasing our potential to experience joy in our lives—a birthright we all share.

And the more resourced we are in body, heart, mind, and spirit, the more prepared we can be to endure moments of difficulty, even moments of suffering. But knowing *how* to handle our suffering is vital for ensuring that the systemic violence we face does not become internalized violence.

In the next chapter, we will take a look at a pivotal moment in history when courageous individuals, working together, found strength amidst their suffering in the quest for freedom. We will then examine the role of voluntary suffering in our work as educators and explore how it can support us in the urgent work of teaching and learning for justice.

CHAPTER 8

Honoring Suffering

Bernard LaFayette was a young college student at American Baptist Theological Seminary in the fall of 1958 when his roommate and best friend, John Lewis, told him about a nonviolence workshop he had recently attended. Lewis implored LaFayette to attend another upcoming workshop, but he was initially uninterested. "I was so busy with my courses," recalled LaFayette. "I said, 'Listen, I don't have time for that.' But he [Lewis] kept badgering me, and lo and behold, I got hooked" (Porter 2020).

Led by a graduate student named James Lawson, the workshops focused on how nonviolence, as a philosophy and disciplined practice, could transform oppressive conditions and engender a society that reflected a higher standard of moral values. Lawson was well-versed in the Gandhian tradition, having visited and studied nonviolence in India. He introduced the Nashville students to the Sanskrit word ahimsa, which refers to the absence of violence in thought, word, and deed and the Gandhian concept satyagraha, which translates to "truth force," "soul force," or "steadfastness in truth" (Kashtan 2010). As well, he trained the young people in nonviolent tactics, organizing, and philosophical underpinnings including agape love and voluntary suffering. The students were deeply inspired and felt moved to act, urgently, to dismantle the humiliating and unjust reality of segregation.

After some deliberation, the group's consensus was to desegregate Downtown Nashville by targeting lunch counters at department stores. The need to act felt urgent but required diligent strategizing and planning. And so, Lawson led the students in role-plays, engaging in intense physical and psychological preparation.

The students alternated taking on the roles of agitators—name-calling, cursing, shoving, pushing, blowing cigarette smoke—and of demonstrators, trying to withstand harassment and assault without retaliating. In attempting to "test" and "break" each other, they prepared their bodies, minds, hearts, and spirits for the violence they anticipated would be directed toward them (Lewis, Aydin, and Powell 2013, 80).

There were a number of individuals, including Bernard LaFayette, John Lewis, and others, who embraced the concept of nonviolence as a way of life and manifestation of love for humanity, which they believed was the most effective way to create the kind of society they yearned for. They also understood the educational power that voluntary suffering could have on garnering sympathy and support from the masses, and, by extension, changing unjust laws.

Not everyone was willing to put their bodies on the line, however; some medical students and athletes, for example, worried about losing employment opportunities and scholarships, respectively. Others did not think they could take a beating without fighting back or fleeing. No one was forced to nor shamed into suffering; it was *voluntary*. "Many of these people stepped aside, and no one held it against them," wrote John Lewis in his memoir, *Walking with the Wind: A Memoir of the Movement* (Lewis and D'Orso 1998, 91). "Many more offered behind-the-battle-lines help," assisting in other, indispensable ways, such as: transporting demonstrators to the sit-ins; handling logistics at meeting centers like churches; relaying communication among students and organizers; helping prepare food; communicating with the press; and painting protest posters. There was something for everyone who wanted to be involved in the movement.

Part of the group's training also entailed minimizing the degree to which those who voluntarily suffered endured harm. The students practiced "how to curl [their] bodies so that [their] internal organs would escape direct blows" and "how if one person [was] taking a beating, others could put their bodies in the way, diluting the force of the attack" (1999, 85). Such training was critical when, during one of the sit-ins, a white agitator lit a match to the hair of a Black woman seated next to LaFayette.

"You could hear her hair sizzling, burning," LaFayette recounted during a conversation we had (LaFayette 2023a). When he turned to see if she was aware of what was happening, he saw that "she was very stoic, did not move, and looked straight ahead." Concerned for the woman's safety, LaFayette "reached over and tried to put the fire out" quickly with his hand. But her reaction to his doing so took him somewhat aback: "She turned around and looked at me, right in my eyes, as if I was out of order, and said, 'Don't interfere with my suffering'" (2023a).

LaFayette notes that while the woman "was accepting *her* suffering," she was likely "completely unaware of how [he] was suffering" in bearing witness to her hair being set afire. Such an extreme display of suffering seemed "unnecessary" to LaFayette for the purposes of desegregating lunch counters. He wanted the group to call attention to their plight, yes, but did not want anyone to die, become gravely injured, or have "permanent damage." Noticing that the woman's hair was still burning, he again attempted to put it out with his hand. "We both were suffering [and] so I thought, *Maybe my actions would reduce the suffering for both of us*" (2023a).

In recounting this experience, LaFayette admits that he still "wrestle[s] with that intellectually and emotionally" and questions "whether or not [he] took away her freedom and suffering, which she had already decided to do for herself." He wanted to respect her autonomy as an individual. At the same time, he said, "We were there as a group" and felt a responsibility for them to look out for one another. "They didn't try to burn *my* head. They did this only because she was a girl," he added, recognizing the sexist, misogynistic nature of the violent attack toward the woman. He added that, having grown up with several sisters, he felt somewhat protective. "Would I do it again?" he asked rhetorically, reflecting on the decision over sixty years after the fact. "The answer is," he paused for a moment before responding, resoundingly, "*yes*" (2023a).

LaFayette's conflicted feelings about intervening notwithstanding, he understands well the depth of such willingness to suffer for the sake of a cause. He has been arrested and jailed, beaten, and held at gunpoint multiple times. He risked his life participating in the Freedom Rides to desegregate interstate bus terminals [Figure 8.1], sustaining three broken ribs by an angry white mob during one attack and being confronted by the Ku Klux Klan during a separate encounter. He and John Lewis even wrote out their wills—at just *twenty years old*—in the event they did not make it back home from the Freedom Rides. He was badly pistol whipped and nearly shot in front of his home when running a voter registration project in Selma, Alabama.

LaFayette's staunch commitment to nonviolence and unwavering resolve to put his life on the line for freedom were undergirded by an empowering decision he had made early on: "I had already given my life to the movement. They can't take from you what you've already given away" (LaFayette 2017). For LaFayette, the willingness to give up his life transcended any singular protest and campaign; it reflected a shared sacrifice for and vision of the Beloved Community of which he and everyone else were an integral part.

Bernard LaFayette (left of center with arms crossed), John Lewis, and others at the
Greyhound bus station in Birmingham, Alabama during the Freedom Rides in 1961.

Moreover, in reflecting on the lunch counter sit-ins in Nashville,
LaFayette said, "We protested because *we* had changed. We continued to
give them the opportunity to also change because we believed that it was
possible" (Porter 2020). Nonviolence was as much about changing systems
as it was about personal transformation. Strengthening the capacity to love.
Fueling the will to fight. Nurturing the ability to dream, to hope, and to
create.

This deep-seated devotion to be immersed into the throes of a struggle
larger than oneself was echoed by John Lewis, who, in his memoir, wrote of
the moment immediately following his initial arrest during the sit-ins:

That paddy wagon—crowded, cramped, dirty, with wire cage
windows and doors—seemed like a chariot to me, a freedom
vehicle carrying me across a threshold….Now I had crossed over,

I had stepped through the door into total, unquestioning commitment. This wasn't just about that moment or that day. This was about forever. It was like deliverance….It was the purity and utter certainty of the nonviolent path (1998, 100–101).

Finding strength and hope *through* the struggle helped fortify the spirit and nourish the heart, very much so as the young leaders of the Nashville sit-in movement were faced with numerous setbacks.

When the sit-ins themselves and arrests did not initially lead to integration, the activists said no to paying bail and instead filled the jails. When filling the jails did not produce their desired outcome, they boycotted white-owned downtown stores. When their boycotts did not lead to their desired change and the house of one of their attorneys was bombed, they marched en masse to city hall [Figure 8.2], where Diane Nash pointedly asked Mayor Ben West, "Do you recommend the lunch counters be desegregated?" (Lewis, Aydin, and Powell 2013, 110). The rest is, as they say, history.

8.2

Reverend C.T. Vivian (left, front row), Diane Nash (center), and Bernard LaFayette (right, front row) marching to Nashville's City Hall after a bombing of attorney Z. Alexander Looby's home in April of 1960. Looby had been representing a group of students following sit-in demonstrations in Nashville.

With the benefit of hindsight, it can be easy to gloss over this historical moment and forget that it was the refusal to stop fighting and the willingness to endure suffering that led to some of the change they fought for. Were the activists 100 percent *certain* that they would be successful? Maybe not every moment of every day, but they were empowered by the fact that it was *themselves*—ordinary young people—and not solely politicians, who were the vanguards of bettering their society. They consistently showed up and had resolute faith that their efforts would not be in vain.

Many of us educators, too, see our work as part of a sacred calling we feel enormously dedicated to. To serve, learn from, teach, build with, and be alongside other human beings every day are gifts in and of themselves. And with those gifts, of course, come disappointment, heartbreak, rage, and suffering, especially if we are doing antiracist, anti-oppressive, and liberatory work. But we don't *have* to avoid the difficult emotions in order to thrive and keep our flame aglow.

Even when we are in the thick of the struggle, perhaps even feeling defeated, and unsure whether our efforts will pay off, unsure whether we'll have the kind of impact we yearn for, we can still find strength amidst our setbacks and suffering. So much of our work and capacity to endure setbacks rests on faith. Maintaining ongoing awareness of our (un)met needs, especially in fighting for justice and during times that test our spirit, can nurture our faith and be the difference between suffering that destroys and suffering that liberates.

In this chapter, we will explore how voluntary suffering, when grounded in awareness of our needs and guided by intentional boundaries, can empower and sustain us as we act for justice.

Reflecting on this Historical Moment

- How does Bernard LaFayette's story influence, challenge, or align with your understanding of (voluntary) suffering?

VOLUNTARY SUFFERING AND THE URGENCY OF OUR WORK

It goes without saying that what we do as educators is tremendously challenging even in the best of times. Anyone who authentically cares about children and works in a system that is capable of suppressing our humanity and enacting violence will inevitably experience despair, hurt, and suffering. And while people's suffering varies in degree, depending on circumstances, lived experience, identities, and privilege, ultimately, suffering is universal. That said, one may wonder: *Is it appropriate to draw lessons from the suffering of those who fought against overt and brutal racism of the Jim Crow South and apply them to our modern-day teaching contexts?*

In my view, it is not a question of whether to compare the nature of our suffering to that of those who've come before us. Their fight may have been different in form, but the substance of what they were resisting endures today. We are still up against the same and other compounding, violent forces that are harming both teachers and students: white supremacy, anti-Blackness, poverty, militarism, LGBTQIA+ phobia, Islamophobia, anti-Asian hate, police brutality, a global climate crisis, and more. The stakes can feel insurmountably high when we step back and consider the magnitude of it all.

I know for myself, fighting for and protecting an education rooted in love, hope, and justice is of the utmost urgency. I have students who are no longer here. Some have lost their lives to violence and drugs. I've lost count of the number who have confided in me that they no longer want to live. Some of my students and families have been unhoused. Others have been or still are incarcerated. Some, including their parents and relatives, are enmeshed in gangs, pitted against some of their own people because of allegiances to red and blue. These realities are utterly heartbreaking and overwhelming at times, and while they are not unique to my teaching context, they are heightened by historical and sociopolitical factors.

Approximately half of my student population is Vietnamese, and nearly the other half is Latinx, with families hailing largely from Mexico and Central America. A smaller percentage of students at my school identify as Cambodian, Pilipinx, Black, Laotian, Native American, Palestinian, Indian, Chinese, Samoan, white, among other races, comprising a culturally rich and racially diverse student body.

A large number of my Vietnamese students' grandparents and parents fled Vietnam to the United States as refugees during and following the Fall of Saigon. In fact, our city has the largest Vietnamese population outside of Vietnam (Visit San Jose n.d.). Needless to say, the catastrophic conflict between the United States and Vietnam has resulted in high rates of mental illness including depression, anxiety, and post traumatic stress disorder (Wang 2022). More recently, the term complex-PTSD has grown in usage to more accurately reflect how, in some instances, people's trauma is not a result of a single traumatic episode but multiple, recurring traumatic experiences over time.

Many of my Latinx students and their parents are undocumented, and I have heard them share stories of extremely difficult journeys to the United States. Countless other students have witnessed loved ones being arrested and deported. Some have gone years without seeing—or ever meeting—their parents and other family members.

The effects of highly traumatic experiences could be significant for anyone, let alone a youth, but there is some research that suggests that traumatic events in a person's life can alter how their genes are expressed and passed down to the next generation(s) (Henriques 2019; PBS News 2015). Students whose parents, grandparents, or ancestors have experienced historical trauma could be impacted without even realizing it.

I share some of my context not to sensationalize the realities that my community lives through nor to suggest that my students and families are "broken." My students and families are deeply resilient and come from generations of fighters steeped in cultural pride, activism, and resistance.

For example, Figure 8.3 shows the opening celebration of the Vietnamese American Service Center, the first of its kind in the United States, which provides wellness programs, mental and physical health services, and other resources to address "health and social disparities in the Vietnamese American and local

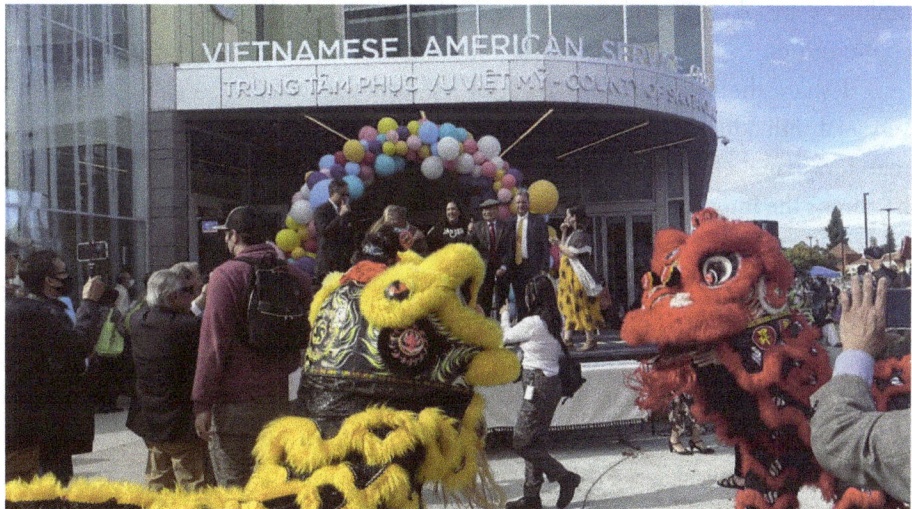

8.3

Opening celebration of the Vietnamese American Service Center located in East San José.

8.4
—

McDonnell Hall, located on the grounds of Our Lady of Guadalupe Parish in East San José. The building was declared a national landmark in 2017. Personal collection.

communities" (Nguyen 2021). Figure 8.4 depicts McDonnell Hall, located on the grounds of Our Lady of Guadalupe Parish in East San José, where César Chávez organized Mexican American farm workers and community activists. Both of these buildings are physical representations of the strength and beauty of our San José communities.

I share the more difficult parts of my teaching context to call attention to very real individual, collective, and intergenerational trauma that exists. I imagine that for many of us, such trauma compounds the challenges *of* teaching and heightens the importance and urgency for *what*, *how*, and *why* we teach.

But does that mean it is on teachers to make up for systemic and societal failings? That we must suffer endlessly in order to solve the world's problems? No. We are not machines nor saviors. But neither are we *just* teachers who help students learn skills and content. Our impact, often immeasurable, can be the difference between literal and spiritual life and death for students, and naming that reality is not hyperbole. Many of us are ardently fighting against oppressive conditions and issues that are way bigger than the school system itself. It makes sense, then, that some of our efforts be proportional to the magnitude of the issues we are fighting against. There is a fine line, though, between feeding into the (white) savior trope and being of service to and in solidarity with our students.

> **A Moment for Reflection**
>
> - What are some cultural or familial assets that your students and their families possess?
> - How do collective challenges or hardships shared by your students and families impact your school community?

SAVING OURSELVES FROM SAVING

To borrow from Dr. Victor Rios, professor of sociology at UC Santa Barbara and author of several books, if we label certain populations as "at-risk," we ourselves risk viewing and treating students through deficit framing, even if we have the best of intentions. He would know—he was a former gang member who was labeled and treated as at-risk as a youth.

Rios' story of childhood and adolescence contains the hallmarks often associated with "troubled" young people: his father abandoned the family before Victor was born; his mother was pregnant with him while she was incarcerated; he grew up in dire poverty; witnessed his uncle get shot and bleed to death; joined a gang at age fourteen; got arrested and incarcerated in juvenile hall three times by the time he was fifteen; had poor relationships with many of his teachers; was put on probation; dropped out of school multiple times; and his best friend was killed.

In his Ted Talk "Help for Kids the Education System Ignores," Rios says, "I had lost faith and hope in the world, and I had given up on the system because the system had given up on me. I had nothing to offer, and no one had anything to offer me. I was fatalistic. I didn't even think I could make it to my eighteenth birthday" (2015, 2:23). But he would soon meet someone who did believe in him and who did not treat him as a problem to fix. It was one of his teachers, Ms. Russ, who Rios says, "cared, reached out, and managed to tap into my soul," despite his initial pushing her away. He described his memory of her with fondness:

> Ms. Russ was there for me. She was culturally relevant. She respected my community, my people, my family....[She] listened to my story, welcomed it into the classroom and said: 'Victor, this is your power. This is your potential. Your family, your culture, your community have taught you a hard work ethic, and you will use it to empower yourself in the academic world so you can come back and empower your community' (2015, 2:40).

Russ connected Victor with mentors and helped him return home to himself. He ended up graduating on time with his class and subsequently attended UC Berkeley. Rios credits Russ, who was an educator for fifty years before retiring, for his being alive today but not because she saved him per se. She saw, respected, and nurtured the promise of who he already was, enabling Victor to liberate himself *through* the unconditional love and support he received from her and others—love and support he now puts back into the universe [Figure 8.5].

The 2018 documentary *The Pushouts* follows the stories of several young people, ages 16–24, in Watts, Los Angeles who were pushed out of their schools and subsequently joined an alternative education program. In this program, they receive support from mentors including Rios, whose story is also featured prominently throughout the film. In one scene, as the group is building rapport and community, Rios says to the kids: "We're not here to tell you we're going to save you. We're here to ask your permission to share our stories with you and for you to share your stories with us....We're not here to give you the power—you've already got it. We're just here to *facilitate*, to see that power grow" (Galloway 2018).

To "save" in the context of teaching implies that I am an empowered subject who liberates disempowered objects, that I am somehow distant to or removed from the brunt of the struggle. But if, instead, I see and treat my students as

8.5

Victor Rios with his teacher Flora Russ at Berkeley High, where Rios was invited to guest speak about his experience as a student, nearly twenty years after graduating.

powerful, whole people and save myself from the illusion that I am superior to, separate from, or more powerful than them; if I can facilitate the cultivation of what is already present and share my story alongside theirs; if the fight for collective liberation and fruition of the Beloved Community is done through companionship—*then* I allow myself to be bound up in the struggle from a place of love, humility, and interdependence.

> ## A Moment for Reflection
>
> • How do you navigate supporting your students without "saving" them?

HONORING OUR NEEDS, BOUNDARIES, AND CHOICE

Without a doubt, building learning communities that let down walls, build up love, and surface young people's brilliance is not easy and invariably requires sacrifice. Some of us dedicate evenings or weekends to designing relevant lessons because it meets our needs for *creativity* and *joy*. Some of us invest substantial energy and time into building, sustaining, and repairing relationships because it meets our needs for *connection* and *care*. Some of us may even use our own money to purchase materials and supplies for our kids because it meets our need for *contribution*.

Having said that, I want to be unequivocal here: no one should ever be exploited for their labor, feel pressured to do more than they are willing, or have to toil in order to simply earn a livelihood. If being a "good employee" means that one is guilted or coerced to "take one for the team" or do something that does not align with their values, needs, or capacity, I can only hope that they get different school leaders or find an alternate school to work in.

I completely understand and respect the choice to set firm boundaries between one's teaching career and personal life, especially for educators who are already doing and carrying so much as it is: BIPOC, LGBTQIA+, parents and caregivers, folks with multiple jobs, etc. Working in environments saturated with white supremacy culture and LGBTQIA+ hate and phobia while trying to undo their harm on ourselves and our kids weighs on the spirit—especially when done in isolation.

Teachers of color, in particular, are hit with an "invisible tax" when additional responsibilities or expectations are placed upon them, such as being the go-to person for students with behavioral challenges, acting as a liaison or advocate for families of color, leading Diversity, Equity and Inclusion (DEI) work, and other emotional and mental labor not shared by (white) colleagues (Pottiger 2022). For some, setting hard boundaries, be it with time, emotional capacity, physical energy, etc., is a matter of self-preservation and survival.

I *also* understand that while we share the same universal needs as human beings, we don't all meet our needs in the same way. Nor is our capacity static; it will ebb and flow depending on our internal state and external factors, though over time and with supportive practices, our capacity *can* expand. Furthermore, even within a particular demographic, we are each unique organisms with our own constitution, personality, and proclivity toward meeting our needs.

One way of conceptualizing needs is non-hierarchically, which challenges the conventional view that groups of certain needs are contingent upon others. Leading Nonviolent Communication trainer Miki Kashtan writes that "people regularly override certain needs in order to fulfill others" such as "in the willingness to die for a cause, or the capacity to choose to go on a hunger strike" (Kashtan 2013). She adds that some "people and groups who are suffering from oppression and harsh conditions nonetheless find outlets for art and personal expression which would not be possible if their basic survival needs were a prerequisite to other needs being pursued" (2013).

Although her examples may seem extreme, the underlying logic helps explain why, for instance, some students completely check out of school after a parent or close family member passes away, while other students in the same situation double down on school for consistency and stability. Or why an educator is willing to risk their job over teaching a banned book title or censored topic.

Viewing needs as non-hierarchical also complicates the simplistic view that teachers who are "ride or die" for their kids have a martyr complex. If we are doing something that diminishes our own spiritual, emotional, physical, or mental well-being, then that is one thing. And if we're noticing that a colleague is not doing well, it's important that we or someone else check in on them and offer support if possible. If, however, we have a vision we are striving for that transcends the job description and are willing to endure some degree of suffering in pursuit of fulfilling that vision because it empowers us, strengthens our spirit, and meets our needs, then who is to tell us otherwise?

This is not about subjecting ourselves to suffer more than we have to. It is about having the awareness and internal spaciousness to slow down when we *do* suffer to discern whether such suffering truly serves our needs or undermines them. I know that when I don't dedicate the time to pause, I tend to function from a reactive place of "I *have* to"; this can leave me feeling less free, less willing, and sometimes even resentful. In contrast, when I do dedicate the time to pause, breathe, and discern, I am more likely to operate from a place of "I am choosing to

___ because it meets my needs for ___." That doesn't make the suffering *easy* but it does make it *easier*. Without fail, the latter approach helps me feel more free, more engaged, and open because I am caring for myself from an intentional and empowered place.

Dr. Pooja Lakshmin, psychiatrist and author of *Real Self-Care: A Transformative Program for Redefining Wellness*, says that dedicating time to pause—even if just for a moment—in order to make an informed choice is a boundary. Pausing gives us the space to decide whether to say yes, say no, or negotiate when a request is made of us, whether by someone else or ourselves. The boundary is "in the space between" the request and our decision, she says, which allows us "to decide how [we're] going to move. It's not a brick wall" (2023b). Pausing in this manner is part of practicing *real* self-care, which she defines as "the internal process of setting boundaries, learning to treat yourself with compassion, making choices that bring you closer to yourself, and living a life aligned with your values" (2023a, xx). When we practice real self-care, "it has the potential to shift our relationships, our workplace culture, and even our social systems," Lakshmin says (2023a, xx).

Although Lakshmin wrote her book specifically for women, I think all of us can benefit from the wisdom of pausing and sitting "in the space between" what is asked of us and how we want to respond. Setting boundaries in the form of pausing gives us the space to choose, with clarity and intention, how to make difficult decisions amidst difficult circumstances. We cannot always control when we suffer; that is part of life. But being able to choose the extent to which we are *willing* to endure some degree of suffering helps us retain our power. It must be emphasized here, however, that doing so is a *choice* and should always be **voluntary**.

In his magnificent book *The Art of Living: Peace and Freedom in the Here and Now*, Thich Nhat Hanh writes, "Handling our suffering is an art" (2017, 173). He opines that it is not suffering itself that we should be afraid of, but rather, "not knowing how to deal with our suffering" (2017, 172). It weighs on me when students feel ashamed of or hate who they are. It weighs on me when students tell me they are hopeless and want to end their lives. It weighs on me when students stop coming to school or engage in self-sabotaging behavior and push me away despite my love for them and earnest attempts to help. It weighs on me when students are failing every class and seem resigned to have completely given up. It weighs on me when teachers' efforts and impact go unrecognized by school leaders. It weighs on me when lawmakers pass violent legislation that assaults the souls, hearts, and bodies of trans, queer, Black, Brown, Asian, and Indigenous teachers and youth.

But my spirit is also lifted up and strengthened by how I deal with my suffering. I remember to pause and breathe. I identify my unmet needs and determine what strategies would be most helpful to meet those needs. I remind myself that my willingness to make sacrifices for the sake of the Beloved Community is borne out of love for my students, love for humanity, and love for myself because it is for all of us. Don't get me wrong—I don't *want* to suffer, and I'm not actively looking for it; however, I don't avoid it when it's there.

Moreover, mindfully *feeling* the difficult emotions reminds me that I am in solidarity and communion with my students, staying grounded in the struggle. In this way, there is solace in my suffering, which I strive to handle as "an art." I recognize that as an able-bodied, healthy, straight, cisgendered man of color with medium skin tone, there is some privilege in my saying that. Still, I want to have sovereignty over how I experience my suffering; I don't want anyone or anything to take that power from me.

Pausing as a Boundary

▷ Recalling Pooja Lakshmin's definition of a boundary as a pause, what is a demand, responsibility, or expectation at school that feels challenging for you at the moment?

▷ How would you ideally like to respond to this demand, responsibility, or expectation?

▷ Review the list of needs shared in Chapter 1 (or in Appendix B). What need(s) does/would this response meet for you?

Reflecting on Voluntary Suffering

▷ What tends to cause you suffering in your work as an educator?

▷ To what extent does this affect your day-to-day teaching and/or well-being?

▷ How do you (or would you like to) take care of yourself during such suffering? Is there someone else at your school whom you could lean on (and vice versa) for support?

Extending Support

▷ Think of colleagues of yours from historically targeted groups (BIPOC, LGBTQIA+, etc.). Whose work/efforts stand out to you as particularly important or effective?

▷ With your current capacity, identities, areas of privilege, and lived experience in mind, what are some ways you might be able to support these colleagues, directly or indirectly?

In a 1967 speech given less than a year before his assassination, Dr. Martin Luther King, Jr. said:

> [S]ocial progress never rolls in on the wheels of inevitability. It comes through the tireless efforts and the persistent work of dedicated individuals. And without this hard work, time itself becomes an ally of the primitive forces of social stagnation. And so we must help time, and we must realize that the time is always right to do right (1967b, 0:46).

I know that as individual teachers, there is only so much we can realistically do. Our time and capacity are limited. I also know that, at the end of the day, it is dedicated individuals who make up collective action. However, our tireless and persistent efforts should not come at the expense of honoring our body's wisdom and need for rest.

Almost ten years prior, King recognized the toll of his nonstop work schedule and prominent leadership status following the monumental success of the Montgomery Bus Boycott. He said in an interview with *Jet* magazine in December of 1959:

> For almost four years now, I have been faced with the responsibility of trying to do as one man what five or six people ought to be doing.... What I have been doing is giving, giving, giving, and not stopping to retreat and meditate like I should—to come back. If the situation is not changed, I will be a physical and psychological wreck. I have to reorganize my personality and re-orient [*sic*] my life (*Jet* 1959, 14–15).

The pressure he felt as the movement progressed and splintered, FBA surveilled him, and death threats increased is almost unfathomable. He was treated for exhaustion several times, which his wife Coretta referred to as depression (Eig 2023b). The final eighteen months of his life, in particular, were rife with isolation and turmoil. He was desperate for respite.

Being engaged in the urgent fight to transform our schools does not mean we always have to do more and go faster. Yes, there is plenty that needs to be done, and there is a risk that if we move *too* slowly, "forces of social stagnation" will persist. But the time each of us has on this planet—sacred, precious time—is very brief in the grand scheme of things. We must remember to "come back" to ourselves.

"The work of social change is stressful enough on its best days," writes Kazu Haga in an article titled "The Urgency of Slowing Down," which inspired part of the theme and title of this section. "[I]f we are moving without intention, without mindfulness and without awareness of *how* we are moving, it can easily add to what is already a challenge....We need to learn to slow down while acknowledging the urgency of this moment," he says (2017). That is, we need to be able to learn to slow down without compromising the urgency and need to continually fight for justice.

And in that fight, I do not want to lose myself to grind culture, getting worn to the point where I no longer can nor want to teach. If I am fortunate enough to teach until I am an elder, I want to be able to look back and trust that I did my absolute, honest best to find beauty amidst the chaos. That I gained resolve through the suffering. That I cared for myself and others amidst the struggle. That I remembered to slow down. Pause. Rest. Breathe.

In.
Out.
In.
Out.

OUTER
PRACTICE

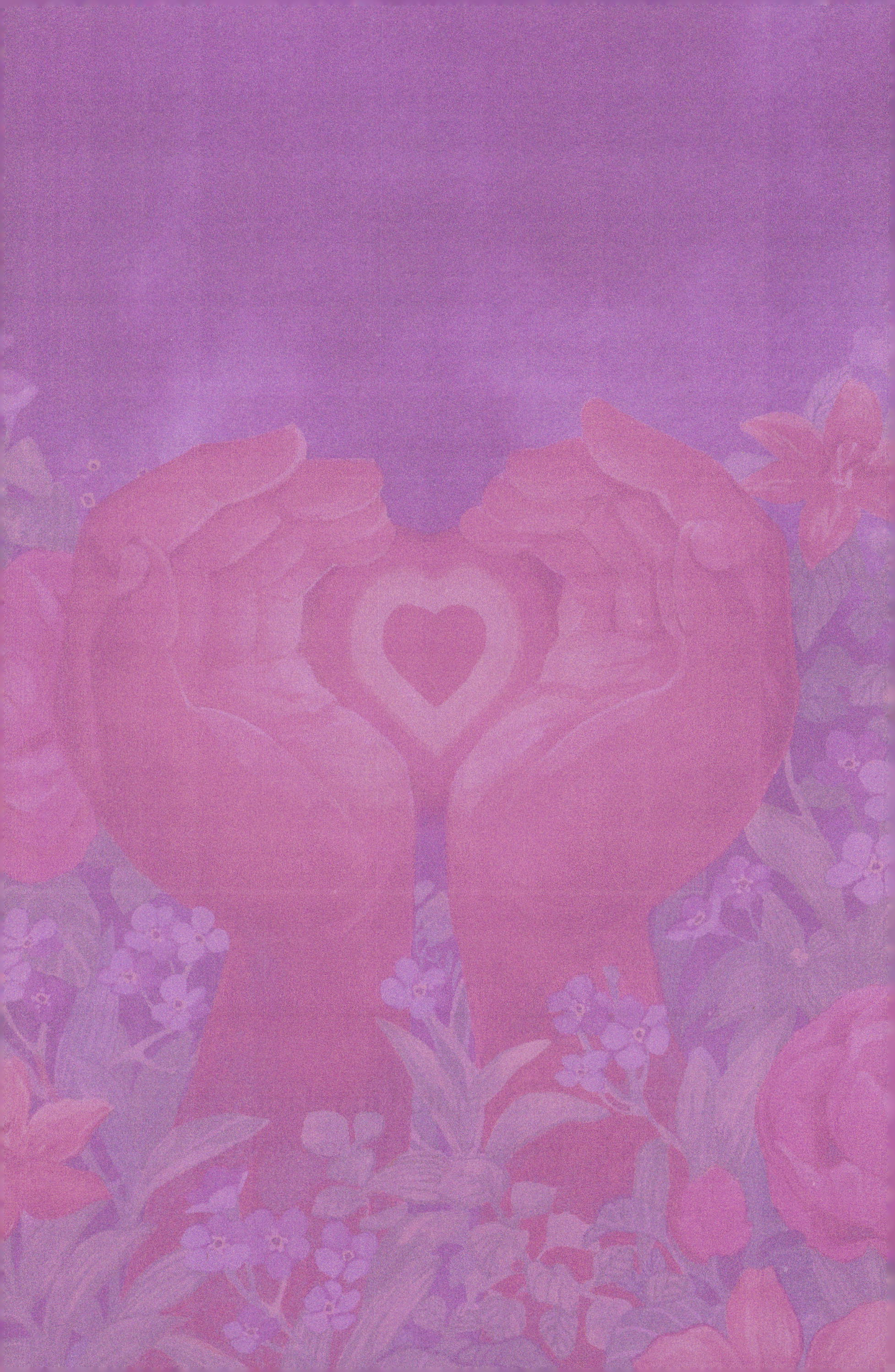

"All gifts are multiplied in relationship.
This is how the world keeps going."

DR. ROBIN WALL KIMMERER, from *Braiding Sweetgrass*

Tending the Whole Garden

CHAPTER 9

Connecting Through Conflict

"Wow," he said with his signature raspy voice, trying to process the breathtaking sight before his eyes.

"It's not as bad as it looks, right?"

"No, Mike—*worse*."

My grandpa furrowed his eyebrows while studying the mess that lay before us: boxes piled atop each other, some without lids, others toppled; scattered CDs and DVDs; laundry strewn across the couch and floor; a microphone, guitar pedals, and snaking cables connected to a huge bass amp still warm from a beatbox session; a makeshift computer station at the coffee table; empty soda cans; and dirty dishes piled in the kitchen.

I had recently moved in, shortly after my twentieth birthday, and just started to unpack. Granted, it was my first time living on my own, and I had intended for the living room to serve as a temporary holding space while I moved stuff into my bedroom and other areas. But the lack of systems in place for organizing my belongings made for a haphazard process and display. I was embarrassed and worried that my grandpa would regret letting me live alone in his house.

Seven years earlier, my grandma Nilda, then a widow, fell in love again and married a man named Leon, also a widower, who would become my step grandpa. After I left Oregon and returned to California to live with my dad the following year at age fourteen, I saw my grandparents periodically but not as much as I wish I had in hindsight. As a moody teenager preoccupied with skateboarding, beatboxing, and video games, I did not always treat the ninety-minute drive to visit them as a priority.

Moreover, my grandma, loving as she was in her own way, had a stern demeanor and, at times, mercurial temperament that did not always make for fun visits. My grandpa could usually assuage her moments of intensity with his unbending lightheartedness, but he had a tendency to talk *a lot*, which my adolescent ears sometimes lacked patience for.

That said, I could tell that my grandpa was sincere in wanting to get to know me. I remember when he took me swimming at a pool where his fellow senior-aged friends congregated (not exactly the hippest place for a young person). I remember when we hiked at Sanborn County Park alongside redwood trees of majestic height. I remember when he made me lunch and asked what I was into and hoped for in life, inquiring with genuine interest and listening with full presence. I remember his stories of watching the Golden Gate Bridge being built, being a record track runner in school, smoking four packs of cigarettes a day for years before quitting cold turkey. I especially remember the surprise I felt when, after I told my grandparents I was planning to move out on my own and was considering college, he offered, unsolicited, for me to live in his house alone.

My grandpa had bought his modest, four-bedroom abode in the mid-1970s and lived there up until he and my grandma married. He then moved in with her while his house subsequently sat unoccupied. By the time I moved into his place, we had certainly become better acquainted, but in my mind, we were still getting to know each other. I was very grateful for his extreme generosity and figured that he wouldn't have made such a gesture if he did not hold a lot of respect for and trust in me.

Which is why I felt regretful when I saw him taking in, with ostensible disappointment, that which I had allowed to become in disarray. While there weren't explicit, agreed-upon terms for my living there, I knew that my grandpa was exceptionally organized. I think we shared a tacit understanding that I'd try to keep his place tidy. So I was prepared to be scolded and presented with an ultimatum to "clean up or move out." I was even prepared to hear, "Maybe it's not such a good idea after all for you to live here on your own."

But neither of those were said. My grandpa didn't scold me. He didn't lecture me. Instead, he let out a raspy sigh of seeming relief, as if whatever he had been initially feeling evaporated, and said, "Okay then. I'll leave you be. But tomorrow, I'd like you to help me with some watering."

Huh? I thought. *Where did watering come from?* But I was not about to question or argue. "Okay, Grandpa," I said. "Sounds good."

* * *

"These are called hybrid tea roses. Have you ever watered a rose bush before?" my grandpa, donning a wide-brimmed straw hat, asked while handing me a green garden hose.

"Uh, I don't remember," I replied. I then waved running water over the top of the red flowers. "Like *this*?" I asked.

"Woah! Hang on," he interjected before gently pushing the hose out of the way. "We always want to water at the base, where the roots are. That way the entire plant will receive what it needs. The rose petals are very delicate."

"Oh—whoops." I felt foolish for not knowing better. "Sorry."

"That's okay," my grandpa said while nodding his head, apparently sensing my embarrassment. "Try again."

I then watered the base of the bush, as he had instructed, allowing the dirt to absorb enough water without becoming overly saturated.

"*Good.* That's the way," he said.

I watered the remaining rose bushes before moving on to the camellias, geraniums, and other flowers and plants in the front yard. "Well done, Mike," he said when I finished. "Now let's move on to the backyard."

I had been in his backyard several times prior to moving in but hadn't quite noticed just how large the garden was. He introduced me to nearly every plant, flower, and tree. There were several fruit trees—pomegranate, orange, lemon, quince—and a humongous incense cedar that stood in the middle of the yard.

"The city designated this cedar as a heritage tree," he told me as we looked up at its stunning size. "That's why it hasn't been cut down. Beautiful, isn't it?"

He showed me bright yellow crown daisies, thick shrimp plants that attracted gigantic carpenter bees, an oleander with hot pink blooms, and dozens of spider plants, lilies, aloe vera, and cacti that lined the side and rear of the house [Figure 9.1].

After I finished the watering, my grandpa gave me a satisfied smile and said, "Thanks, Mike. Now, if you could please do that a few times a week, I would appreciate it."

At first, it felt like a real chore. It was time-consuming, and, early on, I rushed through the process. *Why does he care so much about these things, anyway?* I thought. *They just sit there.* The fruit trees I could understand, as they actually gave something tangible to eat. But I did not get nor appreciate—yet—why my grandpa caressed the plant leaves, smiled as he pruned the rose bushes, and seemed in a meditative state amidst the silent greenery.

Although I did not ever directly ask him why, he provided answers through his ceaseless respect for the garden. Once, we had planted tomato

9.1

Crown daisy (left) and hybrid tea roses (right) from my grandpa's garden.
Personal collection.

seeds, and after some time, they began to flower. But despite months of watering and waiting, the plant did not bear any fruit.

"What if it never grows any tomatoes?" I asked him. "Should we even water it still?"

"Yes, what if?" he questioned in return. "Would that make it any less beautiful? Any less worthy of our attention and care?" Eventually, the tomato plant did, in fact, bear delicious fruit. But to my grandpa, it wasn't deemed more valuable because of how it "performed."

For the longest time, I had thought of vegetation primarily in terms of its utility, placing value on what it could offer and be used for: oxygen, food, pollen, decorations, gifts, etc. But slowly, my grandpa's words and example shifted my thinking. I started to realize that it didn't have to "give" anything in order for me to appreciate and enjoy its being alive.

I was reminded of when I was in the first grade and my teacher gave each student a packet of seeds to take home and plant, water, and watch grow. I recall the pride I took in gently caring for my little green friend and the excitement I felt in witnessing it sprout, grow vines, and ascend over the days and weeks. I was fascinated by knowing that it, like me, was unequivocally *alive*.

It saddened me to realize that I hadn't had that kind of fondness for nor relationship with a plant, flower, or tree since childhood. Soon after, I started moving a little more slowly whenever watering the garden. I enjoyed hearing the water and dirt touch. Sometimes, I would place my hand on the ground just to *feel* the earth. I looked forward to seeing the spectacular colors. I developed an appreciation for being in the midst of so much beauty, so much life.

Eventually, tending the garden ceased to feel like an obligation and became a serene experience that I, like my grandpa, relished. I found being in nature to be one of my favorite activities and started hiking regularly at Fremont Older, Alum Rock, Mission Peak, Rancho San Antonio, Mount Umunhum, Castle Rock, among other parks and trails.

In learning to feel connected with the land, I also learned to appreciate what came before me. Long before my grandpa planted his garden; long before he had his house; long before there were city-designated parks; long before there was a Silicon Valley; long before there were orchards; long before land was stolen from Native Americans, who were subjected to genocide, abuse, and loss of culture, religion, and identity; there were—and still are—the Tamien Nation, Muwekma Ohlone Tribe, and other indigenous peoples who knew how to be in relationship with the land and who lived in sustainable ways.

I also came to understand that our relationship with plants, flowers, trees, and land can guide us in how to treat one another. My grandpa's reverence for his garden reflected how he treated those around him—and how he treated himself. He adored my grandma and helped her find happiness. He listened when I had doubts about college, helped me to recognize and nurture my own brilliance, and was there to watch me walk the stage and journey toward becoming a teacher [Figure 9.2]. He was generous with what he had and sought to help others reap joy. He lived in spiritual and emotional abundance, expressing gratitude for his blessings and possessing an unshakably affable disposition even when his health deteriorated.

My grandpa, an unpretentious and sweet, sweet man of a different generation, political orientation, and racial and cultural background than I, embodied and radiated love that truly knew no bounds. A well-known proverb says that "blood is thicker than water." Maybe sometimes. But it is water that cleanses when blood stains. It is water that nourishes and sustains life. It is water that allows a garden to flourish.

Like plants and flowers, we thrive when we are treated with care and receive what we need. Thus, gardens are a helpful metaphor for what schools *can* be: spaces where everyone—students, teachers, support staff, administrators—is treated as sacred. No one above, no one below. Unfortunately, the reality for most of us in schools is that some plots of the garden blossom while others are left to wither. Who among us has seen someone be chastised, humiliated, or arbitrarily pushed out, as if they were undesirable weeds to be plucked? Who hasn't felt disrespected, belittled, or demoralized at times, perhaps to the point of questioning whether they want to continue teaching?

9.2

Me, my siblings, and our grandpa at my college graduation. Personal collection.

The existing power hierarchy in schools makes it such that, without effective guidance and strong support from and positive influence of leaders, creating a schoolwide culture grounded in humanization, love, and justice can feel futile, if not impossible. Consequently, it may be tempting to throw our hands up and think there's little to nothing we individual teachers can do unless *others* change. We may feel compelled to just keep our classroom door shut and tend to our own area of the garden, with our students, where we know we have the most direct influence and impact.

But we should not have to put up with environments that are toxic, dehumanizing, and inhibit our ability to fully *be*. We should not have to wait for others to lead us toward creating the kind of schools we deserve and

like plants and flowers, we thrive when we are treated with care and receive what we need

need. Shifting culture and changing systems is arduous, ongoing work and requires collective effort and will, including from traditional school leaders. But individual efforts make a difference and matter.

In this chapter, we will explore how to maintain connection with self and others amidst conflict. This is an important way of tapping into our *own* leadership, beyond our classrooms, for the well-being of ourselves and fellow members of our school communities. The more that we can come together and draw out the best in one another, fostering a kind of mutual steward-ship, the more likely our respective gardens will flourish.

RHYMING HISTORY

Before we look at how to maintain connection with ourselves and others amidst conflict in an educational context, I would first like to draw a striking, eerie parallel between what is currently playing out in today's sociopolitical climate and schools and that of over half a century ago. Oftentimes, in the thick of a struggle, it can be difficult to zoom out and know how to best navigate it. It is my hope that drawing such a parallel will guide us through our current moment, offering us inspiration and resolve.

Given our highly polarized and politicized landscape, where schools, school board meetings, and libraries are increasingly serving as battlegrounds for some of America's culture wars, the idea that our educational environments can be akin to beautiful, thriving gardens may seem like a pipe dream. After all, a growing number of teachers, librarians, and even administrators have experienced alarming blowback in response to advocating for just, equitable, and humanizing education.

A social studies teacher in Tennessee was fired for teaching his students that white privilege is a fact; the teacher himself was white (Natanson 2021).

An English teacher in Oklahoma who shared a QR code for her students to access banned books, including *Gender Queer*, at the public library was accused by a parent of providing access to "porn." The complaint eventually led to the state department of education applying to revoke her teaching certificate (Tolin 2023).

After the killing of George Floyd, a Black principal of a Texas high school—the school's first in its twenty-five-year history—sent an email out to colleagues and friends, stating that systemic racism is "alive and well" and that education is "a necessary conduit to get liberty and justice for all." Despite initially receiving "overwhelmingly positive" responses and support from his community, the school board voted to end his contract and he was placed on administrative leave before ultimately quitting (Lawrence 2022).

Not surprisingly, proponents of legislation targeting critical race theory, LGBTQIA+ issues, social-emotional learning often cite Dr. Martin Luther King Jr.'s "I Have a Dream" speech as an attempt to defend their opposition to said topics. For instance, when Florida's governor signed the "Stop W.O.K.E. Act" in July of 2022, he invoked King, saying of the civil rights leader, "'He said he didn't want people judged on the color of their skin but on the content of their character'" (Blest 2021).

The cherry-picking of such lines from the "I Have a Dream" speech invariably perpetuates a distorted and sanitized image of King that has come to permeate much of the collective imagination: that he was a calm, benevolent, and saint-like martyr who advocated for colorblind peace and holding hands. In reality, King consistently and vehemently argued that it was absolutely necessary to reckon with the nation's ugly history and existing reality of racism in order for children to "not be judged by the color of their skin but by the content of their character."

Moreover, as his years as a leader of the civil rights movement continued, King came to recognize the interconnected nature of injustice and oppression, believing that the fight against racism was intertwined with the struggle against extreme materialism and poverty, which was inextricably linked to the fight against militarism and war. We could not build the Beloved Community without confronting all of these existential threats.

In an interview with NBC News in May of 1967, King said of the dream he spoke of at the 1963 March on Washington: "I must confess that that dream I had that day has, at many points, turned into a nightmare." He added that he had "gone through a lot of soul-searching and agonizing moments" in analyzing the "triple evils" of racism, economic exploitation, and militarism plaguing the United States. From this difficult period emerged a sobering realization: "Some of the old optimism was a little superficial, and now it must be tempered with a solid realism" (1967a, 22:31).

THE RADICAL KING

The white-washing of King's radical nonviolence and legacy conveniently ignores how he himself was vilified mercilessly as a result of condemning the United States for inflicting catastrophic, devastating violence and suffering in Vietnam—vilified for speaking out and doing what was morally right.

On April 4, 1967, exactly one year to the day before his assassination, he gave his "Beyond Vietnam" speech at Riverside Church in New York, in which he said, "I knew that I could never again raise my voice against the violence of the oppressed in the ghettos without having first spoken clearly to the greatest purveyor of violence in the world today—my own government" (2015b, 204). Throughout the speech, he lambasted the United States and called out its hypocrisy of espousing freedom, justice, and democracy yet failing to uphold these ideals for all of its people.

It should be noted that while King was personally against the war, he was initially reluctant to issue his opposition publicly, for concern, shared by many of his civil rights colleagues, that doing so would strain his budding relationship with President Lyndon B. Johnson and undermine the movement's recent legislative victories. But it was difficult for King to remain quiet while others spoke out. Celebrities like Muhammad Ali refused to be drafted and many young people, such as members of the Student Nonviolent Coordinating Committee, denounced the war.

Perhaps most influential on King was his wife, Coretta Scott King, a humanitarian and activist in her own right [Figure 9.3]. She was a longtime member of the NAACP and in her lifetime fought for women's rights, world peace, economic and racial justice, gay rights, and against apartheid in Africa, among other issues. She was particularly outspoken against war and militarism before, during, and after her husband's apex in the civil rights movement. As stated in an article from *The Atlantic*:

> She was present at the creation of the National Committee for a Sane Nuclear Policy in 1957 and represented Women's [*sic*] Strike for Peace at a nuclear-disarmament conference in Geneva in 1962. When her husband received the Nobel Peace Prize, in 1964, she impressed upon him the role he must play in pursuing world peace (Theoharis 2018).

After giving his scathing "Beyond Vietnam" speech, King's words ricocheted throughout the country, and the backlash was swift and harsh.

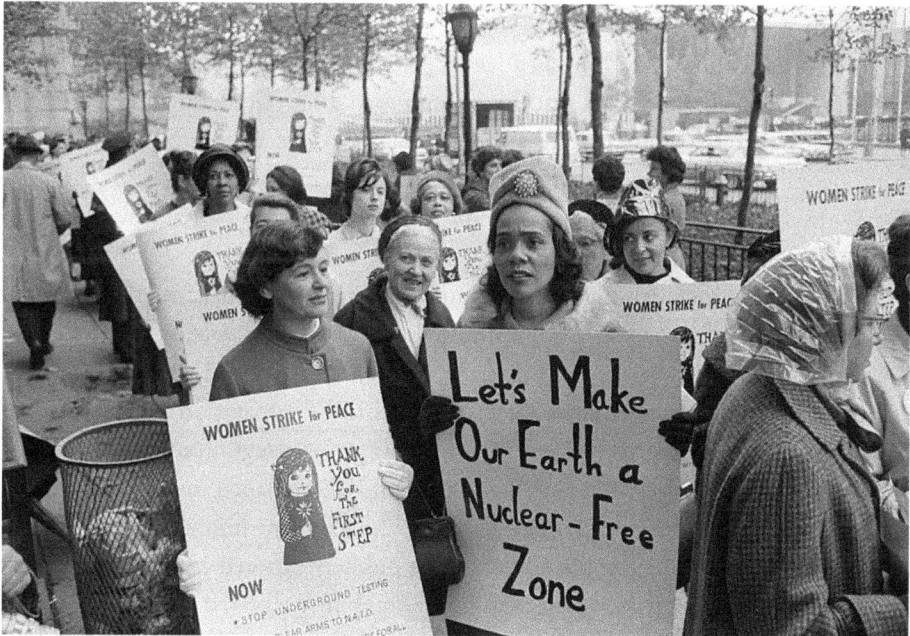

9.3

Coretta Scott King with Dagmar Wilson, founder of Women Strike for Peace, at a march in New York in November of 1963.

The Washington Post wrote that King "has diminished his usefulness to his cause, to his country and to his people" (Krieg 2018).

The New York Times opined that "uniting the peace movement and the civil rights movement could very well be disastrous for both causes," claiming that racial equality and the war were "two public problems that are distinct and separate." It added that "to divert the energies of the civil rights movement to the Vietnam issue is both wasteful and self-defeating" (*The New York Times* 1967).

Life magazine argued that "King has gone off on a tangent suggesting that American Negroes boycott the war. By characterizing it as a colonialist war, he introduces matters that have nothing to do with the legitimate battle for equal rights here in America." The article added, "Much of his speech was a demagogic slander that sounded like a script for Radio Hanoi" (*Life* 1967).

King's relationship with President Johnson, with whom he had previously worked to pass the Civil Rights Act of 1964 and the Voting Rights Act of 1965, crumbled (The Martin Luther King, Jr. Research and Education Institute n.d.c).

He was even criticized by friends, religious leaders, and allies from within the movement, who believed that he was jeopardizing gains made in the civil rights movement (Kunhardt 2018). Many distanced themselves from King's firm stance on the war, including the NAACP, who issued a public statement opposing merging the civil rights movement and the anti-war, peace movement.

Public support for King, which had already been waning, dropped significantly. In a Gallup Poll from August of 1966, 63 percent of respondents gave an unfavorable opinion of him as a leader (Jones 2011). By early 1968, a Harris poll showed that he had a 75 percent *disapproval* rating (Cobb and Zócalo Public Square 2018). His denunciation of the war between the United States and Vietnam, people's growing skepticism of nonviolence as a means for liberation, and the rise of the Black Power movement all contributed to an image of a growingly outdated, "irrelevant" King (Smiley 2014, 4:10).

King's unpopularity and negative image were, no doubt, fueled in part by frequent charges that he was a communist "extremist" and "outside agitator" who "instigated violence." An assistant director of the FBI, who had secretly surveilled King for several years as part of their COINTELPRO operation under J. Edgar Hoover's watch, referred to him as "the most dangerous Negro leader of the future in this Nation" (Blow 2013). After wiretaps and surveillance revealed that King had engaged in numerous extramarital affairs, the FBI sent him a letter pressuring him to take his own life, lest his infidelities be publicly exposed (Prokop 2018).

In the final analysis, King was anything but well-liked and lionized the way he is today. Seldom mentioned in the history books is how the last eighteen months of his life were extremely isolating and taxing, taking a toll on his emotional, physical, and mental health. When his autopsy was performed, the condition of his heart was said to be that of a *sixty*-year-old; he was only thirty-nine (Bagwell and Walker 2004).

And yet, King's spiritual resolve did not waver; his stance against the war remained unequivocal for the remainder of his life [Figure 9.4], as did his belief that we had a stark choice: "nonviolent coexistence or violent co-annihilation." It is remarkable to consider that, despite the massive amount of criticism, opposition, and vitriol directed at him, he still had faith in the nation and in humanity. Still had faith, up until the very night before his untimely death, "that we, as a people, will get to the promised land" (2015c, 275).

It's hard to imagine what it must have been like to experience the level of scrutiny, number of threats, and degree of isolation as King. And while his struggle and historical moment were certainly unique in many respects, we can still learn from his example of having radical faith for a better present and future.

The ability to not lose hope for what can be is critical to our being able to dream. And it is dreaming that enables us to envision and create something different than what currently exists. Even if the conditions of the garden seem poor, we can still create beauty, find abundance, and help each other thrive.

9.4

Martin Luther King Jr. speaking at Vermont Avenue Baptist Church in Washington, February of 1968. In his speech, King gave several reasons for ongoing violence and riots, including the conflict between the United States and Vietnam.

Across the United States, teachers and students are dreaming of and fighting for education that affirms, loves, and resists. As the culture wars rage on, many refuse to adopt a view of the past and present that ignores race, racism, gender, queerness, and are, instead, acting in solidarity with those in regions who are being restricted from teaching and learning the truth.

But dreams can also be stifled, even snuffed out, when people are exploited, treated as expendable, and not valued. It's disheartening that some schools, the institution entrusted with the sacred duty of educating our precious young people, have leaders who weaponize their power, do not model empathy, nor go to bat for their staff who teach and fight for justice. I have no doubt that most folks' hearts are in the right place. But, as mentioned in previous chapters, there is a big difference between one's intentions and one's impact—especially for a school leader who sets the tone for a school's culture.

What kind of example is set for the youth when adults are "put in their place" because they spoke up for what they believed was right? What kind of schools do we have when adults disrespect, resent, distrust, and even hate each other? What happens to our own heart and spirit when we encounter people who do not agree that Black Lives Matter and that migrants, religious minorities, youth of color, and gender queer kids are whole and beautiful human beings? Even schools in regions not strongly demarcated along ideological lines aren't immune from such harmful patterns of behavior.

Regardless of where and what we teach, we can choose to embody an alternate way of being, particularly during times of strife, so that we don't lose connection to ourselves. Maintaining self-connection is vital for ensuring that we don't lose our ability to hold compassion for our very real experience. And if we have capacity and willingness, we may also choose to stay connected to those with whom we are in conflict; in so doing, we model a powerful form of leadership that emerges from within.

A Moment for Reflection

- What characteristics of leadership are valued in your school context?
- Whose perspectives and voices tend to be valued, elevated? Whose perspectives and voices tend to be shut down, minimized, undervalued?
- In your view, what does it mean to be a leader? Whom at your school (or a different teaching site or context) do you see exhibiting such leadership qualities?

CHALLENGING OUR MODE OF (CO)EXISTENCE

Reverend Ronald English grew up in Ebenezer Baptist Church in Atlanta—the same church, in fact, that Martin Luther King Jr.'s family attended and was an integral part of. King's mother, Alberta Williams King aka Mama King, introduced English's parents, who sang in the choir together. The two families became close, and as a young man, English was Ministerial Assistant to King Jr. [Figure 9.5], who served as co-pastor with his father King Sr. aka Daddy King.

After King Jr. was assassinated, English, then just twenty-four years old, delivered a prayer at his funeral. He said, in part:

> Inspire us to accept the imperative that [King's] life so fully exemplifies—that we would not judge the worth of our lives by their physical longevity, but by the quality of their service to [human]kind....He has shown us how to live, oh God. He has shown us how to love....And so, like Jesus, not only did Martin Luther King challenge the status quo, but he challenged our mode of existence (1968, 2:43).

9.5

Ronald English, seated in the first row on the far left, looks on as King delivers a sermon at Ebenezer Baptist Church in 1960.

English shared King's conviction that nonviolence was a powerful tool to fight against oppression and injustice. He participated in lunch counter sit-ins as a youth, attended the March on Washington, and helped organize striking sanitation workers. English also believed, like King, that nonviolence was more than just a tactic; it was a philosophy and way of life.

While growing up in Ebenezer and knowing King profoundly shaped English's orientation toward nonviolence, he gained an even "deeper understanding" of its potency and methodology when he met prominent Nonviolent Communication teacher Miki Kashtan later in life and began practicing NVC (English 2023).

"Nonviolence is always something on the inside working on the outside in order for the stuff on the outside not to get to the inside and corrupt our consciousness," English told me during a conversation we had. NVC, in particular, serves as a conscious and embodied practice, offering a different mode of engaging with himself and others. "I don't have to only respond in a way that *increases* the tension; I can also respond in a way that *resolves* the tension," he said (2023).

An elder who has tirelessly dedicated his life to pastoring, being a community leader, and fighting for social and racial justice [Figure 9.6], English has had his share of enduring setbacks, experiencing disappointment, receiving criticism, and having righteous rage. But prayer, mindfulness, NVC, and other practices have enabled him to stay spiritually resourced and *engaged* in the struggle for as long as he has.

English shared that when he is in conflict with someone and feeling charged emotions such as anger and frustration, he first takes a moment to *pause* to "become aware" of his internal experience. As a Pisces, he said he sometimes envisions the two fishes "talking" to each other: "I can put my anger on one side and my calm to the other side. When the angry Pisces starts shouting, that is a time frame that the other Pisces can speak to the pain."

Connecting with himself in this creative way decreases the likelihood of succumbing to the whims of his anger, frustration, and pain. "I'm really doing harm to myself" and "disturbing my own psyche" when speaking or acting from an uncentered and reactive place, he said. However, taking "a brief pause," connecting, and discerning how to respond, especially when in conflict with someone, allows for the heart to "register some caution."

This is not to say that rage and anger are not helpful. Valarie Kaur, activist, writer, and author of *See No Stranger: A Memoir and Manifesto of Revolutionary Love* writes that "There are many ways to confront one's opponent without anger. But in the case of ongoing social injustices," for some people, "expressing outrage is often the only way to be heard" (2020, 134). Outrage can raise awareness, garner support, and be a healthy expression toward that which belies what we stand for

Ronald English with Coretta Scott King and Ruth Norma at First Baptist Church in Charleston, SC in 1976. Norma was the oldest congregant of First Baptist and Chairperson of a Women's Day event for which Scott King was invited as guest speaker. Photo courtesy of Ronald English.

and love. But, if left unchecked, outrage can also extinguish our internal flame—or morph it into a conflagration that ultimately hurts ourselves and those around us.

Bayard Rustin, a civil rights leader who was instrumental in organizing the 1963 March on Washington, viewed rage as a force that could either be channeled toward constructive, political action or destruction. He once said that if "rage is not expressed politically, if it is not devoted towards achieving constructive goals, then it will be self-defeating and ultimately self-destructive. Let us be enraged by injustice, but let us not be destroyed by it" (1969). Similarly, Kaur says that we should not "suppress our rage or let it explode" but "find safe containers" for it that allow us "to express our body's impulses without shame and without harming ourselves or others" (2020, 131). That is, safe containers support people in speaking their truths and expressing the rawness of their emotions while being held with and maintaining care and safety. For some, a safe container might be an affinity group who shares a common identity, struggle, or interest. For others, a safe container might be dialoguing with or receiving empathy from a sole confidant. (In Chapter 10, we'll look at an example of what a safe container can look like among teachers.)

Once we have a safe container for our outrage, Kaur adds that we can "choose to harness that energy in a way that creates a new world for *all* of us" (2020, 133). When I met English at an NVC retreat several years ago, I was inspired by his wholehearted commitment to nonviolence in a society that breeds violence. Inspired by how he held care for everyone in the group that was navigating conflict and pain. Inspired by his humility and being a lifelong learner, exemplified by the fact that, despite living through the civil rights movement, he was still expanding his repertoire of nonviolent practices and ways of being [Figure 9.7].

> ### Reflecting on this Historical Moment
>
> - With Ronald English's story in mind, what practices do (or would) you find helpful for experiencing and expressing strong emotions, e.g., rage, frustration, etc.?

9.7

Me, Ronald English, and my partner, Rachelle, at the Nonviolent Leadership for Social Justice retreat in 2018. Personal collection.

I've known many educators from different schools who unquestionably loved teaching but who ultimately left. Some were fed up with being perpetually unsupported, unseen, and isolated. Others felt disillusioned and harmed by dysfunction and toxicity. I know that sometimes, the right choice for some people is to leave a particular school or the classroom altogether. I, myself, have had moments when I questioned whether I could continue teaching. I also know that expanding my own repertoire of nonviolent practices during difficult moments has fortified my heart and sustained my teaching.

English told me, "Oftentimes, you find out how strong a virtue is when it's being tested" (2023). His examples of leading from the heart and continually learning have helped guide me when I myself have been in conflict, when my commitment to nonviolence has been tested. I would like to share one such example with you, and then invite you to reflect on and write about a conflict you have encountered or are currently experiencing with a colleague. In the story I am about to share, the names of the individuals involved have been changed, but those with whom I was in conflict gave their full support for its inclusion in this book.

GROWING THROUGH CONFLICT

A few years ago, I taught a writing workshop as part of a summer program designed for young writers. During our two weeks together, students wrote and shared powerful poems, narratives, empathy letters, and other pieces that supported them in owning their stories. They appreciated having space to bond and express themselves, and I was deeply moved by their courage to lean into vulnerability. It was truly an amazing experience.

The staff, fellow teachers, and program directors, Sarah and Taryn, were also a pleasure to work with, and we were all there because we shared a passion for writing and teaching writing. That there was something for nearly everyone—novel and creative writing, how to write powerful personal statements, advanced essay writing, and more—made for a diverse and joyful experience for both the kids and adults.

One concern I had, however, was that teachers' compensation was tied to the number of students enrolled in and attending our respective workshops. The compensation model was introduced during our planning meetings prior to the start of the program, but I did not think much of it initially, as I was preoccupied with and excited about preparing for my workshop; I assumed that each teacher would have, more or less, similar numbers of students enrolled. But in practice, it struck me as problematic when, after the first couple of days, some parents switched their child(ren) out of creative writing-themed workshops, like mine, and enrolled them into ones deemed "more academic." Consequently, some workshops ended up with more students than others, which, at the end of the day, determined our compensation.

Of course, parents had that prerogative; they were, after all, paying for the program. I took issue not with the parents' choice or even the number of students I had but rather, the *process* itself. In particular, I felt concerned about the apparent lack of safeguards in place to mitigate negative impact and minimize inequitable compensation. Adding a layer of complexity was the fact that two of the workshops with the highest student enrollment by the end of the first week were taught by Sarah and Taryn. I wasn't sure if, as Program Directors, they potentially had an unfair advantage.

I wanted to hear how others were feeling and whether anyone else shared my concerns. Even if it was not possible to remedy the situation for the remainder of the program that summer, which I recognized was likely, at the very least, I hoped we could discuss it as a team. However, broaching the topic was a challenge in and of itself, as we did not have a meeting structure conducive for such dialogue. We had informal check-ins during lunch most days, but these tended to cover multiple topics within a short period of time, making it difficult to have a sustained conversation about one particular thing.

I did attempt to bring it up a few times to Sarah, who was present for and led most meetings. Although she partially acknowledged my concern, she said that it was essentially decided already. Her response was matter-of-fact, nothing rude or malicious, though I did find it a bit dismissive. That said, I wanted to give her and Taryn the benefit of the doubt since they were swamped with juggling duties as co-directors and teaching. I knew they had dedicated significant time and energy into planning and running the writing program; I also figured that my bringing up something they presumed we were all in agreement about, after the program had already started, was not something they had anticipated nor had much capacity to think about. Still, I wanted to ensure that my concerns were fully heard, so I tried a different route: email.

Raising the Concern

Let me first say that email is not my preferred way of communicating. However, when circumstances are such that it is difficult to hold a conversation in-person, emailing does allow me to carefully and thoughtfully express my ideas. And so, at the end of the first week, on Saturday morning, I sent a message to Sarah and Taryn. (For the sake of clarity and length, I am including only the most relevant excerpts from our correspondence while trying to accurately preserve the content and tone of our communication.)

> Hi Sarah and Taryn,
>
> I'm noticing that I'm feeling uncertain about whether the concerns/ wonders I've named regarding fluctuations in numbers have provided awareness of its impact on me (and potentially other people). I say this because I've noticed on a few occasions when I've raised a concern or wonder, particularly about the compensation model, the response tends to focus on why things are the way they are rather than actually sitting with and unpacking the initial concern. To be clear this doesn't always happen, and it's not a critical judgment toward anyone; it's just an observation I'm naming.
>
> I think it would help meet my needs for being seen and heard if we could devote some more time next week talking about the student course switches and the impact(s) they're having on the members of our group. Even if we don't necessarily "fix it," having some spaciousness to slow down and fully acknowledge how folks are feeling would provide me with some mutual recognition and assurance that we're catching folks where they're at.

I appreciate the conversations we've been having so far and how open you both are at receiving feedback from us teachers. I know there's a lot we've been discussing, sometimes multiple things at once, so thank you for being patient and gracious with hearing ideas, concerns, and suggestions. Hopefully we can continue having opportunities to brainstorm/strategize ideas that meet multiple needs.

Thanks,
Mike

The following day, a Sunday, Taryn responded with a short message that assured me that my message had been read, at least by one of the directors.

Hi Mike,

I am happy to sit down and listen to you as I know that Sarah has already had several conversations with you regarding students moving classes. When would be a good time for you to have this conversation? I am definitely willing to try to find a time that works with you. Let me know.

Best,
Taryn

I appreciated Taryn's offer to meet with me individually, and, in hindsight, perhaps that was a route that would have been worthwhile. At the time, though, the strategy I was really yearning for was to meet as a group. But I realized that I did not actually pose that request clearly in my initial email, so I tried again.

Thanks for your response, Taryn. I've shared with the group a couple of times during informal check-ins some wonders/concerns I have about students moving classes and the impact it has on me, though as I mentioned in my previous email, there are often several things we end up discussing simultaneously, which makes it difficult for me to know the extent to which there's awareness of the actual impact. It's also challenging for me to track what we're discussing when there are multiple topics and ideas being exchanged simultaneously.

I'm not actually asking to meet one-on-one. Rather, my request is for us to continue to converse as a group, preferably picking back up with the topic of schedule switches because the conversation still seems incomplete to me. And to be clear, I'm not necessarily requesting for a "solution" to the concerns themselves (although I'd appreciate the continued openness to different ideas). Rather, I'm really just wanting the *impact* of the student switches to be acknowledged.

I then offered a couple of concrete strategies that I thought would support me and perhaps the rest of the group. The first was seeing if we could reduce the number of topics to discuss during the informal check-ins to allow for deeper dialogue and sustained attention on fewer things. The second was seeing if we might be open to reflect back the underlying feelings and needs when someone raises concerns (e.g., "It sounds like you're feeling/wanting/needing…"). In retrospect, I cringe at the framing of the latter strategy, which may have come off as mansplaining and condescending. I also recognize, now, the futility of asking folks to try out NVC without knowing whether they have seen or practiced it first.

That said, I wasn't sure what else to do and was trying to offer anything that could move us toward constructive dialogue. I closed my email by saying, "I share these in the spirit of helping our discussions meet various needs (e.g., being seen/heard, ease, understanding) while also wanting to respect both of your own unique approaches to facilitating our discussions. What do you both think? Do these requests seem reasonable?"

It was not until the following day, late Monday morning, that I received a response from Sarah, her first time chiming in. I was completely unprepared for her message.

Hi Mike,

Taryn and I read through your email last night, took time to think about it and discuss it. Please know that your concerns have consumed hours of our time and have not been ignored or treated lightly. You should also know that no other faculty member has required so much time of us. As busy people managing multiple responsibilities, partners, children, friends, and our own health and wellbeing, the time dedicated to your individual concerns has been significant and out of line with our own needs for the program.

At this point, Taryn and I agree that any continuing conversation on this issue is unproductive and draining to both of us. Personally, I'm sad that so much energy and conversation between staff members have revolved around this topic rather than teaching and learning strategies.

We are not open to discussing this topic any further and trust that you will honor the boundaries we are setting here.

Best,
Sarah

Self-connection

I was floored. Livid. Confused. I had attempted to lay out, with great thoughtfulness and care, my concerns and hopes for how we might respond as a group. I was also baffled at the tone of Sarah's response. We had known each other for several years; in fact, we first met through the writing program itself some years prior. I considered her a friend and thought we held mutual respect for one another. It seemed uncharacteristic of her to communicate with me—or anyone—in that way, and I thought she would have called me or talked to me in-person if she felt that strongly. Thus, her words cut deep, leaving me hurt. It also made for an intensely uncomfortable and awkward start to our second week, as we had already begun teaching for the day and I was *with students* when she sent her message.

I avoided engaging with both Sarah and Taryn that day to provide myself space and emotional safety. Admittedly, some judgments initially surfaced when I first read their response. *What the fuck?!? What gives them the right to talk to me like that? They must not care about what I think or how I feel. This is just another instance of people paying lip service to equity and not actually doing the work nor engaging in dialogue when they feel inconvenienced.* And while it was important that I gave myself space to honor my initial reaction, I did not want that reaction to consume me. I knew that beneath those judgments were real needs, and it was important to me that I connect with those needs—not just feel the visceral reaction.

So, I prioritized empathizing with myself by connecting with my feelings of *disappointment*, *anger*, and *confusion* and corresponding unmet needs of *safety*, being *heard* and *seen*, and *respect*. Going for a long run that afternoon helped, as I was able to release some of the stress I was holding in my body. I also received support from my partner, who offered her loving presence and patient ear.

Initially, I wasn't sure if I wanted to expend more emotional and mental labor composing a response only to have it be potentially minimized or ignored. Moreover, we were already halfway done with the program. *What does it matter at this point?* I thought at one point. *There's less than a week left.* But I also thought about what could happen if I *didn't* respond. *Are they even aware of how that message came across? What's to say that this wouldn't happen to someone else?*

Ultimately, I decided that I would respond for two reasons. One, I wanted to make known that I was hurt and offended by the tenor of Sarah's words. I was not necessarily interested in an apology; I just wanted the impact to be known. I wanted my humanity to be seen. Second, I wanted to call out the deeply problematic way in which two white women in a position of power treated a person of color. I hoped that my doing so would be a catalyst for self-reflection and prevent them from ever doing that again to anyone else.

Even if my message did not lead to any immediate, tangible changes for the remainder of our time together that week, at least I could find solace in knowing that I acted from a place of truth, integrity, and love, living in alignment with my values of and commitment to nonviolence. That does not mean we "have" to respond in moments such as this, but having the clarity for myself that doing so in that moment would alleviate the weight I felt in my body and heart seemed like the right thing for me. And so, later that evening, I wrote the following message:

Sarah and Taryn,

I feel so disappointed and concerned after reading what you wrote since I do not sense any respect for the issues I've been trying to bring up. All I was asking for was to be heard. Your unwillingness to actually hear how I am impacted by aspects of our program is, in effect, a form of silencing me. As the only person of color on our team, I feel deeply disturbed by your response and no longer trust that you are holding me with care and respect.

I put a painstaking amount of time and thought into crafting my previous emails out of care for both of you, myself, and our team, and I was taken aback when I read your response. I received it as callous and dismissive, and it struck me as not reflecting the degree of care and respect I've attempted to show you.

I, too, have tons of other commitments. You are not the only people who are busy, and I don't appreciate the implication that your time is more valuable and that my concerns are either inconvenient, too time consuming, or "unproductive." I am a member of this team with legitimate ideas and concerns, and I would hope that my input, like anyone else's, would be welcomed by leadership—regardless of whether you actually agree with the input or not. How else am I supposed to make known to you as leaders how my experience is going? How would you feel if your concerns were dismissed as casually as you've dismissed mine? I am baffled and at a loss as to how to even give you feedback, which both of you have asked for, if it's going to be met with resistance.

I am not sure what hours you are referring to, Sarah. The few times we've talked about student schedule switches has been minutes at most because it's been but a fraction of so many other topics that come up in conversation. It's not as though we've already devoted an entire conversation to this; it's been in bits and pieces at best, and then we quickly move onto something different without ever checking to see if there's clarity or closure about the previous topic.

I haven't once asked for us to discuss anything outside the structure of our regular day; I simply asked if we could more intentionally and strategically structure our time during lunch and at the end of the day. That's why I reached out in the first place—to see if we could have a better process for helping the members of our team feel fully acknowledged. If either of you spent hours discussing this, that was not at my request.

The irony of this whole situation is that you say my concerns "have not been ignored or treated lightly," but as the person who has been impacted, I am telling you very clearly that my needs for being seen and heard are not being met. Instead, I feel hurt after vulnerably and compassionately reaching out to both of you only to be shut down with callousness.

Receiving Additional Support

At that point, I was prepared for the possibility that the situation would not improve, which saddened me because I did not want a breakdown in communication to spoil an otherwise pleasant experience and dissolve a friendship. But, at the same time, I recognized that I had reached my emotional capacity and did not want to engage further until or unless they showed willingness to repair the damage and took initiative to reach out to me.

For their part, Taryn did respond shortly afterward, letting me know she and Sarah had read my message "carefully, several times through" and that it was clear to them I felt hurt by their words. She added, "we want to assure you that we do not take your concern at not being heard as the only person of color on our team lightly. Sarah and I will reflect upon this." They, too, seemed to recognize the limits of their own capacity and perhaps their insufficient skills to mediate the situation at hand. They invited me to meet individually with Dr. Lee, a dear mutual friend of ours who was also the director of the regional branch of a national writing program of which the youth summer workshops were part.

They knew that Lee, with whom I had been acquainted for nearly a decade at that point, held me in very high regard. He epitomized being a lifelong learner, taking genuine interest in and showing enthusiasm for others' ideas, and listened compassionately with full presence. I was unclear whether or when Sarah and Taryn would follow up with me, but I figured that meeting with Lee privately, before attempting a mediation, was probably a prudent step. Taryn closed her email by writing, "We would like to find a common ground from which to move forward so that all of our teachers can have a positive week together." I, too, hoped for a positive experience for the remainder of our time, though, for me, that was entirely dependent on whether the three of us repaired the rupture in communication.

Due to scheduling conflicts, I would not get to meet with Lee until Wednesday late afternoon. This meant that the first few days of the week were excruciatingly awkward, as I could sense that Sarah and Taryn did not know how to engage with me. For my part, I kept my interactions with them to an absolute minimum, only discussing necessary work-related matters and mostly via text message. The ball was in their court, as far as I was concerned. I was not going to initiate a mediation—not out of spite or pride, but rather, because I was setting a boundary for myself to not do more labor than I thought was appropriate under the circumstances. If that meant the week would end as it started, then so be it.

But I was willing to meet with Lee as a next step. With complete presence, non-judgment, and soft energy, he listened carefully. Nodding along, reflecting back what he heard, holding space, maintaining empathic presence. He committed to having a follow-up conversation with Sarah and Taryn with the hope that they would reach out to me so we could begin repair work. And sure enough, they did.

Reconciliation

That Thursday afternoon, after the teaching day had ended, Sarah, Taryn, and I finally sat down in a small circle. It was immediately clear to me that they genuinely cared about how I was impacted. No defensiveness, gaslighting, nor rationalizing—just listening. After I felt assured that they understood the harm their words caused, they apologized and vowed to do better. My heart was already open coming into the meeting, but its capacity in that moment expanded greatly, and I felt willing to hear what was coming up on their end.

Had I not yet felt fully heard and we pivoted the focus to them too abruptly, I doubt I would have had the capacity to be fully present and empathize. They shared how they felt stretched thin from all that they were balancing and did not know how to meet my request in a way that allowed them to attend to everything else on their plates. Taryn shared how she was recovering from a health issue that greatly affected her day-to-day functioning and overall energy level. It sounded like they both had been attempting to meet needs for having spaciousness and maintaining consistency.

Sarah also said that the writing program, of which she had been part for several years, was one of the highlights of her summer. It provided her with immense joy and a break from some of the stressors of regular teaching. She added that she viewed the summer program as a source of ease and that my several attempts to have us discuss the compensation model had made it difficult for her to experience ease. I could completely empathize with her saying that, and I pointed out that it was a privilege for her to be in such a position. As a person of color, I am used to my concerns being silenced, ignored, or minimized. I have often had to double-up my efforts for a concern or issue to be taken seriously *in order* to even access ease. She hadn't considered that until I mentioned it.

What resulted from that conversation was a deepened understanding of each other, more awareness of the relationship between privilege, power, and whiteness and a commitment to sustain our friendship. In fact, my relationships with both Sarah and Taryn have strengthened, and we continue to work together.

CONNECTING WITH WHAT'S ALIVE IN OURSELVES

When a person says or does something that negatively impacts or harms you, how do you generally respond? For the longest time, I often reacted without taking a moment to pause and connect with my feelings and needs. I would say or do things I later regretted. Other times, I would internalize negative self-judgments, minimizing or dismissing my experience (e.g., *It's not that big a deal, I'm over-reacting, It was stupid of me to…*, etc.). Like every human being, I still struggle with these reactions but much less frequently as a result of integrating nonviolence practices such as NVC into my life.

One of the most valuable lessons I've learned through NVC is that I have considerable choice, not only about how to *respond* when I am negatively impacted by or harmed by someone or something, but also about how I want to experience my emotions in the first place. That is, I can view my emotional reaction as a very normal part of being human but accept that it is *mine*; it is not up to the other person to dictate how I feel.

Oftentimes, when we are negatively impacted by the words or behavior of another person, we may think or say something like, "They *made* me feel _____." And we have every right to be angry, hurt, and upset. But if our tendency is to fall into a pattern of blaming others for our own internal experience, then we risk giving our power away by showing up according to how others treat us.

To be very clear, I am *not* saying that we are the source of our pain. I am *not* saying that others don't bear responsibility for their words and actions. I am *not* saying that we need to "pull ourselves up by the bootstraps" and just have grit in the face of problematic, harmful, or abusive behavior.

Because we live in an interdependent world, we will inevitably be affected by other people's behavior—and vice versa. We must have recognition of and care for the impact we have on others and that others have on us if we are to create the Beloved Community. *And,* we can achieve emotional liberation when we pause during conflicts, especially intense ones, to connect with and own what's alive in ourselves.

Doing so enables us to have self-compassion and tap into the beauty of what's beneath the pain or rage. It also helps us recognize why certain things trigger us and how previous experiences (e.g., childhood, trauma, etc.) may shape how we feel and respond during conflict. This is especially critical whenever we may feel alone in our experience, which, unfortunately, is commonplace for teachers in schools where antiracism and social justice work are not universally valued. Just because others do not share what we value or feel what we are feeling in a given moment does not make our experience any less real or important.

Practicing Self-empathy

I now invite you to think through a conflict you have had or are having with someone in your school context and practice empathizing with yourself. While not a prerequisite for working through interpersonal conflict, practicing self-empathy is often a helpful starting point, especially if we were the ones negatively impacted, as it increases our capacity for engagement with the other if we so choose. Additionally, although the story with Sarah and Taryn I've shared is outlined in great detail, my practice of self-empathy and eventual response to them were done by engaging in the same process that follows.

Observation of the Conflict

▷ What is something that a person you work/interact with has recently said or done that is not in harmony with your values or needs? What do you remember happening?

Unfiltered Statement

▷ We all know what it's like to commiserate and vent with a confidant; there can be immense relief in speaking rawly. But there's a risk in habitually doing so, as it can eclipse our underlying needs if we express them without attempting to understand and connect with what it is we truly yearn for. Doing so also decreases the possibility of (re)connecting with the other person, should we choose to do so. That said, writing out an unfiltered statement can still be a valuable way of expressing ourselves without holding self-judgment.

What is something you want to say, or have said, to this person, unfiltered?

Feelings

▷ What feelings emerged during (or after) the conflict with the person?

Needs

▷ What core needs or values of yours underlay the feelings you experienced? That is, what needs were unmet as a result of the conflict?

Authentic Expression

▷ Drawing from NVC, how might you express what's alive in you? Even if you don't actually end up talking to the person, it can still be valuable to do this practice for yourself. It is authentic in that what we are feeling is connected to our identified needs.

When I saw/heard you ____ I felt ____ because I really value...

I am concerned that my need for/value of ____ was not met in that moment because...

CONNECTING WITH WHAT'S ALIVE IN OTHERS

Some may wonder: *Is it really necessary to engage with people I'm in conflict with? And why should I bother engaging with those who have caused me harm, especially if they do not respect nor value me?*

These are valid questions, and I think it is important to emphasize here that we do not *have* to do anything that doesn't meet our capacity or align with our needs or values. It is not always possible nor practical to engage in conversation with people we are in conflict with or who have harmed us, especially if the other party is unwilling or uninterested. Not every plant, flower, or organism in the same garden has to be in close proximity to one another in order for them to live and grow. Sometimes, it might not even be wise to engage, such as if we are at odds with someone who holds more institutional power that can be wielded in unfavorable, even destructive ways.

I have heard shocking stories of administrators acting hostilely, even vindictively, toward teachers, at times for inane reasons. Some teachers are not even comfortable talking to an administrator without the presence of a union representative. I fully understand and respect such a choice. When a person is acting harmfully or even abusively, sometimes the healthiest and safest thing to do is distance oneself and avoid any further interaction. To do otherwise without support or resources is to subject oneself to violence.

I also know of several schools where staff, some of whom were close, shared a vision and *believed in* each other but fell apart due to internal strife. These were touted as progressive schools that nonetheless succumbed to broken relationships and high staff turnover. No school, or group, for that matter, is immune from the reality of conflict.

Even prominent organizations in the civil rights movement, such as the Southern Christian Leadership Conference (SCLC) and the Student Nonviolent Coordinating Committee (SNCC) endured, at times, contentious and searing conflicts. For example, during a heated SNCC meeting in May of 1966, when the group had begun splintering over conflicting views about nonviolence and the role of white members, John Lewis was notably replaced by Stokely Carmichael as chairperson. Lewis subsequently left SNCC.

But it is not always conflict, in and of itself, that causes relationships to disintegrate; typically, the lack of processes in place to help people navigate conflict and hold each other with care is where breakdowns occur.

Maintaining Relationality

Doubtless, there may be occasions when the impact is so great, so painful that we just don't have the capacity, willingness, or maybe even desire to reconcile. No one can be blamed for wanting to maintain safety and avoid potentially subjecting themself to more pain. If or when we choose not to engage, it is important to hold ourselves with immense care by connecting with our underlying needs, avoiding self-judgment, and reminding ourselves that we are not weak.

And, I think it is also helpful to reflect on how we generally respond to conflict. Here are some self-reflection questions for consideration:

- What patterns of thinking or behavior do I tend to engage in during conflict?
- What need(s) am I attempting to meet through such patterns?
- Do these patterns leave me feeling expansive or depleted?
- Do these patterns guide me toward emotional liberation or emotional confinement?
- What are other strategies I can use to fulfill needs that I am otherwise attempting to meet through said patterns?
- In the aftermath of conflict, do my relationships tend to fall apart or mend?

Ultimately, if we value transforming relationships and building communities, then it is important to keep open the possibility for repair and healing if and when we have capacity and willingness.

As mentioned in the Introduction, one way we can think of violence is as "the result of the collapse of relationality, whether the relationship is human or ecological, physical or psychic, material or spiritual" (Wang 2014, 494). This is not to say that all conflicts are violent or lead to violence, but if relationality collapses as a result of conflict, the possibility for violence—within oneself, between people and other living things, or through systems—increases.

Viewing oneself as separate from the other—whether the other is a fellow person, creature, or nature itself—is, according to Buddhism, at the root of violence. Moreover, the political polarization and dualistic thinking (e.g., good/bad, right/wrong, us/them, human/nature) that has become so embedded in our collective consciousness is not only tearing apart the social fabric of the United States and other parts of the world, but it has very real immediate and long-term consequences on our lives and the sustainability of the planet. Finding ways to nurture our individual and collective capacity to maintain relationality, I would argue, is a matter of survival.

In the martial art aikido, relationality is sustained and harmony is sought through the mutual creation of circular and blended movements in the midst of conflict. During a "fight" between two individuals, a nage (*nah-gay*) and a uke (*ooh-kay*) take turns giving and receiving attacks, engaging in a kind of fluid dance together. Nage's role is to execute the attack while uke's role is to receive it, whether it be a throw, roll, strike, etc.

I remember one particular class at the dojo when a partner and I took turns giving and receiving attacks. As nage, I would stand directly in front of my partner, step in, and strike at them. Uke, in turn, would catch my wrist, step inward and spin to redirect the momentum of the attack, bringing me along in the process. Through the movement, our positions then switched, where I became uke and they nage. We continuously revolved around each other, taking turns centering and decentering ourselves, our fight forming an ever-flowing circle [Figure 9.8].

9.8

A representation of two individuals centering and decentering themselves through circular movements. Illustration by my former student Keilani Mae Jasmin.

Without question, sustaining relationality amidst conflict can be extraordinarily challenging, but when there is shared open-heartedness, curiosity, and willingness to listen and possibly even learn and grow, the likelihood for repair and connection increases significantly. Even when those conditions are not present, though, we can still choose to hold care for the other person's humanity. And doing so does not have to come at our own expense. Our capacity for open-heartedness is not contingent upon how others show up.

My friend Rebecca once said, "Wouldn't we want for each other the same kind of healing we'd want for ourselves?" The moment my heart closes off to another human being is the moment I must ask myself: *At what point are people no longer worthy of my care and love? Will I only keep my heart open toward those who are easy to love? Those who agree with me? How do I want others to hold me for what I think, say, and do?*

Moreover, engagement does not always have to be in the form of dialogue. We can still choose to hold care for the other person by engaging from the heart and maintaining an empathic presence from afar.

Practicing Empathy for Others

As discussed in Chapter 4, one way of thinking about empathy is that it is not something we "give." It is something that we feel and experience inside of ourselves. In the case of being in conflict with someone, we can have empathic presence for them by connecting with their feelings and needs.

I now invite you to revisit the conflict you wrote about on pages 256–257 and try to connect with what the other person may have been experiencing using the following guiding questions.

Feelings

▷ What feeling(s) might this person have been experiencing or expressing in the midst of your conflict with them?

Needs

▷ What need(s) might have underlay this person's feeling(s)? What need(s) do you imagine were driving what they said or did?

NVC in Action

▷ With the other person's feelings and needs in mind, what might a real or imagined conversation with them sound like, ideally one that includes connecting with their experience and sharing your own?

I'm wondering if you were feeling [possible feelings] when you said/did...

Were you feeling this way because you were wanting [possible needs]?

I am concerned that my need for/value of ___ was not met in that moment because...

A FEW CAVEATS

There are some caveats I want to offer when practicing or considering practicing NVC with someone we're in conflict with.

First, if we do not have capacity or willingness to dialogue with someone with whom we are in conflict, we can lean on others to assist us if we so choose. One of my friends heard a comment from a colleague that was likely not intended to cause harm but was nonetheless racist in nature and negatively impacted her. Rather than feeling as though it was on her to fix, school leaders intervened and talked to the person who did the harm, all the while ensuring that my friend was held with care. If trusted colleagues have the skill and will to dialogue on our behalf, that might be worth considering if we don't have sufficient internal resources or desire to do so. Alternatively, if we know someone who has experience with NVC and mediating conflicts, it might be a good idea to ask for their support.

Second, if the person we are attempting to (re)connect with does not have or loses the capacity to show up in the moment, is not making a good faith effort to dialogue, or they seem primarily concerned with their own experience and not ours as well, we won't get far. Capacity and a sincere effort to listen on the part of the person who caused the negative impact or harm are necessary. If that does not seem, or no longer seems, present, then there is nothing wrong with either of the following responses, depending on the situation:

- **If they dismiss or minimize your experience or become defensive, you might say:** "I was hoping we could begin some repair work, but I am not feeling confident that what I am sharing with you is being received with sufficient care. I'm disappointed about this, but the best thing for me is to not engage further at this time."
- **If they jump in and center themselves before you are done sharing, you might say:** "I'm hearing that there is a lot coming up for you, and I can tell that you really want your experience to be known. But I am struggling to stay present right now and would feel more willing and able to listen if I could trust that what I'm sharing with you is also being fully received. It feels very vulnerable for me to even engage in this conversation. Are you willing to hear me out some more and share what it is you are understanding is important to me?"

In my experience, I find that people often *do* care about the impact they've had on others. Many just don't know how to hear it without feeling defensive and centering their intentions. It's understandable; we're human, and we want to be known for our truth and be seen as good-intentioned people. But having to redirect the conversation while staying connected to ourselves and the other person can be taxing and takes practice, which leads me to the third caveat.

The practices offered here for self-empathy and having empathy for others is more of a starting point for preparing for and possibly initiating dialogue. There are other elements of the Nonviolent Communication process that we have not explored here. For more on practicing NVC in the midst of conflict, particularly when privilege and power are in the mix, I strongly recommend Dr. Roxy Manning's powerful and inspiring *How to Have Antiracist Conversations: Embracing Our Full Humanity to Challenge White Supremacy*. I also highly recommend Miki Kashtan's paradigm-shifting *Spinning Threads of Radical Aliveness: Transcending the Legacy of Separation in Our Individual Lives*.

ALL GIFTS MULTIPLIED IN RELATIONSHIP

In her groundbreaking book *Braiding Sweetgrass: Indigenous Wisdom, Scientific Knowledge and the Teachings of Plants*, botanist, professor, and writer Dr. Robin Wall Kimmerer, who is a member of the Citizen Potawatomi Nation, writes beautifully of how we can (re)learn to live more sustainably and in more spiritual abundance. In particular, she explores how we can restore our relationship with Mother Earth, which, in turn, can guide us in deepening our relationships with each other.

In the chapter "The Three Sisters," Kimmerer writes of the reciprocal, interdependent relationship that can flourish between beans, squash, and corn when they are grown together, following indigenous wisdom. The plants, whom she refers to as "sisters," actually bear more food when they intertwine and support each other than if they were to exist among only their own.

Specifically, the corn stalks provide structural support for the beans to grow and get more sunlight. The beans, in turn, take nitrogen from the air and, with the help of Rhizobium bacteria, create a nitrogen fertilizer that helps the corn and squash grow. The squash's broad leaves serve as a ground cover to prevent weedier plants from competing for nutrients; they also provide shade and help keep moisture in soil, thereby supporting the growth of the sister plants. Kimmerer says of the symbiotic relationship of the three sisters:

> Of all the wise teachers who have come into my life, none are more eloquent than these, who wordlessly in leaf and vine embody the knowledge of relationship. Alone, a bean is just a vine, squash an oversize leaf.

Only when standing together with corn does a whole emerge which transcends the individual. The gifts of each are more fully expressed when they are nurtured together than alone. In ripe ears and swelling fruit, they counsel us that all gifts are multiplied in relationship. This is how the world keeps going (2013, 140).

Three sisters exemplify reciprocity and serve as a "visible manifestation of what a community can become when its members understand and share their gifts" (2013, 134). Doubtless, amidst any beautiful garden also exists conflict and decay. Plants and flowers can ensnare each other as they vie for space, sunlight, water, and nutrients. Crops can be destroyed by pests. Weeds can choke nearby plants and rob them of sustenance.

But there can still be beauty amidst chaos, joy amidst struggle, blossoming amidst withering. Tending to our wonderful and imperfect relationships with one another is an act of love that benefits the whole garden of our school. And the more that we find ways to come together and grow through struggle, the more we bring out the best in ourselves and each other, multiplying our gifts and chances for keeping the world going.

In the following chapter, we will take a look at the extraordinary freedom fighter Ella Baker, whose powerful example of fostering grassroots, group leadership can serve as a model for us teachers. We will then explore how we can tap into our own power and leadership in order to co-create opportunities for professional growth that support collective care.

CHAPTER 10

Leading Together

Although her name may not be well-known by many, Ella Josephine Baker is considered one of the mothers of the civil rights movement (Gates Jr. 2020). She possessed an indomitable spirit to fight alongside oppressed peoples, engaged in grassroots organizing, and fostered group leadership, all of which contributed to her enormous influence and impact as a leader.

According to Dr. Cornel West, "There is no civil rights movement without the example, the witness of Ella Baker" and "there is no Martin [Luther] King's movement without an Ella Baker's intelligence, imagination, and courageous witness" (West 2014).

A grandchild of formerly enslaved people, Baker was born in Virginia in 1903. She was influenced tremendously by her grandmother's stories of resistance during slavery and by the "activist spirit of her mother," who "called on women to act as agents of social change in their communities" (The Martin Luther King, Jr. Research and Education Institute n.d.a).

Baker attended Shaw University, where her activism began to flourish. She challenged unfair school policies, and after graduating, she became involved in several organizations focused on social and racial justice. She was a field secretary for the NAACP and later became a director of branches; she co-founded In Friendship with Bayard Rustin and Stanley Levison to support activists in the South fighting against Jim Crow; and she helped spearhead Martin Luther King Jr.'s nascent organization, the Southern Christian Leadership Conference (SCLC), where she ran the Crusade for Citizenship, a voting rights campaign for Black people.

Although Baker and King were both engaged in the cause for enfranchisement and equality for Black people, their respective styles of leadership could not have been more different. King once said that "leadership never ascends from the pew to the pulpit" but "invariably descends from the pulpit to the pew" (1954). King's top-down, charismatic leadership style bothered Baker, who was not treated as an equal by King and other male ministers, according to historian, professor, and writer Dr. Barbara Ransby.

In her book *Ella Baker and the Black Freedom Movement: A Radical Democratic Vision*, Ransby writes that "King kept Baker at arm's length and never treated her as a political or intellectual peer" (2003, 173). Baker felt insulted and frustrated by her treatment and understood well the sexism at play.

In contrast to King's top-down authoritative leadership style, Baker fervently believed "in the right of the people who were under the heel to be the ones to decide what action they were going to take to get [out] from under their oppression" (2003, 195). Regardless of "their level of formal education," Baker felt that oppressed people had "the ability to understand and interpret the world around them, to see the world for what it is, and move to transform it" (2003, 7). She believed that "strong people don't need strong leaders" because they already possess within themselves the power to transform their conditions (Payne 1989, 893).

Moreover, although Baker had a penchant for bringing together people of diverse backgrounds and perspectives and worked tirelessly with different groups, she did not feel loyal to any particular organization. She once said, "I was never working for an organization. I always tried to work for a cause. And that cause was bigger than any organization" (Ransby 2003, 281) [Figure 10.1].

10.1

Ella Baker speaking in Atlantic City in 1964.

Wanting to see more group leadership emerge, Baker, along with King, brought together a large gathering of emerging student activists at Shaw University in April of 1960, following the lunch counter sit-ins in Greensboro, North Carolina that February. From that conference emerged a student-run organization that would name itself the Student Nonviolent Coordinating Committee, or SNCC (pronounced "snick"). Baker believed that the group would be most successful if it maintained its autonomy and did not fall under the purview of the SCLC (National Archives 2022).

Although Baker, herself, did not believe in nonviolence as a way of life, she respected the fact that some students in SNCC did, and she understood its value as a strategy and tactic. She served as an advisor for the group and helped them to tap into their collective power, which was instrumental during the Freedom Rides and Freedom Summer in Mississippi.

Baker also helped the group navigate heated moments, such as during one SNCC meeting when students became divided over priorities. Some wanted to focus on nonviolent direct action whereas others wanted to focus on registering and educating Black voters about their rights. As Ransby writes in her book: "[Baker] stood up and spoke forcefully in the meeting, calling for the formation of two wings of one organization. Rather than two organizations, one wing would focus on direct action and the other on voter education and registration" (2003, 270). It was a compromise that students ultimately agreed with, even if they were not 100 percent happy about the idea of there being two wings of the organization. They understood that two wings of the same bird was better than two separate birds.

Moreover, Baker helped the students to eschew the male-dominated leadership tendency that was ubiquitous in many other civil rights organizations at the time. According to Ransby:

> The SNCC activists always had to struggle against the tendencies toward elitism and male domination, but SNCC did enable women, workers, farmers, and youth to emerge as strong, effective, and publicly recognized leaders of the movement....As architect of SNCC's democratic approach, [Baker] in effect widened the space of leadership, so that those most marginalized or excluded from the centers of power in society and in civil rights politics could stand up and be heard (2003, 298).

In essence, Baker helped scores of people—young and older alike—emerge as leaders, helping them harness their individual and collective power in pursuit of a shared vision. She taught them to believe in their own capacity to change conditions, and they looked up to her with enormous respect and admiration.

Bernard LaFayette, who was present at the conference at Shaw University and helped co-found SNCC, credits Baker with helping him develop invaluable skills that greatly aided him as a leader in the civil rights movement. In particular, LaFayette says that Baker "helped [him] be successful in Selma," when he served as the director of SNCC's Alabama Voter Registration Project in 1962 (LaFayette 2023b).

Initially, after arriving to Selma, LaFayette faced avoidance from many Black folks, who feared that associating with a SNCC member would bring about retaliation and violence at the hands of white people. As he recounts in his book, *In Peace and Freedom: My Journey in Selma*, some people "would not wave or even make eye contact." Others would cross the street or "walk in another direction" to avoid interaction. The fear he noticed seemed visceral and palpable in that it "caused [people's] shoulders to rise and stiffen as they'd quietly but swiftly move away from me." He described it as "a lonely, isolated time" (LaFayette and Johnson 2015, 27).

However, LaFayette told me that due to Baker teaching him and other SNCC members about "building coalitions" and "helping groups come together," he made significant gains in helping amass interest and involvement in voter registration (2023b). As he writes in his book:

> I was well aware that to be effective in bringing about positive change in a community, I needed to garner support from the constituencies in various organizations. These included churches, educational institutions, teacher unions, and civic clubs. I further identified pastors, principals, teachers, business professionals, and club leaders. It was my job to mobilize these community leaders into skilled organizers so that their groups and organizations would follow them (LaFayette and Johnson 2015, 29).

That is, rather than positioning himself as leader of the people in Selma, LaFayette identified and tapped into the *existing* leadership in the community. LaFayette added during our conversation:

> [Baker] knew that if you were going to be effective, it wasn't just your personal commitment—it had to be having some *skills* that were necessary. She didn't just bring us together as students; she helped to provide us with the kind of leadership training that we needed in order to be effective (2023b).

We do not have to, nor should we, reject conventional leaders (e.g., administrators, district leaders, etc.) in our efforts to transform public education. But neither should we dismiss or underplay the enormous power that each of us has to effect change. Every adult in a school can—and must—do their part in tending the whole garden. But it is often teachers who are the ones on the ground leading the charge.

We've seen this power of teachers coming together in recent times, such as with the LAUSD teacher strike in 2019. Approximately 30,000 teachers, with the support of students and families, went on a six-day strike to fight for increased pay, reduced class sizes, and more support staff in schools, among other concerns (Medina 2019).

Similarly, the Red for Ed movement, sparked in West Virginia in 2018, was led by teachers who sought higher wages, reduced class sizes, improved benefits, larger school budgets, and more (Mehta 2023). The protests spread to other "red" states like Kentucky, Oklahoma, and Arizona, where students and families overwhelmingly expressed their support.

In February of 2022, the Oakland Unified School District controversially decided to close or merge eleven schools, citing declining student enrollment and a "growing budget deficit" (Lara and Nguyen 2023). The closures would have disproportionately impacted low-income, emergent bilingual, foster, Black, and youth of color, and the decision was met with outrage (Finney 2022). Teachers, support staff, students, and families vociferously fought against the move via walkouts, a hunger strike, occupancy of a shuttered school, and other forms of protest.

Our power, when multiplied, *can* and *does* create change. And even less dramatic action can still have a great impact on us and our students. In this chapter, we will take a look at how we teachers can exercise our own power and leadership, creating opportunities for professional growth that also foster collective care. I will share two concrete examples from my own experience (my friends' and colleagues' names and stories are shared with their consent) and then invite you to think about ways you might co-create opportunities with your own colleagues.

GRASSROOTS PD: TEACHER INQUIRY GROUPS

Many educators can relate to feeling woefully underwhelmed by and dissatisfied with how their school's collaboration time is used. Few things are more dreadful for a teacher than sitting through poorly facilitated professional development (PD), being talked at for over an hour, and lacking choice and input. Nearly all teachers I know crave effective professional development, yet many of us are seldom *asked* what we actually need in order to support our growth.

Educator Jennifer Gonzalez, who runs the *Cult of Pedagogy* podcast and website, says that there are multiple reasons why so many schools fail at providing meaningful PD. She writes:

> One [reason] is that our PD is often designed to be one-size-fits-all, which means a lot of people in attendance will feel that the content isn't relevant to their work. Another is that PD is often structured in a top-down fashion, where participants are passively receiving information, with little acknowledgement or use of their personal expertise. And another is that hardly any effort is made to ensure that the people in the room — the adult learners — feel physically and emotionally comfortable enough to give their full participation (Gonzalez 2022).

I want to call particular attention to her last point. Intentions and expertise aside, if the person(s) leading the PD or meeting comes off as intimidating, defensive, or fixed in their thinking and averse to differing ideas, there is little chance that the people in the room will fully or authentically engage.

To be sure, when large groups of people with diverse perspectives and experiences work together, there are bound to be moments when misunderstandings happen and egos get bruised. But if the general climate is such that there is a consistent lack of safety and people feel fearful of individuals in leadership, then there is a real problem. Some of the most hostile, disrespectful, and disturbing interactions I have seen among adults is during school PD and staff meetings.

Educator, coach, and co-author of *The PD Book: 7 Habits that Transform Professional Development*, Elena Aguilar, whom Gonzalez interviewed on the *Cult of Pedagogy* podcast, says that "psychological safety is a prerequisite for transformative learning to occur" (Aguilar 2022). When safety is absent and "we feel like someone, especially someone in power poses a threat to our well-being," then we may go into "protection mode," she says. For some, this can mean shutting down or checking out; others may have a palpable emotional response (e.g., anger, frustration, fear).

Professional development should be just that: ongoing opportunities to develop our craft, receive and offer support, and continue to learn. But even if we are not experiencing invigorating PD in our schools, we don't have to settle for less.

Years ago, feeling dissatisfied with my own school's PD and departmental meetings, I reached out to my friend and fellow educator Ray Ramirez and proposed an idea: "What if we provided ourselves with the kind of support and development that we want and deserve?" Ray was immediately interested.

Wanting to hold our own space did not mean we wanted to disengage from or be immutably resistant to learning what we could during our schools' PD. In fact, we were both committed to pushing harder for training and discussions at our schools that were more responsive to our needs and those of our students. In the meantime, though, we weren't going to just sit and wait for change to happen.

A Moment for Reflection

- How has your experience been with PD at your school? What needs are/aren't being met?

Critical Friends

Given that Ray and I had done our teacher education together in a progressive graduate program and shared a commitment to social and racial justice, we had a keen sense about what had helped us grow when we first started teaching and what would continue to support our learning and ability to thrive. We wanted to engage in rich dialogue about our practice by staying grounded in vulnerability, critical reflection, and collective wisdom.

We both knew many educators in the area who taught in different schools and districts and thought that bringing together teachers from various contexts would enrich our discussions, meet needs for being seen and heard, and provide mutual support. Thus, we generated a list of folks who we thought might be interested and whose educational philosophies, practices, and values aligned or were proximate to each other's.

While we wanted the space to be diverse and open to anyone who wanted to learn and grow in community, we felt it was important to have some common ground. We knew that establishing trust and having mutual understanding would be more likely to happen, and more quickly, if people agreed from the outset that antiracism and humanizing, liberatory education were important, even if we had different notions of what that looked like.

We decided that the best way to support one another would be through a teacher-led inquiry process we learned about while still in graduate school. We drew from the Critical Friends Group (CFG) model and protocol, developed by the National School Reform Faculty, to support us in creating the kind of space we envisioned. What sets CFGs apart from other group structures is that they focus on "intentional cultivation of safety and trust between the members" and "on solving problems and accomplishing goals brought by its participants" (NSRF n.d.).

Although our schools had a similar, common group structure in place already, called Professional Learning Communities (PLCs), we wanted to be able to have an ongoing cycle of inquiry that allowed for *multiple* topics to be explored. PLCs, in contrast, generally have a cycle of inquiry in which the same topic is discussed over a prolonged period of time and is heavily data-driven. While certain kinds of data can, no doubt, be indispensable for informing one's practice, we did not want to concern ourselves with "measurables" and "deliverables," which is often the case in schools' collaborative settings; we wanted to let the *process* of inquiry take its own shape while still having guiding questions and goals in mind.

Preparing an Inquiry

One of the strengths of holding teacher-led inquiry cycles is that everyone gets a chance to lead the whole group through something they are passionate or curious about or struggling with. For our group, the process has remained virtually unchanged over the years.

Early in the school year, someone from the group will choose a date for their inquiry session. They will then send an email out to the group a week or two before the date of the inquiry session, usually consisting of the following information:

- **Overview** of a question, idea, or problem they would like to explore. Over the years, inquiry topics have run the gamut, some of which have included: (re)humanizing mathematics; leveraging organizing power via unions; healing from generational trauma; defining our dream schools; teaching critical media literacy through a feminist lens; planning for retirement beyond traditional financial investing; addressing inequities of AP classes; and redefining academic rigor.
- **Guiding question(s)** for the group to discuss when it meets in-person or virtually (e.g., What can it look like to have justice-centered classrooms that don't impose our own beliefs/morals but are also not "neutral"?).

- **Text(s)** to help frame the issue or problem and to support the group's initial understanding. Examples of texts have included poems, journal articles, YouTube videos, book chapters, testimonios, and more.

Facilitating an Inquiry Session

When it is time for the group to meet, whoever's leading the inquiry session will generally host in their classroom, with chairs or desks forming a circle. It is such a joy to visit other people's classrooms, beyond our own schools, and see spaces adorned with beautiful posters, student art, shelves filled with books, and personal items that give a glimpse into the human beings who fill the room each day.

Although we aim to begin our meetings at the start of the hour, we are intentional about disrupting how so many schools treat starting meetings "right on time" as inviolable (yet frequently run long past the supposed end time). We honor the fact that some folks have longer drives, traffic, or personal matters. We want our experience together to feel relaxed and to have an organic flow within the two-hour window we have, and treating time as more fluid than fixed allows for this. That said, our space is not a "drop-in" one per se. We all respect the goal of arriving close to our start time and breaking bread together, and we hold that intention as a group.

Check-ins

Once the group feels ready to start, we'll begin with a check-in question (e.g., something from the week we're celebrating, a rose or a thorn, etc.). I have lost count of how many meetings I have been in where there is *no* check-in, where the first thing on the agenda is a "business item" to discuss. Or, if there is a check-in, sometimes the prompt and accompanying responses are shallow and superficial, making the check-in seem more obligatory than purposeful.

For our critical friends group, check-ins are not an item to check off a box; they are integral to helping us ground, connect, and be present. Even if the question is simple in nature, the *intention* of the check-in process is what matters. Being able to share authentically how one is doing and feeling engenders mutual trust and safety, which allow for vulnerable and deep discussions. Whether folks are coming in feeling elated, exhausted, or upset, the container we have built together can hold all that is alive in the room. Also, we don't set a timer when people are speaking from the heart, as we strive to balance what is real in the moment with what is planned for our discussion. That said, smaller groups (four–six) do allow for fluid check-ins more easily than larger groups (ten+).

Group Norms

After the group has checked in, we will take turns reading our norms, which are ever-evolving. While we had some norms when the space first formed, we did not fully appreciate their importance in holding people together amidst conflict—not until an inquiry discussion went sideways and contributed to some falling-outs. Prior to that, we had assumed that folks were more or less on the same page, and we did not anticipate that rifts would surface among some of our own. Our norms of valuing differing opinions and speaking one's truth with care for others were not upheld in the moment. It was a valuable learning experience for us in realizing that without having norms that *everyone* agrees to and *collectively* upholds, it is difficult to work through such conflict. Following that inquiry session, we reflected on and recreated our norms, committing ourselves to being more intentional about putting them into practice. Here is the current iteration of our Meeting Norms.

Critical Friends Meeting Norms

- What's said here stays here
- Devote time and space to building community
- Move up, move back
- Value everyone's voice
- Honor the time and creative flow
- Experience discomfort in the effort to grow
- Critique with the intention of growing constructively and avoiding alienating forms of language
- Honor discussion of and attention to inquiry topic
- Maintain space for teachers of color and white allies to hold equitable conversations with the intention of stretching ourselves, supporting our students, growing the profession, and transforming oppressive systems
- Continually challenge ourselves to practice and promote liberatory, antiracist, humanizing teaching and learning rooted in love and justice for all people

---

Having said that, we do not always agree nor share the same perspectives during inquiry discussions. In fact, some of our richest conversations have stemmed from conflicting viewpoints. But we are intentional about practicing humility and openness to ideas different from our own, understanding that, as Paulo Freire wrote in *Pedagogy of the Oppressed*, we are "unfinished, incomplete beings" for whom education must be "an ongoing activity" (2010, 84). Similarly, our commitment to "critique with the intention of growing constructively and avoiding alienating forms of language" is not about tone policing but about supporting our being critical with *love*. When individuals are treated as the problem, it is easy to lose sight of the issues and conditions we're trying to change.

Moreover, as a living document, our norms are not static. For example, "Step up, step back" to hold awareness of equity of voice was changed to "Move up, move back" to be more inclusive of folks with disabilities, including one of our own members. To note another likely shift, many of us have increasingly noticed the terms accomplice and co-conspirator, sometimes in place of or in addition to ally. Accomplice and co-conspirator emphasize solidarity, action, and risk over performative gestures and having little skin in the game that can come with mere allyship. Such language highlights important distinctions and varying degrees of engagement in antiracist, social change work. When our group reconvenes for the new school year, we'll be able to discuss and decide together what feels right.

It is a healthy practice to review and revise norms as language evolves and new learnings emerge. Our goal is not to be perfect but to be in a continual state of reflection and learning, as we recognize that we're not going to get it right all of the time. It's important to have language that captures, as accurately as possible, what we value while holding abundant care and awareness for people of diverse backgrounds, identities, and experiences. And it is equally important that we continually evolve together.

A Moment for Reflection

- When have you seen group norms work well? What has allowed for this?
- When have you seen them not work well? Why?

Dialogue

The inquiry discussion itself is the heart of our time together. It is where, as a community, consciousness expands, new practices develop, and knowledge is constructed. Early on, inquiry sessions were chunked into distinct parts (i.e., overview of inquiry, clarifying questions, probing questions, group discussion, facilitator reflection, group reflection). While it was somewhat helpful to have an agenda, time-keeper, and process checker, the group soon realized that such a format felt too rigid for our purposes. That is not to diminish the value of designating roles and having an agenda; those can be especially useful for groups that are new or need more structure. But we preferred allowing questions, connections, and ideas to emerge organically.

After the facilitator/presenter reviews the guiding question, idea, or problem they would like support with, the group will engage in dialogue and share wonderings, relatable experiences, pushbacks, insights, and more. An important note about dialogue here. For our critical friends group, we exchange and receive diverse ideas without knowing where the discussion will lead.

In his book *Education for Critical Consciousness*, writing of the liberatory literacy work he did with oppressed adults in Brazil in the 1960s, Paulo Freire says that true dialogue happens when people are engaged in a generative process, a shared search where the outcome is not predetermined. By valuing others' ideas equally as one's own, the interaction becomes horizontalized and fosters a relation of empathy. When people in dialogue are "thus linked by love, hope, and mutual trust," writes Freire, "they can join in a critical search for something. Only dialogue truly communicates" (2005, 40) [Figure 10.2].

A with B

Communication is sustained through relation of empathy

10.2

Visual representation of Freire's model of dialogue.

Freire contrasts his model of dialogue with a model of anti-dialogue, wherein a person or group imposes their ideas, beliefs, or reality onto another [Figure 10.3]. Rather than allowing for the mutual exchange and receipt of ideas, anti-dialogue "issues communiqués," that is, it transmits statements or ideas without care for the other. Anti-dialogue is "loveless, arrogant, hopeless, mistrustful, and acritical" that results in "a vertical relationship between persons," Freire writes (2005, 41). Without love, hope, trust, humility, and a critical attitude, the relation of empathy becomes "broken."

So often in school meetings, people are talked *at* and information is treated as something to deliver and impart. Certainly, there is a place for announcements, special training, and the like, where it might be practical to communicate in such a way. However, if school meetings and PD are generally marked by rigid, predetermined agendas and passive receiving of information, then there will be fewer opportunities to create meaning and understanding together.

When, instead, dialogue is prioritized and everyone's ideas are treated with care, people are more likely to engage authentically and willingly. It is through dialogue and our commitment to devote time and space to build community regularly that our critical friends group has been able to create a vulnerable and brave space so rare in schools. We are able to show up with our full humanity—laughing, crying, rejoicing, despairing, hoping, dreaming together. And in that process, we hold one another with exquisite care.

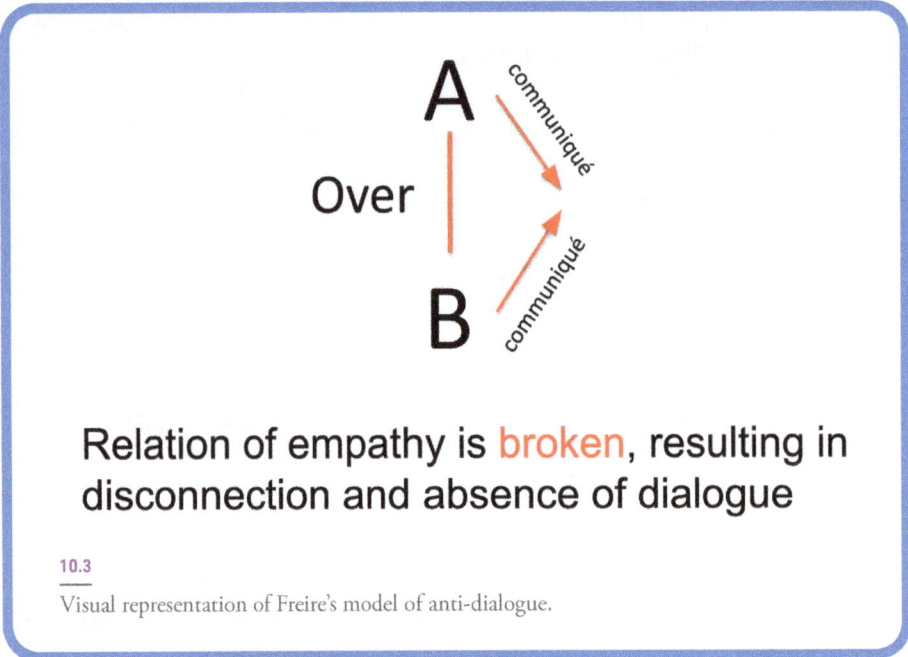

Relation of empathy is broken, resulting in disconnection and absence of dialogue

10.3

Visual representation of Freire's model of anti-dialogue.

Reflections and Appreciations

Toward the end of the inquiry session, the facilitator/presenter will share their takeaways from the discussion, and then the rest of the group will take turns doing the same, usually by going around in a circle. In sharing our reflections, we also express appreciation for people in the space. Sometimes, it's gratitude for the support or contributions someone made to the discussion. Other times, it's appreciation for a new member who dedicated time to be and build with us.

Without exception, a recurring and shared sentiment is that folks feel rejuvenated, inspired, and held after our time together. Although people have come and gone and the size of our inquiry sessions sometimes fluctuate, there is a steady core who sustain the flow. That folks have continued to meet monthly on Fridays for nearly ten years speaks to the power of community. Without the support of our critical friends space, I'm not sure I would still be in the classroom today.

Kickbacks

In addition to the inquiry sessions, we try to hold social gatherings (what we call kickbacks) a few times a year. Kickbacks are generally sandwiched between inquiry sessions so that we have time for recreation and connecting that don't necessarily involve teaching.

Over the years, our kickbacks have included breaking bread, hiking, bowling, hanging out at parks, meeting for happy hour, and more. Although these were more frequent before some of us had children, moved away, or took on new responsibilities, they still happen and nourish our relationships with each other [Figure 10.4].

10.4

Some of the South Bay Critical Friends crew: (from left to right) Ray Ramirez, Rachel deLahunta, Jessica Cohen, Mike Espinoza, Dani Wadlington, me, and Carl Ponzio. Personal collection.

A Moment for Reflection

- What education space(s) have you been part of where dialogue felt rich, organic, or generative?
- Thinking about your own school or teaching context, what are the possibilities for, and obstacles in the way of, this kind of dialogue?
- Who are educators you know, either at your school or beyond, with whom you could see yourself forming a teacher inquiry or support group?

GROWING OUR OWN PATHWAYS ON THE GROUND

Depending on one's capacity and other commitments, it might not always be possible to form or be part of a teacher inquiry group that meets outside of school hours. If one has some administrative support and colleagues who are willing, however, we can still do some of the collaborative and mutually supportive work we yearn for, from the ground up.

For a few years, my good friend and colleague Rachel deLahunta, a math teacher, and I taught groups of students who were part of a Nonviolence Education Pathway that we created. We wanted to provide additional support for students with multiple unmet needs, and we thought that our having a shared belief in nonviolence and similar teaching practices would result in fruitful collaboration. Overall, it proved to be a wonderful experience for us and the students, and it all started with an invitation.

Reaching Out

Before Rachel and I became friends, I had seen her facilitate a few staff meetings and sensed that we shared similar teaching philosophies and practices. At the time, I had been attending nonviolence trainings outside of school and was inviting friends and colleagues I thought might be interested. Although the nascent idea of creating a nonviolence pathway had not yet crystalized, I was hoping that the nonviolence-centered teaching and learning I was doing with my students would happen beyond my own classroom and potentially lead to shifting school culture. I yearned to find folks who were willing to learn alongside me and with whom I might be able to collaborate in some form.

One day during lunch, I stopped by Rachel's classroom and invited her to an upcoming two-day introductory workshop on Kingian Nonviolence. I invited a few other colleagues as well, most of whom attended the training, which fell on a weekend. Rachel seemed particularly enthusiastic about her experience from the workshop and expressed an eagerness to learn more.

I then told her about the Nonviolent Leadership for Social Justice retreat, an annual summer event that I had attended previously and found to be life-changing. It specifically focused on integrating NVC consciousness and practices with social and racial justice work. Rachel attended the retreat with me and was also impacted profoundly by her immersive experience with NVC. Our initial conversations were the genesis of our nonviolence pathway for students.

Building Bridges

From the outset, Rachel and I shared a conviction that nonviolence, as an antidote to violence, held the potential to transform our school culture by strengthening relationships between and among teachers and staff, centering needs, and celebrating the unique gifts of each member of our school. We both believed in the Beloved Community as our North Star and aspired to create classroom communities that reflected such a vision.

But in order to do this in a more unified fashion beyond our two classrooms, we felt we needed an actual way to collaborate and, ideally, with the same groups of students. One limitation was that the existing structure of our PLCs during staff collaboration time only allowed for collaboration *within* departments; this was in addition to separate department-wide meetings. While we valued meeting with the people in our departments, we also recognized the importance of building strong, supportive relationships with teachers of different subject areas.

We decided to solicit the help of an instructional coach from a prominent teacher development organization who was working closely with some first- and second-year teachers at our school. They had a budding relationship with one of our administrators at the time and were willing to support us in making a case for an interdisciplinary cohort program. It was still early in the spring, and we hoped to get something off the ground in time for the following school year.

Our administrator was open to the idea but wanted there to be four of us teachers to work together instead of just two. Specifically, the administrator wanted four subject areas covered: history, science, math, and English. So, the instructional coach, Rachel, and I reached out to a history and science teacher who we thought and hoped would be interested in working with us.

Admittedly, it took some coaxing for the two other teachers to get on board. One was about to be a new parent, and the other was a beginning teacher also balancing graduate school. Neither of them had nonviolence training and both acknowledged that, aside from having a general understanding of the concept, nonviolence in the classroom was new. Rachel and I shared that we, too, were still ever-learning about nonviolence and its application in the classroom, and neither of us thought nor wanted to convey that we had all the answers.

That said, we recognized that our prior training gave us an advantage. Thus, we tried our best to support the other two teachers, providing resources (e.g., readings, websites, trainings), sharing our experiences, and answering whatever questions we could.

Harvesting Ideas

One of the most helpful and generative meetings the four of us had was during a brainstorming session late in the spring, ideating what our collaboration together could look like [Figure 10.5]. During this discussion, we asked ourselves three questions:

1. **What** does nonviolence education/pedagogy look like?
2. **How** can we practice nonviolence education/pedagogy (together)?
3. **Why** should we practice and promote nonviolence education/ pedagogy?

From these three questions emerged a fourth one: Given all this [that we have brainstormed together], what **binds** us together? This question helped us get clarity on our shared values and provided everyone a chance to express what was most important to us as teachers. Some of our shared values and practices included

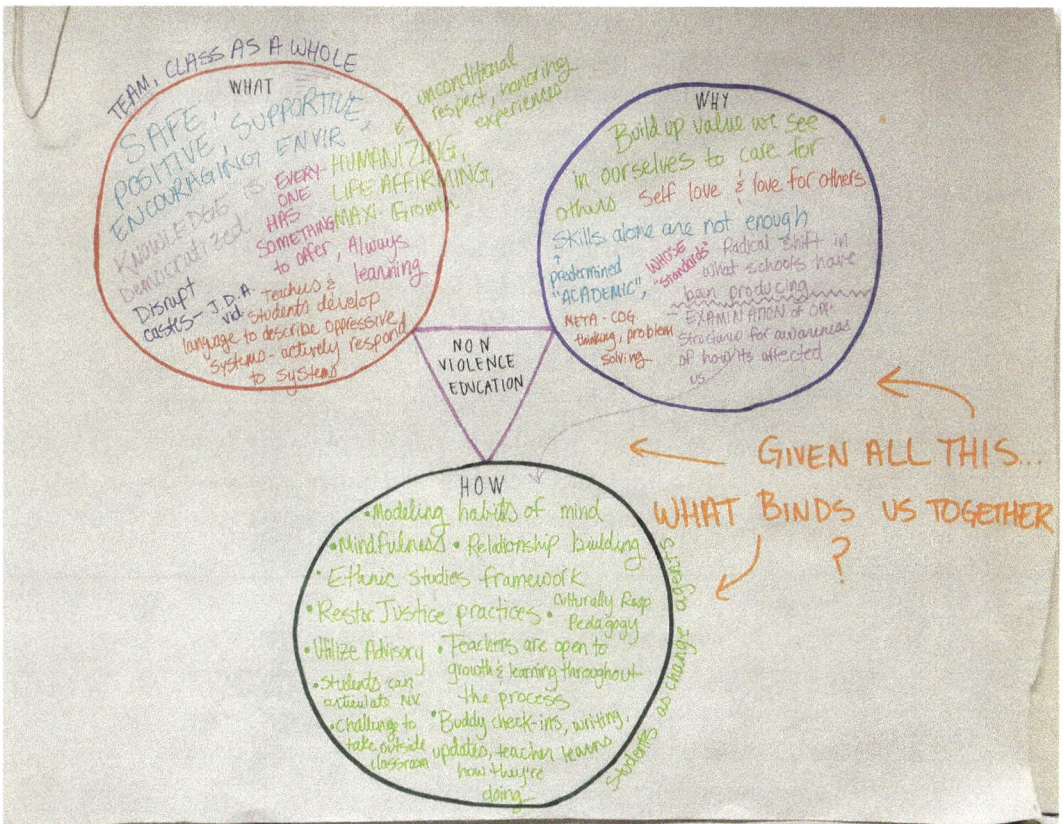

10.5

Brainstorming session for the formation of the Nonviolence Education Pathway.

mindfulness, community building, compassion, empathy, humanizing teaching and learning, interconnectedness, honoring lived experience, culturally relevant education, and critical awareness of systems of power and oppression.

We also developed a description of our vision and mission to articulate what we wanted to bring to our school community:

Vision

Our vision is to cultivate the academic, social, emotional, and spiritual growth of our learning community through nonviolence education, which we believe can fundamentally transform our school into a more loving, just, and equitable environment for all.

Mission

As collaborators in the Nonviolence Education Pathway, we aim to address institutional practices, policies, and structures that reinforce social stratification and inequity, and which result in violence. By acknowledging that opportunity gaps exist within an educational system designed to maintain unequal outcomes, we will collaborate to design and implement humanizing, empowering, and culturally sustaining curricula that supports students across subject areas and honors and elevates students' experiences and funds of knowledge. Grounded in this purpose, teachers and students will work together to build and maintain safe, positive, and supportive classroom communities that promote love, learning, and growth for all.

Some of our areas of focus include building social emotional learning into our respective curricula; coordinating interventions with one another for individual students; disrupting ways in which certain practices in schools and classrooms perpetuate harm in systemic, measurable ways toward low-income students of color; and positioning education as a tool for social change and community development. Therefore, our central commitments in working with this cohort include:

- Building relationships that center human needs and requests
- Providing access to rigorous, meaningful, and culturally sustaining learning experiences
- Utilizing instructional practices that inspire, excite, and engage students in learning
- Creating opportunities for self-reflection that support students in seeing themselves and each other as brilliant young scholars

Early on, we envisioned creating a multiyear pathway in which some of us would loop with the students. Our administrator, while open to the idea, pointed out that doing so would involve time-sensitive and potentially time-consuming steps. If it were to be a traditional academic pathway, or academy, we would need to ensure that our core subject area, theme-based classes were part of the University of California's approved high school course list; if not, we would have to petition to have them added. Furthermore, having an academic pathway would necessitate recruiting eighth graders who would be incoming freshmen. Viability ultimately seemed to be a numbers game.

Given the timing and tasks required to create an "official" pathway, we decided to just focus our energy on preparing for the upcoming school year. And rather than concerning ourselves with recruiting incoming freshmen, sophomore students were selected based on grades and attendance from their ninth-grade year. We specifically asked for kids who performed poorly in their core classes, had attendance issues, and behavioral challenges. Once we were told we would have two cohorts of students for the upcoming school year, the pieces were in place for the start of the Nonviolence Education Pathway.

Co-creating Teaching and Learning Opportunities

▷ What's a program, pathway, or approach you would love to see exist at your school? What might this look like?

▷ Who might your closest champions, co-conspirators, or allies be?

▷ If you were to create an outline or proposal for a project, pathway, or approach you'd like to see at your school, how would you pitch it to people unfamiliar with the kind of work you are practicing or interested in?

▷ Whom could you lean on for support and advocacy if you do not yet have sufficient support from administration?

More than One Path:
Convergence and Divergence

During the pilot year of the Nonviolence Education Pathway, there were several things that went well. The four of us held an orientation early in the year where students got to know us and each other, connecting over food and dialogue. We had designated time during some of our PLCs to meet together, where we shared best practices, challenges, and stories from our classrooms. Talking with other teachers who had the same students was invaluable, which allowed kids to see parallels in some of what was happening across our classes (e.g., centering needs and relationship building). We brought the kids together again at the end of the year, celebrating the teaching and learning we had done together.

Admittedly, there were also some hard growing pains during that first year. The two other teachers Rachel and I were collaborating with did not always attend our meetings; the tentative interest they initially had appeared to wane as the year wore on, as did their involvement. Our hope of creating an interdisciplinary culminating project didn't pan out. Our relationship with the instructional coach we had been working with soured over disagreement about collecting student data.

But our efforts were not in vain. Sometimes, people can start out with similar goals and hopes and then realize that they have different priorities, and that's completely okay. When a group faces setbacks, it doesn't mean that the efforts have to stop or the group failed in fulfilling its vision and mission. Sometimes, all that is needed is a different approach.

Rachel and I decided to continue with the pathway for the following year, except this time, we thought it might be easier if it were just the two of us collaborating. Thankfully, our administrator supported our preference and we gave it another go. Our second year of collaboration was incredibly fruitful and fulfilling. Students repeatedly shared that they enjoyed being in our classes and appreciated the similarities in how we built classrooms that centered love, joy, and community. Many students who had poor grades and low attendance their freshmen year excelled and thrived in our classes their sophomore year. They saw themselves as mathematicians, as writers, as readers, as thinkers, as worthy human beings.

Also supportive for me and Rachel were our weekly informal meetings. We always started with a check-in, holding space for each other to share how we were doing in heart, body, mind, or spirit to ensure we were tending to our friendship in addition to our collaborative work. During our meetings, we celebrated lessons, discussions, and activities that went well and shared our disappointment when things fell flat. We talked about students who we connected easily with and asked each other for support when we struggled to connect with others. We kept track of who called so-and-so's caregiver/guardian as well as students with whom we wanted to follow up.

We also had our own challenging moments that we worked through with great care for each other. For example, one year we had a student who was struggling heavily to keep up with their classes and attend school. I had regular check-ins with them, but I wanted to see if Rachel and I could strategize on how to better support the student. I initiated a parent conference with the student, their guardian, our school's social worker, Rachel, and myself present. At one point, when emotions were raw and the meeting was winding down, Rachel said to the student, "I'm here for you." While I was thankful that she expressed and embodied such authentic care, I also felt slightly hurt that her words were not framed as "*We* are here for you." Rachel and I talked about that subsequently, and she expressed regret for not being more mindful about her choice of words and their impact on me.

On another occasion, when we had a particularly high-needs cohort, I remember feeling exceptionally exhausted from attending to multiple student crises unfolding around the same time. Many students were opening up and choosing to write about or privately discuss traumatic experiences they had endured or were enduring. I was feeling compassion fatigue and didn't know whether Rachel was having similar kinds of conversations with our kids. When Rachel and I checked in, she shared that she was not privy to the information I knew about some of our students.

I initially felt frustrated and wondered whether she was dedicating the same kind of time and energy as I. After a few subsequent conversations where I vented about how drained I was, she asked me, "Mike, do I not seem tired enough? Is that what you want to see? I'm not entirely clear what you're requesting." I think I was yearning for some companionship in how we were holding space for our students, but I did not have clarity, until we spoke, that there are different ways of holding space. I did not fully appreciate how our respective approaches to building relationships and classroom community, while different in many ways, were strengthened by their complementary dynamic. Our approaches did not need to look exactly the same.

That said, Rachel and I also discussed how our identities and racialized experiences—mine as a person of color and hers as a white person—undoubtedly shaped how we taught. We both expressed a desire to learn more about each other's approach to building relationships with students and centering joy in our classrooms; we also committed to reflecting on and sharing with each other how our own privileges and identities informed our positionality as teachers.

We continued with the pathway a third year, but the realities of distance learning made it extraordinarily challenging. That said, we did our honest best to bring the same approach and love and were committed to seeing the year through together with our kids. We would have loved to continue for a fourth year and beyond, but we were only willing to do so if we could have common planning time or be compensated for meeting outside of contractual hours. When we were told there was no guarantee that our requests would be honored, we respectfully declined to continue.

Hopefully, Rachel and I (and possibly others) can resume the pathway we started, or create a different one, at some point in the future. Even if not, though, the teaching and learning we did together meant the world to us and our kids and has left a lasting impact. Toward the end of this past school year, two former students, Alejandra and Leslie, randomly stopped by my classroom after school. We reminisced about our experiences in the Nonviolence Education Pathway. Now in college, they shared how much they missed being in our and their other classes, which felt like "home." They were grateful for our helping them feel safe and seen, which bolstered their courage to share their stories with raw truth and power. They appreciated how we, together, forged classroom communities watered by love, hope, and joy. They have chosen the way of the Warrior Scholar, and their stories and journeys sustain my faith for the future [Figure 10.6].

10.6

Alejandra, Leslie, and me. Personal collection.

FOR LIFE

"Water is the blood of the earth," says Ann-Marie Sayers, a Mutsun Ohlone who has fought to protect and preserve her ancestral lands, Indian Canyon, the only federally recognized sovereign Indian Country along California's Northern Central Coast (2019, 5:35). Indian Canyon has been home to Sayers' people for generations and served as a safe haven for Native Americans who fled capture and persecution from colonizers.

In a visually stunning video about Indian Canyon, there is a moment when Sayers describes the sights and sounds of water flowing. She says that "there is no word in the English language" that encapsulates the spiritual and multifaceted nature of water. "[It] is not just H_2O," says Sayers.

> It's a movement of the water; it's a sound of the water; it's a creek that contains the water. They are one and inseparable. And if you take the time to listen, you can actually hear the water talk to you, whisper to you. It's just taking the time to listen (2019, 5:40).

Through listening, we water our capacity to be more in touch with ourselves, with each other, with life. In doing so, we allow our internal gardens to bloom and reap beauty. As teachers, we cannot capture the essence of each other in fleeting moments in the halls and copy room; we must make time to build community, sustain relationships, and create opportunities for growth. And that work begins and continues through listening—to one another's stories, to our inner wisdom and that of each other, to our hopes and dreams. And from listening emerges action.

Sayers adds that, according to indigenous wisdom, our decisions should always have in mind the welfare of future generations. When young people visit Indian Canyon, she tells them:

> Each and every one of you are going to be in a position that you're going to be making very, very important decisions. Before you make a decision, ask yourself: *How will this affect seven generations in the future?* When you answer that question, then make your decision (2019, 7:58).

When we act in concert to create the kinds of schools—the kind of world—we dream of, we do so not only for ourselves but for all other beings who will be here long after we are gone [Figure 10.7]. Every thought, word, and deed has the potential to sustain life even when chaos, violence, and destruction are all around us. To know that we carry that power is nothing short of remarkable. And when we teach, learn, live, and love with our hearts at the center, we become the Beloved Community.

10.7

A photo I took at a retreat for educators of color in the Santa Cruz mountains of an art piece representing the seven generations teaching. Personal collection.

Epilogue

I first learned about living roots bridges when I attended my initial Kingian Non-violence training years ago. My friend Kazu Haga, who was the lead facilitator, had just distributed certificates for everyone who attended the workshop. We were all standing in a circle, our hearts moved and minds stimulated from a weekend full of energizing, generative discussions.

"When I think of the work it takes to create Dr. King's vision of Beloved Community, I often think of Meghalaya," Kazu said. "Meghalaya is one of the wettest regions on the planet. Because of heavy rainfall, it is impossible to access parts of the village without bridges—*living* bridges, woven by hand."

The bridges are built by first planting rubber fig trees on either side of a riverbank. After several years of growth, the aerial roots, elastic and pliable in nature, are then woven together and scaffolded, often with bamboo. Eventually, once the roots from both trees become long enough, they are tied together to form a pedestrian bridge. The process takes decades, even generations. When taken care of, the bridges can become stronger over years as the trees continue to grow aerial roots that reinforce the bridge (Yadav 2020).

Kazu then referenced a documentary that featured living root bridges in Meghalaya. In the footage, which I subsequently watched, an uncle is teaching his niece how to weave together roots from a sapling. The uncle tells his niece, "This living bridge will grow for 500 years. Your children will use it—and your children's children" (Flowers 2011). Interspersed are a series of close-up and wide shots of people crossing the ingeniously designed, gorgeous bridges, which are absolutely breathtaking.

"Building the Beloved Community will not happen tomorrow. It may take us five hundred years," Kazu said. "But when we tend our portion of the bridge, building off of the previous generation and trusting that the next one will do the same, we relieve ourselves of the burden of feeling as though we must do everything."

*   *   *

Mateo, a student of mine from a few years ago, started off the school year on a high note. He enjoyed class discussions and possessed an outspokenness that reflected strong conviction in his opinions. Although his attendance was spotty from the first week of school, he seemed to enjoy our class as best as I could tell. Except when it came to writing.

Whether we were analyzing a poem, responding to a question, or crafting an essay, writing seemed to be a real sore spot for Mateo. With cajoling and substantial one-on-one support, he'd put his pencil to the page or fingers to the keyboard. But other times, he would check out, put on his headphones, and leave the classroom, sometimes returning, sometimes not.

I stayed in regular contact with his mom, who I could tell was doing her best to keep her son on track. "He's got a lot of pain," she told me. "He's been through *so much* and I think it's really hard for him to focus on school with all that's going on in his life." I knew bits and pieces of his story but did not have a full picture.

Sometimes, whatever Mateo was bottling up would seep through the hard shell he wore at school. Once, when the class was brainstorming topics for a writing assignment, I sat next to him, trying to help him generate some ideas. The class had already read some student examples and had several optional prompts to choose from. Nothing landed for him. I then recalled that he had previously started, but did not finish, a piece on a topic that he had chosen to write about. It was one of his only writing pieces that had more than a few lines down. So I gave it a shot.

"I remember you started writing about the time you reunited with a family member. Would you be interested in revisiting that?"

He stared at me for a moment. "What the fuck makes you think I wanna write about that?" he asked, annoyed. I didn't know it would strike such a nerve.

I waited a beat before responding. "Alright, then," I said, my hopes of helping him find a way into the assignment dimming. "You don't have to write about anything you don't want to write about. If there's something else you'd be open to exploring, let's try." Still nothing.

Mateo's attendance became more infrequent. My classroom door is usually propped open, so I would occasionally catch glimpses of him and his homies walking around during class time. When he was present, I always made it a point to check in and ask how he was doing before bringing up school. I didn't hound him about missing assignments but neither did I give the impression that they would go unnoticed. I wanted him to know that he was believed in, smart, and capable, but I gave space when I sensed he needed it.

He rarely asked for help but often took it when offered. Even if he did not finish an assignment, he usually made an effort to at least try it. I did my best to lift up those tiny wins and encouraged him to keep going. Despite my consistent, earnest attempts to support him, though, he increasingly seemed preoccupied with other priorities. For a while, our English class was the only one he was passing until, eventually, he stopped passing it as well.

Late that spring, Mateo was involved in a gang-affiliated altercation that resulted in a young person being shot. Fortunately, the individual survived, and while the exact details of what happened are unclear, Mateo allegedly fired the gun. He was arrested and subsequently incarcerated.

I was thankful that the young person shot was not killed but dismayed that it even happened, apparently at the hands of one of my students.

What could I have done differently? I remember asking myself. *Could I have— should I have—done more?*

A few months prior, we had read Jason Reynolds' award-winning book *Long Way Down* about a teenager who contemplates getting revenge for the murder of his brother. Our class had powerful, nuanced discussions about the harm of cyclical violence—and what it takes to disrupt it. On the days when Mateo was there, he sometimes preferred to read at his own pace rather than with the class, which was fine with me. He appeared engrossed in the book. Deeply engaged during some discussions; pensive and quiet during others. I remember during a mini debate activity, he shared his conviction that violence was necessary in order to fight violence, but he seemed to listen carefully when his peers disagreed. Perhaps he was questioning some of his own beliefs about revenge, forgiveness, and violence.

But when the shooting happened, admittedly, I wondered whether anything from class had actually counted for something for Mateo. Even though I knew it was not my fault, I felt guilty for not knowing how to better support this young person I genuinely cared about. I felt frustrated that the lure of the streets was such a magnetic force for Mateo and his friends. I felt uncertain whether our classroom community that always welcomed him with love meant much to him.

And then soon after, one of the city's crisis response teams that does youth outreach and gang intervention work came to the school. Chris, one of the team members and a former student of mine from nearly ten years prior, frequently stopped by my classroom whenever there was a crisis involving our students.

"Yo, what's up, Tinoco?" Chris asked as we gave each other a hug.

"Man…I'm shocked by what happened. I'm so relieved no one was killed or seriously injured, but this is really upsetting," I said.

Chris nodded his head. "Yeah, for sure."

We talked some more about what had happened and how we were feeling, and then Chris said, "You know, Tinoco, it wasn't *that* long ago that I was like Mateo."

I knew exactly what he was talking about. When Chris was a student of mine, his brilliance was beyond question. He enjoyed reading, empathized with characters, wrote well, and told me that he appreciated our class and the books I gave him. But he was also getting into all kinds of trouble due to his affiliation with gangs. He got into fights left and right, was suspended multiple times, and switched to and from different schools in the district due to safety concerns. He even had an expulsion hearing, but, thankfully, he was given another chance. He told me that he really took that opportunity to heart and vowed to do better. Eventually, he returned to our school to finish off his senior year.

During that year, Chris hung out in my classroom almost every day during lunch and breaks because, as he put it, he did not want to be distracted by the old homies, whom he had distanced himself from. He was on a roll—literally. He made the honor roll, got nearly straight As, and attended all his classes. We talked about what he was learning in government and forensic science. We talked more and more about college, and even though he doubted whether he could or wanted to go, he seemed intrigued by the possibility which had previously never been a consideration.

And then, less than two months before graduating, Chris' life was flipped upside down when his stepbrother was killed two blocks from my home. He had been shot in the head, apparently by a rival gang member.

Chris was shattered. Heartbroken. Enraged. I did my best to console him, holding space and regularly checking in with him, and, thankfully, I was not alone. By that point, he had several adult mentors in his life who propped him up, wrapping him with love and letting him know that we were there for him. It really took a village to help Chris get through that devastating time. With substantial support, he was able to finish out his senior year. He graduated, and I and his other mentors were there to watch him walk the stage [Figure e.1]. And in the years since, Chris and I have stayed in touch and become friends, sharing important moments of our lives with each other [Figure e.2].

e.1

Chris smiling at the camera moments before receiving his high school diploma. Personal collection.

e.2

Me and Chris and at his child's baptismal party. Personal collection.

"It took me time to figure it out. Sometimes, our paths aren't straight," Chris then told me. He was right. Like Chris, Mateo wasn't on a fixed and linear trajectory toward destruction. Even in the midst of his poor attendance and failing grades, there were moments when I sensed he really wanted to turn things around.

One day during class, months before the shooting, Mateo's headphones were nowhere in sight and he had a pencil in hand.

"Hey, Mateo—where're your headphones at?" I asked, playfully.

"In my pocket. I'm gonna do better today. Plus, you and my mom are always on me," he said with a smile.

Chris' words reminded me that our paths aren't fixed; they continue to grow and take shape. But we move along them when we are ready, which requires patience. And that's hard for us educators, who know that the time with our kids is finite, fleeting. That's hard when the stakes feel so high and we may question whether we're doing enough.

But we can let go of our attachment to immediate outcomes *without* letting go of wanting and working toward that which we dream of. Doing so frees us from the burdens of "forcing" results and feeling as though we must carry the weight of the world on our shoulders. And being in the space between desiring an outcome that the present moment is not yet yielding—or may never yield—is an act of humility and faith.

In Thich Nhat Hanh's book *Zen and the Art of Saving the Planet*, Sister True Dedication writes of how we can fight to save the planet amidst the worsening climate crisis *without* despairing that we're not doing enough during the time we are alive:

> We may feel immense pressure to save the planet in this lifetime, and we may be afraid that we can never do enough. The stark truth is that the planet doesn't need to be saved only once; it needs to be saved countless times, for eons to come. It's impossible to save the planet once and for all, or on our own. That the planet can be here now is a miracle, born of countless favorable causes and conditions over billions of years. And the planet will continue to need countless favorable causes and conditions going forward. This realization is good news. We belong to a stream of life, and this moment is our time and our turn to do our part, and to do whatever we can to pass on what we learn to future generations, so they can do theirs (2021, 36).

e.3

Kazu Haga, Bernard LaFayette, and me at the annual International Nonviolence
Summer Institute at the University of Rhode Island. Personal collection.

Although it is not on us to "save" our students, we can do all that we can to create
"favorable causes and conditions" that foster love, hope, and community. And
when we can trust that others, including our students, can and will do the same,
we can find solace in knowing that we did our absolute best to tend to our portion
of the bridge.

Whether we are classroom teachers, elders from the civil rights movement,
social change activists, or just regular everyday people, having humility and faith
can help us trust that the change we strive and live for is in companionship with
others [Figure e.3].

* * *

Recently, Chris, our partners, and I took our kids to a Japanese friendship garden. Our girls were glued to each other as they delighted in the koi fish, ducks, and geese.

Adjacent to the friendship garden is a sprawling park connected by a small footbridge. Holding hands, the girls crossed the bridge and led us to the park, where we found a picnic table. We broke bread, reminisced, and talked about what was happening in our lives. The girls, off in their own world, then began chasing each other around a giant oak tree, some of its roots visible.

At a certain point, our conversation ceased, and the most important thing in that moment was the precious site before our eyes. We looked on as the girls shrieked in excitement, their arms outstretched and tiny feet pounding on the earth and tree's roots. Playing. Rejoicing. Being. Together.

APPENDICES

and

REFERENCES
CREDITS
INDEX

FEELINGS INVENTORY

Peaceful
Calm
Content
Satisfied
Relaxed
Quiet, still
Secure
Tranquil
Centered
Safe
Serene

Happy
Glad
Excited
Joyful
Pleased
Amused
Encouraged
Confident
Hopeful
Proud
Blissful

Compassionate
Affectionate
Warm
Tender
Appreciative
Friendly
Moved
Passionate
Loving
Sympathetic
Open-hearted

Frustrated
Impatient
Annoyed
Irritable
Agitated
Disgusted
Furious
Enraged
Mad/bitter
Anxious
Cranky

Sad
Lonely
Hurt
Heavy
Broken-hearted
Disappointed
Helpless
Hopeless
Discouraged
Overwhelmed
Tired

Scared
Terrified
Afraid
Nervous
Desperate
Cautious
Insecure
Confused
Uncertain
Stressed
Shocked

Appendix B

NEEDS INVENTORY

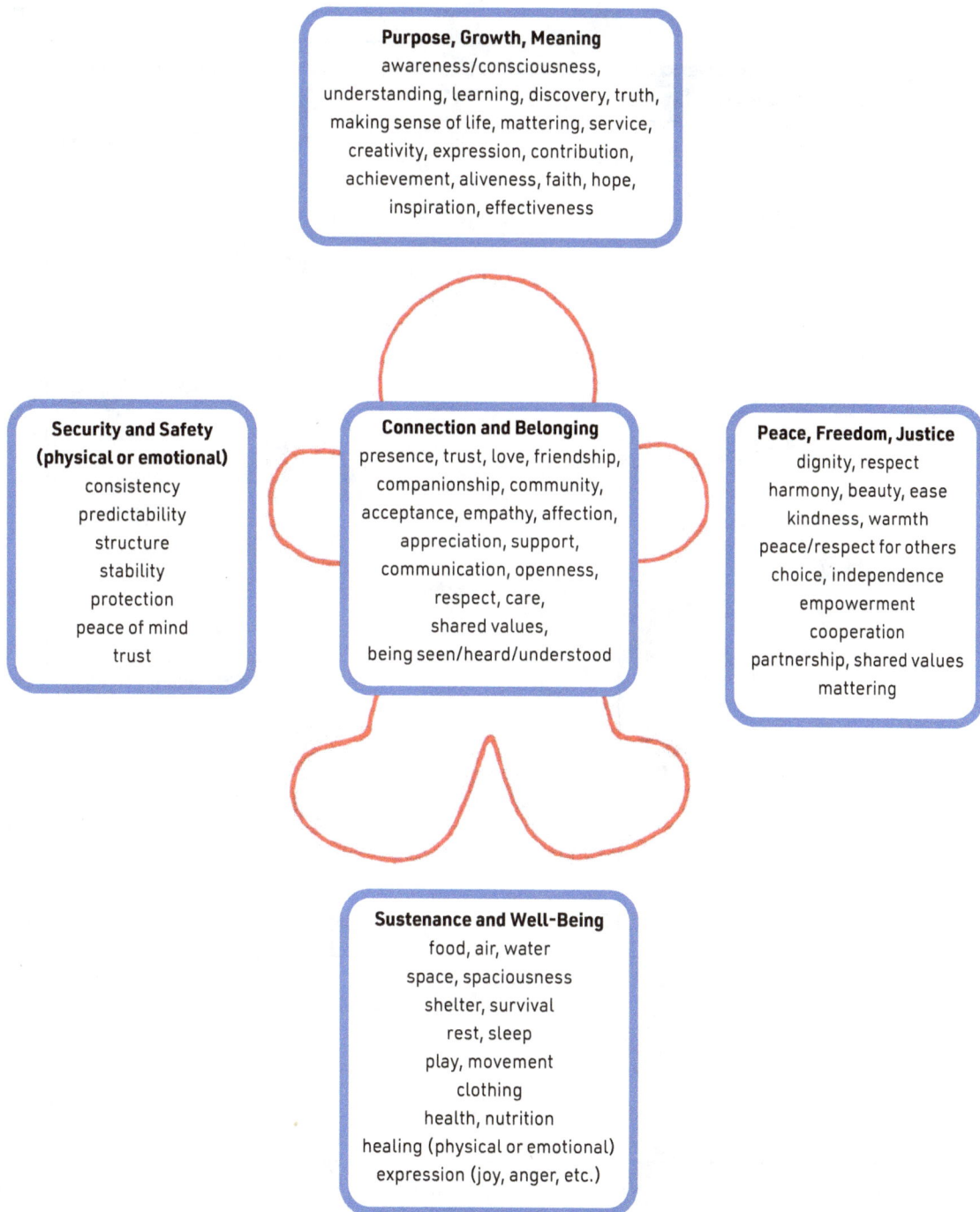

Purpose, Growth, Meaning
awareness/consciousness,
understanding, learning, discovery, truth,
making sense of life, mattering, service,
creativity, expression, contribution,
achievement, aliveness, faith, hope,
inspiration, effectiveness

**Security and Safety
(physical or emotional)**
consistency
predictability
structure
stability
protection
peace of mind
trust

Connection and Belonging
presence, trust, love, friendship,
companionship, community,
acceptance, empathy, affection,
appreciation, support,
communication, openness,
respect, care,
shared values,
being seen/heard/understood

Peace, Freedom, Justice
dignity, respect
harmony, beauty, ease
kindness, warmth
peace/respect for others
choice, independence
empowerment
cooperation
partnership, shared values
mattering

Sustenance and Well-Being
food, air, water
space, spaciousness
shelter, survival
rest, sleep
play, movement
clothing
health, nutrition
healing (physical or emotional)
expression (joy, anger, etc.)

LIFE TRAJECTORY BRAINSTORM

Prompt: What experiences in life and school have shaped your trajectory? What do you envision for your future?		
Elementary School	Middle School	High school (9th grade–current)
		My future
My metaphor (thesis statement)		

Appendix D

FREEDOM'S LIFE TRAJECTORY ESSAY

A New Flame

In the middle of a scenic campground, there lies a pile of twigs. The air is fresh; it's dry and full of oxygen. The sun rises above the sky directing light into a focal point among a patch of grass that has been trampled on by a pack of fawns searching for their breakfast. Smoke rises up like the steam from an evening shower; a patch of inferno spawns out of existence forever changing its surrounding. My life trajectory is like a ball of fire. It started off as a tiny, gentle flame that burned into an unstable and blindingly bright inferno. But just as there are second chances in life, this ball of fire has taken on a different form and is illuminating a new path.

Elementary school was like a clean slate of wild grass at the start of a spring season. The moisture from weeks of precipitation and emergence of greenery makes it a rare occurrence for any wildfire to start, and when there is one, it's usually a spark that extinguishes after a mere second. I remember running across grass fields playing tag and hiding in small shrubs avoiding a seeker. When I moved during second grade to a new school, it wasn't such a big deal. I made friends easily and loved raising my hands when the teacher asked a question.

I remember in third grade, I was introduced to the game of basketball. It was a thrilling experience seeing a ball the size of a watermelon make its way perfectly through a basket suspended ten feet in the air; the satisfying sound the net makes as I throw the ball miles away—"swish…" Elementary school was also when I really began to appreciate science. Every week there was a retired scientist who would come to my class in fifth grade and she would show these amazing experiments, and to a twelve-year-old kid, it was astounding. One time, she brought a container of highly concentrated hydrogen peroxide, and mixed it with a cup of dish soap and salt and the mixture exploded with foam. The entire classroom ended up smelling like the sweet aroma of lemon dish soap. The experience inspired me into an introspective spiral of fantasizing the awesomeness of being a scientist. Elementary school was a time when my fire came into existence. It came with the friendships I made, and it grew with the purpose and empowerment that resulted from my curiosity and my burst of learning. The season passed and the climate began to warm. It set the stage for a larger fire.

Middle school was like a sweltering mix of hundred degree heat. As I changed schools again, my fire grew and grew into a massive ball of inferno. It burned with a desire to shine brighter, enveloping everything around it. Throughout middle school, I made lots of friends. I was the guy who would greet anyone with a smile feeling like he's on cloud 9, and that drew a lot of people toward me. I can't say I didn't enjoy the attention and the recognition from my friends and teachers.

I was getting straight A's in all my classes and was looking forward to going to school every day. At one point, I worked late into the night at school on a science project with a teacher of mine. Things were also working well in my family; I got to see my sister become the first to attend college in my family and I became really close to my mother. Looking back to this period of my life, this is probably one of the highest points of my life. My need for acceptance was fulfilled, and the bonds that were made with the people I loved were inseparable. Homework was no longer dull, but an outlet to grow and share my voice. Home was no longer just a place to relax and pass time, but a lively setting for retrospection. Gradually, my flames shifted from orange to red, and then pale blue. My life trajectory only seemed to be the sky.

High school was like an autumn afternoon with the leaves all dried up and the warm colors of decaying chloroplast. The atmosphere was ideal for the sudden propagation of wildfires. As with the previous years of my education, the transformation between the different stages began with changing schools. This wasn't just a change in where I went, but the people there. I was in a new place, with new people I'd never met in my life. This time, I wasn't able to adapt to the change, which resulted in isolation.

High school was when I became depressed. I mean literally depressed, not the one where you're feeling tired one day and then the next day normal. Every day, there was a cloud over my head preventing me from being happy. I woke up at seven in the morning and I came back home at six in the afternoon. Every day, I would rinse and repeat. When I think back to my freshman year, going through life twelve hours a day in a place I grew to hate with a passion was not a way to live. I started having thoughts on suicide because I thought my life was worthless.

All the trees blackened as my fire struggled to find fuel. At first, I tried coping with depression by running a lot. I would run 2–3 miles a day, and when that wasn't enough, I would join my high school's cross country team and run some more. Sometimes, I would run myself to exhaustion. In a weird way, running was an excuse for my fire to continue burning: it gave me purpose. Somewhere in the middle of my freshmen year, my fire abruptly died. I just stopped coming to school. At first it felt great, being able to break free from an environment that was smothering me. I thought my fire was going to rekindle itself back to life but it never came back.

My parents were extremely disappointed in me, but whenever they brought the topic up for discussion I would shut it down. I didn't want to go back to a place where I felt I lost everything. I lost my pride, my dignity, my sense of belonging. Throughout my hiatus, my way of coping was through video games. It was through video games where I felt like I mattered. The majority of the video games I played involved a protagonist that I was able to empathize with and become, and vicariously, I felt that the imaginary characters cared about me because I had the power to progress their story. Thinking back to this period of my life, I still don't know what happened and why it happened. All I know is that I lost most of the needs that were satisfied when I was little. I no longer had companionship with people, as I spent the majority of my time in my own consciousness. I no longer had the respect for myself and others. I no longer had the peace of mind of being content and happy. My fire no longer existed.

Despite the adversity faced at the beginning of high school, I persevered through the setback. Even though fires ravage through large terrains of forestry, leaving not much behind, where there is life, there will always be regrowth. After some time, I decided to give school another shot, and here I am now, trying to earn missing credits so I can graduate on time. Spruces have begun to grow and animals have returned to dwell. A small, slow-burning fire was emerging from the leftover ashes.

The trajectory of my life has been a fire that went through a variety of intensities. In elementary school, I became passionate about things like basketball and science; I felt excited indulging in these hobbies. My fire sizzled and sparked. In middle school I took those passions and I let them shine. I had friends and teachers who saw potential in me and I felt that I mattered. My fire evolved into flames that matched those which came out of stars. When I started high school, I began to lack human connections and my mental and physical health began to deteriorate. My fire was reduced to ashes. However I recovered from the setback and my fire came back with my wisdom as it burned just as hot but more slowly and stable, just like a campfire: warm and controlled.

As I look back upon my life, I realize that what's kept my fire burning is continuing to aspire to do the things I love. For example, when I was depressed and out-of-school, I turned to video games in order to cope with what I was going through. It was unhealthy at times, and I am not saying I would advocate playing video games all day as part of someone's regimen, even though there are people out there who actually make a living out of it. But at that point in time, I felt that it was something that reflected who I was. It was sort of a self-discovery period for me and I was happy doing it.

Like fire, I am not always going to have the same interests throughout my life; they will change from time to time, and accepting this is what will help me weather life's storms. As I continue on my life trajectory, I see my fire being surrounded by a multitude of friends and family around it keeping themselves warm. I hope to find a job that gets me out of bed every day and contribute to the betterment of other people's lives. I hope to see my fire shining bright as I venture toward my future.

Appendix E

JENAE'S PRECIOUS MOMENT NARRATIVE

My First Bubble

As a kid, I was fascinated by the blowing of bubble gum. I would watch and stare at the chewing and popping, just waiting to see the big balloon-looking bubble explode, as if someone had taken a needle and poked it.

There were always different colored bubbles: pink, red, white, orange, green, yellow, and my all-time favorite, blue. What amazed me the most was the sound it made when it popped. *PAAA!* was like music to my ears.

One day I was sitting in the living room with my mom on our big white couch. She was chewing gum and blowing bubbles.

"Mom, how do you do that?" I asked.

"Do what?"

"You know, blow bubbles, like a balloon. Can you teach me?"

Looking at me with her sweet smile and soft eyes she said, "sure."

My mom took out a packet of Winterfresh gum and handed me one. As I took off the shiny fluorescent paper, out came a thin blue strip of powdery gum that gave off a smell that reminded me of the toothpaste we used and the mints that sat on the table around Christmas time. My excitement was like an expanding balloon about to burst.

I started chewing and instantly tasted the minty, cool flavor. It was delicious and made my mouth feel fresh. But I chewed for so long that my jaw slightly burned like it had been in a marathon.

Ok, I think I'm ready, I thought to myself.

My mom looked at me and said, "Flatten the gum out on your tongue, push, and blow."

"Okaaay," I replied.

I concentrated on her directions, trying not to overthink it, all the while having a bewildered look on my face. I give it a shot despite not feeling entirely confident. With all my might, I attempted to blow a ferocious bubble, but all that effort just resulted in me spitting everywhere and feeling defeated and embarrassed.

With a grim sigh and my head down, I said to my mom, "I can't do it."

"Yes, you can. Just try again. But this time try a little softer."

My mother's encouraging words lifted me back up. With the second try, I blew a bubble but more gently this time. My eyes widened as I began to see the gum inflate.

It's working! I thought to myself.

Inside I felt this rush you get when you're on a rollercoaster, waiting for the drop. As the bubble swelled, I began to anticipate the balloon pop.

"You're doing it!" my mom yelled with excitement.

And then all of a sudden: *PAAA!*

The feeling of accomplishment tasted as sweet as the gum.

Appendix F

JESSE'S FAMILY LEGACY STORY

A note to readers: this story is told from the perspective of my uncle during his time in prison.

Freshly out of high school, I felt as though I could conquer the world. I had no intention of thinking of the future; the smell of a burning blunt and edibles seemed to me like a good enough present. The friends I had seemed like they were ride or die, and for a while they were. However, when those same friends turned a blind eye when they ended up getting me arrested for possession of a firearm, I knew I was in this alone.

Prison wasn't like how they described it in the movies. I didn't feel like some big time gangster. I felt like a little kid, getting scolded for breaking a glass or spilling a cup of juice on a white carpet.

I got incarcerated in the winter of 2012 at the age of eighteen. I was scared of what awaited me. I've seen time and time again people around me getting sent to prison. I thought I was smart and looked at them with pity thinking I would never end up like them. When it was my turn to face the judge, I recognized the trap door they had me step on. The one that led us to an inevitable doom.

I was originally supposed to go in for six months. Those six months sounded like they would fly by quickly, so, out of impulse I ended up sneaking a weapon in. They busted me with it before I could carry out any intentions. *Another slap on the wrist*, I thought. Maybe four months more and I'd be out of here. But the life I once had was pulled out of my grasp when I was given four years.

In those four years, I had to spend seven months in administrative segregation. It's a form of solitary confinement for those with violent and disruptive behavior. This cement box with no light but a little window was going to be my home for the next seven months. It was the most depressing and isolated time in my life. Staring at the same dirty marks on the ceiling and awaiting the next cough or sneeze another human being would make were the only things I really had to do.

I lost privileges to talk to anyone in the outside world. I couldn't talk to any of my family or friends. The only human interaction I had was with the guards, and even then, it was just only through a small metal slot. The minutes turned into hours, the hours to days, and eventually days to months. Time seemed to be against me when I was there.

* * *

Just as I was getting used to administrative segregation, they put me back in the general population. I tried my best not to get into any more trouble. I eventually picked up some hobbies to keep me out of trouble, like exercising and reading. Being in prison is a hostile environment and could get intimidating at times. It is important to treat others with respect and how you want to be treated.

There were never times where I was in a direct line of danger, but there were a lot of gruesome things I saw. I saw men getting stabbed, beaten, and even some deaths. The guards would throw in tear gas and shove inmates back into the cells. The gas getting into your eyes and your lungs made you feel like you were drowning. I was quickly made aware of the potential danger I could be in if I crossed the wrong man.

Besides those violent encounters, it was the same thing every day. Get up at 6:00 AM, go outside, work out, come back and stay until you eat. It felt like I was stuck in a time loop, living the same day over and over slowly driving my sense of time into the ground.

The only thing I really had to look forward to was to wait for my turn to use the phone to contact my family. Hearing their voices was like music to my ears. I got updates on their lives and realized how much I missed. I heard that my nieces and nephews were already celebrating their birthdays when I only had memories of them as newborns.

All I could think about was getting out, my mom's cooking, skateboarding, and hugging and kissing my family members.

A man who had the rest of his life in prison once told me, "If I had one chance to ever make it back to the streets I would become a better man and try to do things differently to provide for my family." It hit me how much I shouldn't take my life for granted. What we do with ourselves and what we do with our time will affect our families if we make the wrong move.

* * *

I was released in the spring of 2016. I was picked up by my sister. Her embrace was something I'll never forget. It felt weird being outside for the first time, with no bars and no schedule. We went to Target for the first time. I stood still while people walked freely around me and felt overwhelmed. I had no sense of belonging there. I felt there was a big red sign above my head that said "Freshly out of prison." The feeling of freedom didn't set in for a while. I kept thinking to myself, *Wow…this is so weird.*

I'm trying my best to stay out of prison. I want to be here for when my family members hit big milestones in their lives. Watching my daughter grow and prepare for school is something I want to be here for. I want to be able to be the father that gave their kids a childhood that they can smile at when they look back.

Student Reflection

I've learned that my uncle, as a father, has chosen to do his best to make a difference and not get incarcerated again. His daughter has impacted him to make a difference in his life. He believes he can and will be a good example for her and be with her for important events in her life like birthdays and school events. He looks at life in a way that he is capable of doing whatever he wants to. His expectations for the future are to never go back to prison and to maybe one day own his own construction company, build a home for his mom in Mexico and be a good role model to his kids. He wishes to grow old with them and to set a good example for them.

EMPATHY LETTER ORGANIZER

Audience Who will you be writing to?	
Description of issue What happened? (For now just write down key points; you'll go in more detail in your letter)	
Impact: your feelings What did you feel during / after this experience? Please explain. (Refer to feelings list)	
Impact: your needs Which of your needs went unmet or were violated from this experience? Please explain. (Refer to needs list)	
Their perspective • Why do you think the person said/did the thing that caused you harm? • What might they have been feeling? • Which needs might they have been trying to meet?	

Appendix H

REMY'S EMPATHY LETTER

Dear Bully,

I am writing this letter to let you know about the way you made me feel when my mom and I were less fortunate.

Here's how I remember it. Same thing, different day coming back from school to my grandma's house always crowded with no privacy. I lived in East Side SJ with my cousins and aunts. It was like an everyday day thing where you would call me out on the clothes I would wear.

I remember one day my friends and I were chilling, minding our own business when I saw you walking towards me. Seeing the look on your face, I could predict what was about to happen. You then called your friends over and pointed out in front of everyone my generic, worn-out clothes, as if I didn't already know what I was wearing. Every time I tried to walk away you would just follow me and continued to make fun of me while laughing. The worst part was that it wasn't only you; more than half of the time it was your friends, too.

I'd go home every day and be upset—not just at the fact that I didn't have nice clothes but because you and your friends didn't understand. You didn't know my mom was a single parent working two jobs who still couldn't afford the clothes we wanted. You didn't see the agony you made me feel. You didn't see the anger I had built from constantly being reminded that I was poor. All the times you and your friends made fun of me it'd make me feel less than and hate myself for who I was.

The way you treated me did not meet my needs for understanding, respect, and being seen. Maybe you would've had some sympathy if you knew what my family and I were going through. I remember waking up sometimes in the morning not wanting to go to school because of you. I wasn't scared; I was just tired and mentally drained from my family not having much money and stability. I never told my mom because I didn't want her to stress over it. But every now and then before going to sleep I'd ask myself: *Should I tell my mom to move me to a different school? Should I ask her to buy me name brand clothes?* And then I would get mad at myself for even thinking that because I knew it would tighten her budget.

I've asked myself: why did you do that to me? Was it because you were white and well off and I was poor Mexican? Was it because you felt insecure about yourself and thought that you'd gain some respect from your friends? Was it because you yourself were hurt from being bullied at some point in your life and projected that pain onto me? I guess I'll never know for sure, but I can't help but wonder.

Do you remember the day when I called you out on it? I remember telling myself after the second to last time, *If he does it again I'm going to stand up for myself.*

You were walking up to me. I was ready because I knew I had it in me. Before you even said something I was already telling you off. I remember saying to you, "I'm done with this bullshit, and if you're not, then let's do something about it right now!" I guess that shocked you because after that you never did it again. The relief of going to school knowing it had ended was great.

I'm choosing to forgive you because I don't want to hold any grudges. What you did to me really hurt at the time, and I hope you understand that you don't have the right to treat anybody like that. You don't know a person's story simply by the clothes they wear. I hope that my letter has helped you reflect on the pain you caused me and learn from your mistakes.

Sincerely,
Remy

REFERENCES

ACLU. 2024. "Mapping Attacks on LGBTQ Rights in U.S. State Legislatures." American Civil Liberties Union. https://www.aclu.org/legislative-attacks-on-lgbtq-rights?state=.

Aguilar, Elena. 2022. "How to Build Psychological Safety in Professional Development." Interview by Jennifer Gonzalez. Episode 201 Transcript. https://www.cultofpedagogy.com/pod/episode-201/.

Bagwell, Orlando, and W. Noland Walker, dirs. 2004. "Citizen King." American Experience, PBS. https://www.pbs.org/wgbh/americanexperience/films/mlk/#transcript.

Baker, Laura and Education Week Staff. 2022. "Forever Changed: A Timeline of How COVID Upended Schools." *Education Week*, April 5. https://www.edweek.org/leadership/forever-changed-a-timeline-of-how-covid-upended-schools/2022/04.

Bates, Karen G. 2013. "While Unsung in '63, Women Weren't Just 'Background Singers'." *NPR*, August 24. https://www.npr.org/sections/codeswitch/2013/08/25/214865982/while-unsung-in-63-women-werent-just-background-singers.

Bigelow, Bill. 2022. "Let's Stop Using Metaphors that Celebrate Extraction, Colonialism, and Violence." *Rethinking Schools* 37 (1): 54–56.

Blest, Paul. 2021. "Ron DeSantis Introduced the 'Stop W.O.K.E. Act'—and Name-Dropped MLK." *Vice News*, December 16. https://www.vice.com/en/article/g5qyqy/ron-desantis-florida-anti-critical-race-theory-bill.

Blow, Charles M. 2013. "'The Most Dangerous Negro.'" *The New York Times*, August 28. https://www.nytimes.com/2013/08/29/opinion/blow-the-most-dangerous-negro.html.

Boyle, Gregory. 2018. "Father Greg Boyle: The Answer to Every Question Is Compassion." Interview by Tami Simon. https://www.resources.soundstrue.com/podcast/father-greg-boyle-the-answer-to-every-question-is-compassion/.

Brown, Brené. 2012. "Listening to Shame." TED. March. Video, 20:22. https://www.ted.com/talks/brene_brown_listening_to_shame.

California Department of Education. 2013. "English Language Arts & Literacy in History/Social Studies, Science, and Technical Subjects." California Department of Education. https://www.cde.ca.gov/be/st/ss/documents/finalelaccssstandards.pdf.

Case, Anne, and Angus Deaton. 2021. "Life Expectancy in Adulthood Is Falling for Those Without a BA Degree, but as Educational Gaps Have Widened, Racial Gaps Have Narrowed." *Proceedings of the National Academy of Sciences of the United States of America* 118 (11). https://doi.org/10.1073/pnas.2024777118.

CDC. 2023. "U.S. Teen Girls Experiencing Increased Sadness and Violence". February 13. Infographic. Centers for Disease Control and Prevention. https://www.cdc.gov/media/releases/2023/p0213-yrbs.html.

Changa, Anoa. 2022. "From Slavery to School Discipline: A Continuum of Control." *Learning for Justice* 2: 43–48.

Clark, Septima Poinsette. n.d. "Non-Violence Speech." Lowcountry Digital Library, Avery Research Center at the College of Charleston. https://lcdl.library.cofc.edu/lcdl/catalog/lcdl:92076.

Clark, Septima. 1964. "Literacy and Liberation." *Freedomways: A Quarterly Review of the Negro Freedom Movement* 4 (1): 113–124.

Clark, Septima Poinsette, and LeGette Blythe. 1962. *Echo In My Soul.* New York: E.P. Dutton & Co, Inc.

Cobb, Charles, and Zócalo Public Square. 2018. "Even Though He Is Revered Today, MLK Was Widely Disliked by the American Public When He Was Killed," April 4. https://www.smithsonianmag.com/history/why-martin-luther-king-had-75-percent-disapproval-rating-year-he-died-180968664/.

Cohen, Li. 2021. "Teacher Placed on Leave after Video Shows Her Wearing Makeshift Headdress and Mimicking Native American Dance during Class." *CBS News*, October 23. https://www.cbsnews.com/news/teacher-video-headdress-mocking-native-american-dance-placed-on-leave/.

Domonoske, Camila. 2017. "When 'Miss' Meant so Much More: How One Woman Fought Alabama — and Won." NPR, November. https://www.npr.org/sections/codeswitch/2017/11/30/567177501/when-miss-meant-so-much-more-how-one-woman-fought-alabama-and-won.

Duncan-Andrade, Jeffrey M.R. 2014. "Jeff Duncan-Andrade PhD – Boys and Men of Color Conference." Foreign Native. April 23. Video, 14:56. https://www.youtube.com/watch?v=0arTbweg5dQ.

———. 2010. *What a Coach Can Teach a Teacher: Lessons Urban Schools Can Learn from a Successful Sports Program.* New York: Peter Lang.

Eig, Jonathan. 2023a. *King: A Life.* New York: Farrar, Straus and Giroux.

———. 2023b. "Martin Luther King Jr.: Challenges in His Final Years and His Message Today" Interview by Scott Tong. *Here & Now*, NPR. June 14. https://www.wbur.org/hereandnow/2023/06/14/martin-luther-king-jr-biography.

Emdin, Christopher. 2023. "Designing for Justice in and Beyond the STEM Classroom: An Interview with Chris Emdin." Interview by Ayva Thomas. *Rethinking Schools* 37 (3):26–31.

English, Ronald. 2023. Interview by author. Telephone, March 14, 2023.

———. 1968. "Rev. Ronald English Prayer at Martin Luther King Jr. Funeral Service." Krise. January 18. Video, 5:42. https://www.c-span.org/video/?c4997241/user-clip-rev-ronald-english-prayer-martin-luther-king-jr-funeral-services.

Finney, Annelise. 2022. "'How Dare You': Oakland School Closure Decision Inspires New Opposition Efforts." *KQED News*. February 21. https://www.kqed.org/news/11905982/how-dare-you-oakland-school-closure-decision-inspires-new-opposition-efforts.

Flowers, Mark, dir. 2011. Human Planet. Episode 7, "Rivers – Friend and Foe." BBC, United Kingdom. 52 min.

Freire, Paulo. 2010. *Pedagogy of the Oppressed: 30th Anniversary Edition*. Translated by Myra Bergman Ramos. New York: The Continuum International Publishing Group Inc.

———. 2005. *Education for Critical Consciousness*. London and New York: Continuum International Publishing Group.

Freire, Paulo, and Donaldo Macedo. 1987. *Literacy: Reading the Word and the World*. Westport, CT: Bergin & Garvey.

Galloway, Katie, dir. 2018. *The Pushouts*. DVD. Good Docs.

Gates Jr., Henry Louis. 2020. "Ella Baker – 'The Mother of the Civil Rights Movement.'" Black History in Two Minutes or So. March 13. Video, 3:01. https://www.youtube.com/watch?v=McneFCdHUn0.

Gilmore, Kim. 2021. "The Birmingham Children's Crusade of 1963." Biography. January 19. https://www.biography.com/activists/black-history-birmingham-childrens-crusade-1963.

Ginwright, Shawn. 2018. "The Future of Healing: Shifting from Trauma Informed Care to Healing Centered Engagement." *Medium*, May 31. https://ginwright.medium.com/the-future-of-healing-shifting-from-trauma-informed-care-to-healing-centered-engagement-634f557ce69c.

Gonzalez, Jennifer. 2022. "How to Build Psychological Safety in Professional Development." Cult of Pedagogy. December 16. https://www.cultofpedagogy.com/psychological-safety/.

Haga, Kazu. 2020. *Healing Resistance: A Radically Different Response to Harm*. Berkeley, CA: Parallax Press.

———. 2017. "The Urgency of Slowing Down." *Waging Nonviolence*, January 25. https://wagingnonviolence.org/2017/01/urgency-slowing-down/.

Hanh, Thich Nhat. 2021. *Zen and the Art of Saving the Planet*. New York: HarperCollins Publishers.

———. 2017. *The Art of Living: Peace and Freedom in the Here and Now*. New York: HarperCollins Publishers.

———. 1995. *Living Buddha, Living Christ*. New York: Riverhead Books.

———. 1993. *The Blooming of a Lotus: Guided Meditation Exercises for Healing and Transformation*. Boston, MA: Beacon Press.

———. 1992. *Peace Is Every Step: The Path of Mindfulness in Everyday Life*. New York: Bantam Books.

Harvard Health. 2019. "Breathing Lessons." May 1. https://www.health.harvard.edu/mind-and-mood/breathing-lessons.

Hathaway, Bill. 2020. "Want to Live Longer? Stay in School, Study Suggests." *YaleNews*, February 20. https://news.yale.edu/2020/02/20/want-live-longer-stay-school-study-suggests.

Hawkins, Edmond, dir. 2018. Season 1, Episode 2, "NRA Problems, Chicken Bone Problems, Birmingham Problems." *Problem Areas*, HBO April 20.

Henriques, Martha. 2019. "Can the Legacy of Trauma Be Passed Down the Generations?" *BBC Future*. BBC News. March 26. https://www.bbc.com/future/article/20190326-what-is-epigenetics.

hooks, bell. 2006. *Outlaw Culture: Resisting Representations*. New York: Routledge Classics.

———. 2001. *All About Love: New Visions*. New York: Harper Perennial.

Houston, Robert, dir. 2005. *Mighty Times: The Children's March*. DVD. Hudson and Hudson, HBO, Learning for Justice.

Jet. 1959. "Why Rev. M.L. King Is Leaving Montgomery: Leader Says Time Is Ripe to Extend Work in Dixie," December 19: 12–17.

Jones, Jeffrey. 2011. "Americans Divided on Whether King's Dream Has Been Realized: Fifty-One Percent Say It Has Been Realized, 49% Say It Has Not." *Gallup*, July 26. https://news.gallup.com/poll/149201/Americans-Divided-Whether-King-Dream-Realized.aspx.

Kashtan, Miki. 2014a. *Reweaving Our Human Fabric: Working Together to Create a Nonviolent Future*. Oakland, CA: Fearless Heart Publications.

———. 2014b. *Spinning Threads of Radical Aliveness: Transcending the Legacy of Separation in Our Individual Lives*. Oakland, CA: Fearless Heart Publications.

———. 2013. "The What and the Why in Human Needs." The Fearless Heart. January 23. https://thefearlessheart.org/the-what-and-the-why-in-human-needs/.

———. 2010. "Nonviolent Communication: Gandhian Principles for Everyday Living." Satyagraha Foundation for Nonviolence Studies. https://www.satyagrahafoundation.org/wp-content/uploads/2013/02/gandhian-principles-for-everyday-living.pdf.

Kashtan, Inbal, and Miki Kashtan. n.d. "Basics of Nonviolent Communication." BayNVC. https://baynvc.org/basics-of-nonviolent-communication/.

Kass, James. 2023. Conversation with the author. Telephone. February 23, 2023.

———. n.d. "History." Youth Speaks. https://youthspeaks.org/about/.

Kaur, Valarie. 2020. *See No Stranger: A Memoir and Manifesto of Revolutionary Love*. Manhattan, NY: One World.

Kawi, Terry, [ms_kawi]. 2020. "What Message Does Our Language Send Students about 'Work'? Our Students Are More than the Work They Produce and They Are Not Workers, so Why Does Our Language Reflect That?" September 18. *Instagram*. https://www.instagram.com/p/CFSAc-TB5Q6hWPnOtwF5Vc078ZkZ72A0ddfVdQ0/.

Kimmerer, Robin Wall. 2013. *Braiding Sweetgrass: Indigenous Wisdom, Scientific Knowledge and the Teachings of Plants*. Minneapolis, MN: Milkweed Editions.

King, Martin Luther. 2015a. "Letter from Birmingham Jail". In *The Radical King*, ed. Cornel West. Boston, MA: Beacon Press.

———. 2015b. "Beyond Vietnam: A Time to Break Silence". In *The Radical King*, ed. Cornel West. Boston, MA: Beacon Press.

———. 2015c. "I've Been to the Mountaintop." In *The Radical King*, ed. Cornel West. Boston, MA: Beacon Press.

———. 1967a. "MLK Talks 'New Phase' of Civil Rights Struggle, 11 Months Before His Assassination." *NBC News*. April 4. Video, 26:50. https://www.youtube.com/watch?v=2xsbt3a7K-8.

———. 1967b. "An excerpt from Martin Luther King, Jr.'s 1967 Stanford visit." Stanford University. January 16. Video, 1:23. https://www.youtube.com/watch?v=sctENM_d77g.

———. 1961. "The Man Who Was a Fool, Sermon Delivered at the Detroit Council of Churches' Noon Lenten Services" Transcript of speech delivered at Central Methodist Church in Detroit, Michigan, March 6. https://kinginstitute.stanford.edu/king-papers/documents/man-who-was-fool-sermon-delivered-detroit-council-churches-noon-lenten.

———. 1958. *Stride Toward Freedom: The Montgomery Story*. New York: Harper & Row.

———. 1956. "'When Peace Becomes Obnoxious' Sermon Delivered on 18 March 1956 at Dexter Avenue Baptist Church." *The Martin Luther King, Jr. Research and Education Institute*, March 18. Stanford University. https://okra.stanford.edu/transcription/document_images/Vol03Scans/207_29-Mar-1956_When%20Peace%20Becomes%20Obnoxious.pdf.

———. 1954. "Recommendations to the Dexter Avenue Baptist Church for the Fiscal Year 1954–1955." Transcript of report delivered in Montgomery, Alabama, September 5. https://kinginstitute.stanford.edu/king-papers/documents/recommendations-dexter-avenue-baptist-church-fiscal-year-1954-1955.

Klein, Alyson. 2021. "1,500 Decisions a Day (At Least!): How Teachers Cope With a Dizzying Array of Questions." *Education Week*. December 6. https://www.edweek.org/teaching-learning/1-500-decisions-a-day-at-least-how-teachers-cope-with-a-dizzying-array-of-questions/2021/12.

Kochiyama, Yuri. 2004. *Passing It On: A Memoir*. Los Angeles, CA: UCLA Asian American Studies Center Press.

Krieg, Gregory. 2018. "When MLK Turned on Vietnam, Even Liberal 'Allies' Turned on Him." *CNN*, April 4. https://www.cnn.com/2018/04/04/politics/martin-luther-king-beyond-vietnam-speech-backlash/index.html.

Kunhardt, Peter, dir. 2018. *King in the Wilderness*. HBO.

Kush, Joseph M., Elena Badillo-Goicoechea, Rashelle J. Musci, and Elizabeth A. Stuart. 2022. "Teachers' Mental Health During the COVID-19 Pandemic." *Educational Researcher* 51 (9): 593–597. https://doi.org/10.3102/0013189x221134281.

LaFayette, Bernard. 2023a. Interview by author. Telephone, February 5.

———. 2023b. Interview by author. Telephone, June 6.

———. 2017. "Intellectual and Emotional Preparation." Group discussion. International Nonviolence Summer Institute, University of Rhode Island, Providence, RI, June 15.

LaFayette, Bernard, and Kathryn L. Johnson. 2015. *In Peace and Freedom: My Journey in Selma*. Lexington: University Press of Kentucky.

Lakshmin, Pooja. 2023a. *Real Self-Care: A Transformative Program for Redefining Wellness.* Manhattan, NY: Penguin Life.

————. 2023b. "The Power of the Pause: Talking to Dr Pooja Lakshmin About Real Self-Care, Boundaries, Postpartum, Creativity and the Patriarchy." Interview by Kaitlin Solimine. *Postpartum Production*, season 2, episode 4, May 3. https://www.postpartumproduction.com/episodes/s2e4.

Lara, Juan Carlos, and Daisy Nguyen. 2023. "Oakland School Board Halts Controversial Closure Plan, Sparing 5 Elementary Schools." *KQED News.* January 12. https://www.kqed.org/news/11937906/oakland-school-board-halts-controversial-closure-plan-sparing-5-elementary-schools.

Lawrence, Andrew. 2022. "'Our Job Is to Present the Truth': The Texas Principal Caught in a 'Critical Race Theory' Firestorm." *The Guardian*, January 13. https://www.theguardian.com/us-news/2022/jan/13/our-job-is-to-present-the-truth-the-texas-principal-caught-in-a-critical-race-theory-firestorm.

Lewis, John, and Michael D'Orso. 1998. *Walking With the Wind: A Memoir of the Movement.* New York: Simon & Schuster.

Lewis, John, Andrew Aydin, and Nate Powell. 2013. *March: Book One.* Marietta, GA: Top Shelf Productions.

Lewis-Randall, Gloria Washington. 2022. Interview by author. Telephone, November 13.

Life. 1967. "Dr. King's Disservice to His Cause." 1967. *Life*, April 21. Google Books. https://books.google.com/books?id=GFYEAAAAMBAJ&pg=PA4&dq=%22dr+kings+disservice+to+his+cause%22:&hl=en&sa=X&ei=OBJ9U62ZO4fUsATQ-YGABg#v=onepage&q&f=true.

Love, Bettina. 2019. "How Schools Are 'Spirit Murdering' Black and Brown Students." *Education Week*, May 23. https://www.edweek.org/leadership/opinion-how-schools-are-spirit-murdering-black-and-brown-students/2019/05.

————. 2016. "Anti-Black State Violence, Classroom Edition: The Spirit Murdering of Black Children." *Journal of Curriculum and Pedagogy* 13 (1): 22–25. https://doi.org/10.1080/15505170.2016.1138258.

Manning, Roxy. 2023. Conversation with the author. Telephone. January 26.

————. 2020. "Nonviolent Communication with Dr. Roxy Manning." SharpLeft. May 9. Educational video, 34:25. https://www.youtube.com/watch?v=IZ0EpkW6Kq8.

McCray, Rebecca. 2013. "In Florida, High School Student Kiera Wilmot's Curiosity Is a Crime?!" *News & Commentary*, ACLU. May 3. https://www.aclu.org/news/criminal-law-reform/florida-high-school-student-kiera-wilmots.

Meckler, Laura. 2022. "In 'Social-Emotional Learning,' Right Sees More Critical Race Theory." *Washington Post*, March 28. https://www.washingtonpost.com/education/2022/03/28/social-emotional-learning-critical-race-theory/.

Medina, Jennifer. 2019. "At Los Angeles Teachers' Strike, a Rallying Cry: More Funding, Fewer Charters." *The New York Times*, January 17. https://www.nytimes.com/2019/01/17/us/lausd-strike-schools.html.

Mehta, Jonaki. 2023. "What Has and Hasn't Changed for Teachers in the 5 Years since 'Red for Ed' Walkouts." *NPR*, May 22. https://www.npr.org/2023/05/22/1177576762/what-has-and-hasnt-changed-for-teachers-in-the-5-years-since-red-for-ed-walkouts.

Moll, Luis C., Cathy Amanti, Deborah Neff, and Norma González. 1992. "Funds of Knowledge for Teaching: Using a Qualitative Approach to Connect Homes and Classrooms." *Theory Into Practice* 31 (2): 132–141. https://doi.org/10.1080/00405849209543534.

Natanson, Hannah. 2021. "A White Teacher Taught White Students about White Privilege. It Cost Him His Job." *Washington Post*, December 6. https://www.washingtonpost.com/education/2021/12/06/tennessee-teacher-fired-critical-race-theory/.

National Archives. 2022. "The Student Nonviolent Coordinating Committee (SNCC)." African American Heritage. June 17. https://www.archives.gov/research/african-americans/black-power/sncc.

National Institutes of Health COVID-19 Research. n.d. "Mental Health During the COVID-19 Pandemic." National Institutes of Health COVID-19 Research. https://covid19.nih.gov/covid-19-topics/mental-health.

NCES. 2022. "U.S. Schools Report Increased Teacher Vacancies Due to COVID-19 Pandemic, New NCES Data Show: Resignations, Retirements Identified as Leading Causes for Unfilled Positions in Nation's Public Schools." *National Center for Education Statistics*. The Institute of Education Sciences. https://nces.ed.gov/whatsnew/press_releases/3_3_2022.asp.

New Oxford American Dictionary. n.d. "Indoctrinate." Computer application.

News & Letters. 1961. "Jackson, Mississippi, U.S.A. Freedom Rider Mary Hamilton," November.

Nguyen, Tran. 2021. "Hundreds Celebrate the Opening of Vietnamese Service Center in San José." *San José Spotlight*, October 23. https://sanjosespotlight.com/hundreds-celebrate-the-opening-of-vietnamese-service-center-in-san-jose/.

Norte, Edmundo. 2018. Conversation with the author. Calistoga, CA. August 1.

NSRF. n.d. "Critical Friends Group Work and CFG Coaches' Training." National School Reform Faculty. https://nsrfharmony.org/.

Odell, Jenny. 2019. *How to Do Nothing: Resisting the Attention Economy*. Brooklyn and London: Melville House.

Orosco, José-Antonio. 2008. *Cesar Chavez and the Common Sense of Nonviolence*. Albuquerque, NM: University of New Mexico Press.

Patterson, Nick. 2014. *Birmingham Foot Soldiers: Voices from the Civil Rights Movement*. Charleston, SC: The History Press. Kindle.

Payne, Charles. 1989. "Ella Baker and Models of Social Change." *Signs* 14 (4): 885–899. https://www.jstor.org/stable/3174689.

PBS News. 2015. "Can Trauma Be Passed to Next Generation through DNA?" *PBS News Classroom*. PBS News. August 31. https://www.pbs.org/newshour/classroom/daily-videos/2015/08/can-trauma-be-passed-to-next-generation-through-dna.

Peeples, Julian. 2022. "Inspiring Love, Empathy, and Compassion: Educator Ryan Brazil and Class Build Awareness with 'Anti-Bias ABC's.'" *California Educator* 26 (6): 38–40.

Pennsylvania State University and Robert Wood Johnson Foundation. 2016. "Teacher Stress and Health: Effects on Teachers, Students, and Schools." Pennsylvania State University. September 1. https://www.rwjf.org/en/insights/our-research/2016/07/teacher-stress-and-health.html.

Perry, Bruce D., and Oprah Winfrey. 2021. *What Happened to You?: Conversations on Trauma, Resilience, and Healing*. New York: Flatiron Books.

Porter, Dawn, dir. 2020. *John Lewis: Good Trouble*. CNN Films, ACG Studios, and TIME Studios.

Posnick-Goodwin, Sherry. 2021. "Making Dreams Possible." *California Educator* 26 (3): 18–19.

———. 2018. "Confidence and Creativity: Art Teacher Is a 'Life Changer' for Compton Kids." *California Educator* 23 (2): 14–15.

Pottiger, Maya. 2022. "The Invisible Tax on Black Teachers." The Washington Informer. September 29. https://www.washingtoninformer.com/the-invisible-tax-on-black-teachers/.

Prokop, Andrew. 2018. "Read the Letter the FBI Sent MLK to Try to Convince Him to Kill Himself." *Vox*, January 15. https://www.vox.com/xpress/2014/11/12/7204453/martin-luther-king-fbi-letter.

Prothero, Arianna. 2023. "Student Behavior Isn't Getting Any Better, Survey Shows." *Education Week*, April 20. https://www.edweek.org/leadership/student-behavior-isnt-getting-any-better-survey-shows/2023/04.

Ransby, Barbara. 2003. *Ella Baker and the Black Freedom Movement: A Radical Democratic Vision*. Chapel Hill, NC: University of North Carolina Press.

Rios, Victor. 2015. "Help for Kids the Education System Ignores." TED. November 2015. Video, 11:53. https://www.ted.com/talks/victor_rios_help_for_kids_the_education_system_ignores.

Roedel, Bodo. 2011. *Aikido: The Basics*. Maidenhead, England: Meyer & Meyer (UK) Ltd.

Rosenberg, Marshall B. 2015. *Nonviolent Communication: A Language of Life*. 3rd ed. Encinitas, CA: PuddleDancer Press.

Roy, Arundhati. 2020. "The Pandemic Is a Portal." *Rethinking Schools* 34 (4): 47.

Rustin, Bayard. 1969. Transcript of remarks delivered to the U.S. House of Representatives. Washington, July 17. Google Books. https://www.google.com/books/edition/Congressional_Record/Ss4Ej_-Z0skC?hl=en&gbpv=1&dq&pg=PA19975.

Sayers, Ann-Marie. 2019. "How This Native American Elder Reclaimed Sacred Land in the Bay Area." KQED Arts. November 20. Video, 9:33. https://www.youtube.com/watch?v=qYgZ1Pxw6aI.

Schwartz, Sarah. 2023. "MAP: Where Critical Race Theory Is under Attack." *Education Week*, June 11. https://www.edweek.org/policy-politics/map-where-critical-race-theory-is-under-attack/2021/06.

Sievers, Caitlin. 2023. "Tom Horne Focused on Test Scores and Discipline, Says 'Race Is Irrelevant' in American Life." *AZ Mirror*, January 11. https://www.azmirror.com/2023/01/11/tom-horne-focused-on-test-scores-and-discipline-says-race-is-irrelevant-in-american-life/.

Simmons, Dena. 2019. "Why We Can't Afford Whitewashed Social-Emotional Learning." Association for Supervision and Curriculum Development. April 19. https://www.ascd.org/el/articles/why-we-cant-afford-whitewashed-social-emotional-learning.

Simonson, Amy. 2022. "Florida Bill to Shield People from Feeling 'Discomfort' Over Historic Actions by Their Race, Nationality or Gender Approved by Senate Committee." *CNN*, January 20. https://www.cnn.com/2022/01/19/us/florida-education-critical-race-theory-bill/index.html.

Smiley, Tavis. 2014. "Tavis Smiley on Dr. Martin Luther King, Jr.'s Final Year." Interview by Brian Lamb. C-SPAN. November 9. Video, 7:41. https://www.c-span.org/video/?c4514175/tavis-smiley-dr-martin-luther-king-jrs-final-year.

Smithsonian. n.d. "An Indomitable Spirit: Autherine Lucy." National Museum of African American History and Culture. https://nmaahc.si.edu/explore/stories/indomitable-spirit-autherine-lucy.

SNCC Digital Gateway. n.d.a "Septima Clark." https://snccdigital.org/people/septima-clark/.

———. n.d.b "Highlander Folk School." https://snccdigital.org/inside-sncc/alliances-relationships/highlander/.

Stanford, Libby. 2022. "Divisions on Race, Gender Intensify a Fight for State Superintendent." *Education Week*, September 30. https://www.edweek.org/policy-politics/divisions-on-race-gender-intensify-a-fight-for-state-superintendent/2022/09.

Stevens, John, and Walther V. Krenner. 2004. *Training with the Master: Lessons with Morihei Ueshiba, Founder of Aikido*. Boston, MA: Shambhala Publications, Incorporated.

StoryCorps. n.d. "About StoryCorps." https://storycorps.org/about/.

Taylor, Drew. 2022. "'Everybody Can Change': Autherine Lucy Discusses Name Added to Alabama Hall alongside Former KKK Leader." *CBS 42*, February 7. https://www.cbs42.com/news/local/everybody-can-change-autherine-lucy-discusses-name-added-to-alabama-hall-alongside-former-kkk-leader/.

The King Center. n.d. "The King Philosophy." https://thekingcenter.org/about-tkc/the-king-philosophy/.

The Martin Luther King, Jr. Research and Education Institute. n.d.a. "Baker, Ella Josephine." Stanford, CA: The Martin Luther King, Jr. Research and Education Institute, Stanford University. https://kinginstitute.stanford.edu/encyclopedia/baker-ella-josephine.

———. n.d.b. "Clark, Septima Poinsette." Stanford, CA: The Martin Luther King, Jr. Research and Education Institute, Stanford University. https://kinginstitute.stanford.edu/encyclopedia/clark-septima-poinsette.

———. n.d.c. "Johnson, Lyndon Baines." Stanford, CA: The Martin Luther King, Jr. Research and Education Institute, Stanford University. https://kinginstitute.stanford.edu/johnson-lyndon-baines.

The New York Times. 1967. "Dr. King's Error." April 7. https://kinginstitute.stanford.edu/sites/mlk/files/kingserror.pdf.

Theoharis, Jeanne. 2018. "Coretta Scott King and the Civil Rights Movement's Hidden Women." *The Atlantic*, April 2. https://www.theatlantic.com/magazine/archive/2018/02/coretta-scott-king/552557/.

Tiel, Tyonie, [TyonieT]. 2021. "John W. North High School Shared This from a 2012 Yearbook. This Teacher Candice Reed Has Been Doing This for Awhile Now." *Twitter.* https://twitter.com/TyonieT/status/1451236812681216001.

Tolin, Lisa. 2023. "Oklahoma Teacher Is Still Fighting Book Bans, Now from Brooklyn." PEN America the Freedom to Write. https://pen.org/oklahoma-teacher-summer-boismier/.

Ueshiba, Morihei. 1996. *Budo: Teachings of the Founder of Aikido.* Translated by John Stevens. New York: Kodansha America, Inc.

———. 1992. *The Art of Peace: Teachings of the Founder of Aikido.* Translated by John Stevens. Boulder, CO: Shambhala Publications.

Visit San Jose. n.d. "Little Saigon." Visit San Jose. https://www.sanjose.org/neighborhoods/little-saigon.

Wang, Claire. 2022. "Wartime Trauma Among Vietnamese Refugees Subject of New Study." *NBC News*, January 24. https://www.nbcnews.com/news/asian-america/wartime-trauma-vietnamese-refugees-subject-new-study-rcna12759.

Wang, Hongyu. 2014. *Nonviolence and Education: Cross-Cultural Pathways.* New York: Routledge.

———. 2013. "A Nonviolent Approach to Social Justice Education." *Educational Studies: A Journal of the American Educational Studies Association* 49 (6) (November): 485–503. http://dx.doi.org/10.1080/00131946.2013.844147.

West, Cornel. 2014. "Cornel West's Thoughts on Ella Baker." *Time.* October 9. Video, 2:12. https://www.youtube.com/watch?v=omyQ6P2SCzo.

World Health Organization (WHO). n.d. "Violence Prevention Alliance Approach." n.d. https://www.who.int/groups/violence-prevention-alliance/approach.

Yadav, Prasenjeet. 2020. "PHOTOS: Living Tree Bridges in a Land of Clouds." NPR, August 1. https://www.npr.org/sections/goatsandsoda/2020/08/01/892983791/photos-living-tree-bridges-in-a-land-of-clouds.

Yeager, Andrew. 2013. "Mary Hamilton, the Woman Who Put the 'Miss' in Court." NPR, July 12. https://www.npr.org/sections/codeswitch/2013/07/12/198012536/summer-of-1963-miss-mary-hamilton.

Yosso, Tara J. 2005. "Whose Culture Has Capital? A Critical Race Theory Discussion of Community Cultural Wealth." *Race Ethnicity and Education* 8 (1): 69–91. https://doi.org/10.1080/1361332052000341006.

Zajacova, Anna, and Elizabeth Lawrence. 2018. "The Relationship between Education and Health: Reducing Disparities through a Contextual Approach." *Annual Review of Public Health* 39 (1): 273–89. https://doi.org/10.1146/annurev-publhealth-031816-044628.

CREDITS

Chapter 1

Feelings and Needs Inventories adapted from the Feelings and Needs Inventories developed by The Center for Nonviolent Communication. Used with permission.

Chapter 2

FIGURE 2.2 Photo of 1963 Children's March in Birmingham, © Michael Ochs Archives / Getty.

FIGURE 2.3 Cover of The Radical King by Dr. Martin Luther King, Jr., edited by Cornel West © 2015. Reprinted with permission from publisher.

Chapter 3

FIGURE 3.1 Photo of Autherine Lucy, © Getty Images.

FIGURE 3.2 Photo of Mary Hamilton from the Mississippi Police Department.

FIGURE 3.3 Photo of March of Our Lives by Olivier Douliery © AP Images.

Chapter 4

FIGURE 4.1 Photo of master-level aikido practitioners creating flow by Alexander Kolbasov. Reprinted with permission.

Chapter 5

FIGURE 5.5 Photo of Brentwood Press newspaper by Mike Tinoco, © The Press.

Chapter 6

FIGURE 6.7 Photo of Septima Clark and Rosa Parks among other activists by John Malone © Special Collections Division of the Nashville Public Library.

FIGURE 6.8 Photo of Septima Clark by Bob Fitch Photography © Department of Special Collections at Stanford University.

FIGURE 6.10 Map: Where Critical Race Theory Is Under Attack (2021, June 11). Education Week. Retrieved August 14, 2023 from http://www.edweek.org/leadership/map-where-critical-race-theory-is-under-attack/2021/06. Used with permission of the publisher.

Chapter 8

FIGURE 8.1 Photo of Bernard Lafayette, John Lewis, and others at the Greyhound bus station in Birmingham, Alabama during the Freedom Rides in 1961, © Alabama Department of Archives and History. Donated by Alabama Media Group. Photo by Robert Adams and Ed Jones, Birmingham News.

FIGURE 8.2 Photo of Reverend C.T. Vivian, Diane Nash, and Bernard Lafayette marching to Nashville's city hall by Jack Corn / The Tennessean, © IMAGN.

FIGURE 8.3 Photo of Vietnamese Service Center opening celebration by Tran Nguyen, © San Jose Spotlight.

FIGURE 8.5 Dr. Victor Rios with his teacher Flora Russ at Berkeley High by Emilie Raguso, © Berkeley Side news site.

Chapter 9

FIGURE 9.3 Photo of Coretta Scott King and Dagmar Wilson in United Nations Plaza, New York City, November 1, 1963 by Bettman © Corbis / Getty Images.

FIGURE 9.4 Photo of Marking Luther King Jr. at Vermont Avenue Baptist Church in Washington, February 1968 by Matthew Lewis © The Washington Post / Getty Images.

FIGURE 9.5 Photo of Dr. King hosting a sermon © Donald Uhrbrock/The LIFE Images Collection/Getty Images.

FIGURE 9.6 Photo of Reverend English with Coretta Scott King and Ruth Norma © Reverend English.

Chapter 10

FIGURE 10.1 Photo of Ella Baker in Atlantic City, 1964 by George Ballis © Take Stock.

INDEX

English, Ronald 9, 241–242, 244, 245

F

Family Legacy Stories 134–135, 311–313
feelings 92–94; connecting with 254–255; identifying 25–27; and needs 5, 23, 25, 92, 95
Feelings Inventory 25, 26, 94, 189, 302
Freedom Rides 1, 73, 74, 208, 268
Freire, Paulo 153, 276, 277–278

H

Haga, Kazu 68, 85, 142, 222–223, 292
Hamilton, Mary 9, 73–75
Hanh, Thich Nhat (Thay) 4, 87, 181, 183, 185–187, 219, 297
healing 120, 122; collective 137, 138, 139–146
healing-centered practices 116–117, 137, 138
Highlander Folk School, Tennessee 150–151
hooks, bell 115, 164
hope: centering 154; projecting 158–161

I

interconnectedness 4, 48, 52, 284
interdependence 4, 41, 50, 72, 139, 142, 217, 254, 264

J

justice 29, 66, 138, 149, 303; being on the side of 48, 52, 59; literacy and 153; restorative 70, 71; science and math as tools for achieving 163–164

K

Kashtan, Inbal 5, 23, 25, 92
Kashtan, Miki 5, 23, 25, 41, 48, 92, 206, 218, 242, 264

Kaur, Valarie 242, 243, 244
King, Coretta Scott 237
King, Jr., Martin Luther 1, 4, 5, 8, 9–10, 34, 35, 43, 222–223, 235–239, 241; agape love 138, 139, 149; vision of Beloved Community 41, 48; leadership style 266–267; "Beyond Vietnam" speech 236, 237–238; "I Have a Dream" speech 235, 236; "Letter from Birmingham Jail" 75; *Stride Toward Freedom* 44; "The Man Who Was a Fool" sermon 4; "When Peace Becomes Obnoxious" sermon 68, 69–70, 75
Kingian Nonviolence 2, 5, 6, 44–46, 47, 242
kissing the earth 181–183

L

LaFayette, Bernard 1–2, 5, 9, 10, 11, 206, 207–209, 269
Lakshmin, Pooja 219
language, of work and time, elimination of 183–185
leadership 265, 267, 270; group 268–269; top-down, Martin Luther King Jr. 266–267
A Letter to My Shadow 139–142
Lewis, John 75, 154, 157–158, 206, 208, 209–210, 258
Lewis-Randall, Gloria Washington 9, 34–39
LGBTQIA+ communities 1, 10, 117, 148, 157, 217, 235
liberation: and literacy 152–153; and love 164; nonviolence as means of 238
Life Maps *123*, 123–126, 124, *125*
"life as primary text" 162–165; guiding questions 162–163
Life Trajectory essays 126–127, 305–308
listening 48, 51, 87, 101, 289

literacy 162; and liberation 152–153

Literacy Maps 127–128

Living Moments *128*, 128–130, *129*

love 4, 7, 27, 47, 48, 50, 66, 114, 115–118, 165; agape 44, 138, 139, 149, 158, 206; definitions of 115; and liberation 164; meeting needs as an act of 119–121

Love, Bettina 119, 120

Lucy, Autherine 9, 68–69

M

Manning, Roxy 23, 121, 264

math, and justice 163–164

meditation, walking 181–183

mental health 71, 72, 117, 120, 178, 179; teachers 199

mindful/conscious breathing 185–187, 199

mindfulness 118, 181, 199

N

Name Plates 193, *194*

Nashville sit-ins (1960) 206–208, 209–211

needs 23, 115; centering 22, 23, 41; and feelings 5, 23, 25, 92, 95; identifying 27–30, 54, 55–57; meeting, as an act of love 119–121; met/meeting 25, 27, 41, 50–52, 55–57, 92, 95, 98, 149, 189, *190*, 217, 218; non-hierarchical view of 218; unseen/unmet 5, 21–22, 23, 25, 27–30, 33, 77, 92, 95, 189, *190*

Needs Inventory 28, 29, 95, 303

neutrality, neutralizing 154–161

nonviolence 37, 43–44, 75, 149, 153, 154, 206–207, 208, 209, 238, 242, 244, 268; commitment to 39, 52; culture of 41; Gandhian 206; modeling 4–5; pedagogy 5–6;

practising 59; understanding 4–5; as a way of life 44; *see also* Kingian Nonviolence

Nonviolence Education Pathway 281–288; convergence and divergence 286–288; harvesting ideas for 283–285; mission 284; vision 284

Nonviolent Communication (NVC) 2, 5, 6, 23, 25, 46, 47, 88, 96–100, 242, 254, 262, 263–264, 281

norms 72; teacher inquiry groups 275–276

O

outrage: expressing 242–243; safe containers for 243–244

P

pausing 218–219, 220

peace 29, 52, 69, 303; culture of 121; negative 7, 70–71, 72, 75; nurturing 100–103; obnoxious 68, 69–70, 75; positive 7, 75–77

Positive Notes 148

power 66, 67, 71, 96, 118, 125

professional development (PD) 271–273, 278; *see also* teacher inquiry groups

punishment 67, 70, 71, 72

R

race/racism 45, 118, 119, 156, 236, 240; anti–racism 70; critical race theory 118, 156–157, 235; systemic racism 235

radical consciousness 41, 48

relationality 4, 24; maintaining 259–261; nondual 4; violence and collapse of 3, 259

relationships, management of 72

Remember Me poems 78–79

remote/distance learning 176, 177–178

requests 96–97; using affirmative language when making 97

resilience 21, 51, 120, 146

restorative justice 70, 71, 116–117

Rios, Victor 215–216

Rosenberg, Marshall 5, 23

rules 71, 72

Rustin, Bayard 243, 266

S

scarcity mindset 180–181

self-care: real 219; teachers 199–205

Silent Conversation 139, *140*

slowing down 174, 179–180, 222–223

slowing down at school 180–198; assignment due dates/deadlines 196–198; community circles 193–196; eliminating metaphors of time and work 183–185; mindful breathing 185–187; opening the week 187–188; walking meditation (kissing the earth) 181–183; wellness checks 189–192

slowing down out of school 199–205; body-feel 201–202; doing nothing 201; resting 203

social-emotional learning (SEL) 70–71, 72, 116–117, 118, 235

spirit murder 119, 120

Student Nonviolent Coordinating Committee (SNCC) 1, 237, 258, 268; Alabama Voter Registration Project (1962) 269

suffering, voluntary 207–208, 211, 212–223

T

teacher inquiry groups 273–279; check-ins 274; dialogue 277–278; facilitating a session 274; group norms 275–276; preparing an inquiry 273–274; reflections and appreciations 279

teachers: autonomy 116; mental health 199; professional development (PD) 271–273, *see also* teacher inquiry groups; self-care 199–205; vacant positions 199

time 175, 176; abundance mindset 180; and assignment due dates/deadlines 196–198; flexibility with 180, 196–198; metaphors of, elimination of 183–185; scarcity mindset 180–181

trauma 86, 120, 138, 213; collective 137, 214; impact of 137; intergenerational 213, 214

trauma-informed care 116–117, 137

U

Ueshiba, Morihei 6, 14, 47, 48, 80, 165

V

violence 117, 154, 155; and collapse of relationality 3, 259; culture of 41, 66, 67, 121; cyclical 294; definitions of 3; engaging with 149; forms of 3; in schools 3; unintentional 3

vision: articulating and putting into practice your 53–58, 58; honoring our 42–47; refining and distilling your 53–54, 58; thinking about your 42

voluntary suffering 207–208, 211, 212–223

W

walking meditation 181–183

Wang, Hongyu 3, 4, 259

warrior scholars 43; principles 48–52, 58, 147

wellness 72, 120, 137, 138, 204

wellness checks 189–192

work, metaphors of, elimination of 183–185

For Product Safety Concerns and Information please contact our EU
representative GPSR@taylorandfrancis.com
Taylor & Francis Verlag GmbH, Kaufingerstraße 24, 80331 München, Germany

www.ingramcontent.com/pod-product-compliance
Lightning Source LLC
Chambersburg PA
CBHW081735270326
41932CB00020B/3284

* 9 7 8 1 6 2 5 3 1 6 2 8 8 *